MARIAN
MAXIMALISM

MARIAN MAXIMALISM

Jonathan A. Fleischmann, Ph.D.

ACADEMY OF THE IMMACULATE
New Bedford, MA

P.O. Box 3003
New Bedford, MA 02741
www.MaryMediatrix.com

ISBN Print: 978-1-60114-074-6
ISBN Kindle: 978-1-60114-374-7
ISBN EPUB: 978-1-60114-574-1

Cum Permissu Superiorum

Printed in the United States of America

Cover art:
Front
Coronation of the Virgin, window in Canterbury Cathedral
Back
Detail from *The Annunciation*, window in Covington Cathedral, KY
Both photos by: Fr. Lawrence Lew, O.P.
Graphic Artist
Mary Flannery, Flannery Studios

First Edition

This work is dedicated to:

the Blessed Virgin Mary, the Mother of God;
and to the images of Mary in my own life:
my wife, Clara Maria Bernadette;
my own mother, Mary Jane;
my mother-in-law, Stella;
and to all women.

De Maria numquam satis!

CONTENTS

CHAPTER ONE

Introduction   1

CHAPTER TWO

Miso-Gyny   7

CHAPTER THREE

Testimony of the Saints   11

CHAPTER FOUR

Marian Heretics?   21

CHAPTER FIVE

Appeal to Vatican II   29

CHAPTER SIX

Transubstantiation   35

CHAPTER SEVEN

A Marian Maximal Principle   47

CHAPTER EIGHT

Potuit, Decuit, Ergo Fecit   67

CHAPTER NINE

Grace and Merit   79

Apoc	*Apocalypse*	*1 Kings*	*1 Kings*
Col	*Colossians*	*Lk*	*Luke*
1 Cor	*1 Corinthians*	*Mk*	*Mark*
Dan	*Daniel*	*Mt*	*Matthew*
Eph	*Ephesians*	*Num*	*Numbers*
Ex	*Exodus*	*2 Pet*	*2 Peter*
Ezek	*Ezekiel*	*Prov*	*Proverbs*
Gal	*Galatians*	*Ps*	*Psalms*
Gen	*Genesis*	*Rom*	*Romans*
Hag	*Haggai*	*Sir*	*Sirach*
Isa	*Isaiah*	*Song*	*Song of Songs*
Jer	*Jeremiah*	*1 Tim*	*1 Timothy*
Jn	*John*	*2 Tim*	*2 Timothy*
1 Jn	*1 John*	*Wis*	*Wisdom*

GOM	*The Glories of Mary*
JDS	*Mariology of Blessed John Duns Scotus*
LG	*Lumen Gentium*
MFC	*Mary and the Fathers of the Church*
MMA	*Mary in the Middle Ages*
OLG	*Mariological Studies in Honor of Our Lady of Guadalupe*
PDF	*St. Maximilian Ma. Kolbe, Martyr of Charity – Pneumatologist*
RAP	*Reading Anselm's Proslogion*
SENT	*Commentarius in IV libros Sententiarum S. Bonaventurae*
SK	*Scritti di Massimiliano Kolbe*
ST	*Summa Theologiae*
TIC	*The Immaculate Conception: Why Thomas Aquinas Denied, while John Duns Scotus, Gregory Palamas, and Mark Eugenicus Professed the Absolute Immaculate Existence of Mary*
TTW	*The Triple Way or The Kindling of Love by St. Bonaventure of Bagnoregio, Doctor Seraphicus*
WOM	*'The Woman Clothed with the Sun' According to St. Lawrence of Brindisi*

FOREWORD

In a Sermon preached on the occasion of the Nativity of the Blessed Virgin Mary, Saint Bernard of Clairvaux wrote: "*de Maria numquam satis*"[1]—about Mary we can never say enough. We can never praise highly enough her who was immaculately conceived, in order that she might become the Mother of the Redeemer and the Mother of all the redeemed. One could also add that from the Blessed Virgin Mary we can never expect enough, that we can never trust too much in her intercession for the salvation of souls and for us in our mission of establishing a civilization of love.

The mystery of the Immaculate Conception, as is true of every mystery of our faith, is essentially connected with the mystery of the Redemptive Incarnation, that is, the mystery of God's incomparable love of us by which He has chosen us, from all time, to be His adopted children in His only-begotten Son. In the first chapter of his Letter to the Ephesians, Saint Paul expresses the great mystery of God's love of us in Jesus Christ, teaching us that God has chosen us in Jesus Christ "before the foundation of the world, that we should be holy and blameless before him" (*Eph* 1:4). He reminds us that God the Father has "destined us in love to be His sons through Jesus Christ, according to the purpose of His will, to the praise of His glorious grace which He freely bestowed on us in the Beloved" (*Eph* 1:5–6). That grace, he declares, is "redemption through His blood, the forgiveness of our trespasses" (*Eph* 1:7). It is a grace for the fulfillment of His saving plan, "to unite all things in Him, things in heaven and things on earth" (*Eph* 1:10). In his Second Letter to

---

[1] S. Bernard of Clairvaux, *Sermo de nativitate Mariae*, PL 183, 437D.

Timothy, Saint Paul urges us not to give way to shame or discouragement, on account of our life in Christ, but, rather, to take up our "share of suffering for the Gospel in the power of God" (2 *Tim* 1:8), remembering that our own call is in view of the fulfillment of God's saving plan or purpose, which is the grace of living in Christ as true sons and daughters of God (cf. 2 *Tim* 1:8–10).

In God's plan for our eternal salvation through the Incarnation of God the Son, He chose and set apart the Blessed Virgin Mary, from the moment of her conception, to be the worthy vessel in which His only-begotten Son would take our human nature. By a wondrous work of His grace, Mary was "full of grace" (*Lk* 1:28), the grace of our election as true sons and daughters of God in Jesus Christ. From the first moment of her life, Mary shared already in the grace of divine sonship which Christ would win for us through His conception in her womb and His Passion, Death, Resurrection and Ascension. Blessed John Duns Scotus, the great teacher of the mystery of the Immaculate Conception, wrote: "*in eodem instanti in quo Deus creavit animam dedit ei gratiam*"—in the same instant in which God created her soul, he gave her grace.[2] Blessed Scotus makes clear that the most wonderful gift of grace, given to Mary from the moment of her conception, was given in view of her Divine Maternity, her vocation and mission of Mother of God the Son Incarnate: "*hoc praecise decuit Matrem Christi*"—This precisely befitted the Mother of the Christ.[3] Saint Ephrem of Syria, deacon, theologian and poet of the 4th century, inspired by the text from the Song of Songs, "You are all fair, my love; there is no flaw in you" (*Song* 4:7), wrote these words to honor the mystery of the Immaculate Conception:

> Only you and your Mother
> are more beautiful than everything.

---

[2] Blessed John Duns Scotus, *Lectura completa*, III, d. 3, q. 1 (*Elementa*, 228), quoted in Ruggero Rosini, *Mariology of Blessed John Duns Scotus* (New Bedford, MA: Academy of the Immaculate, 2008), p. 74.

[3] Blessed John Duns Scotus, quoted in Ruggero Rosini, *Mariology of Blessed John Duns Scotus*, p. 76.

For on you, O Lord, there is no mark;
neither is there any stain in your Mother.[4]

The Blessed Virgin Mary is indeed *tota pulchra*—all beautiful.

The favor of fullness of grace in the Blessed Virgin Mary, like all of the mysteries of the faith, is for our salvation. By her Immaculate Conception, the Virgin Mary was prepared to receive and fulfill her call to be the Mother of God; the Virgin Mary's Heart was totally pure from her conception and thus her womb was the fitting vessel in which God the Son could be received into the world. The purity of her Heart is a sign to us of how our hearts must become pure, with the help of God's grace, in order that we may welcome Our Lord ever more fully into our lives and be ready to meet Him at His Final Coming.

Mary's Immaculate Heart is filled with love of us who are called to be true sons and daughters of God in her Divine Son, Our Lord Jesus Christ. When He was about to die on the Cross, Jesus gave us to His Mother, as our Mother, even as He entrusted her into our hands through the Apostle John (cf. *Jn* 19:26–7). As our Blessed Mother was totally one in heart with our Lord Jesus in His saving mission, so she continues to exercise her maternal care for all who, through Baptism, have come to life in her Divine Son and, indeed, for all mankind for whom her Son died and rose from the dead, and whom He desires to come to life in Him. Our Blessed Mother both teaches us the truth that God became man for our eternal salvation and leads us to experience the same truth: Christ's unfailing and unconditional love of us in the Church.

On December 8, 1854, Blessed Pius IX issued the Apostolic Constitution *Ineffabilis Deus*, in which he definitively proclaimed

---

[4] Saint Ephrem the Syrian, *Carmina Nisibena* 27, 8; CSCO 219, 76, quoted in Luigi Gambero, *Mary and the Fathers of the Church: The Blessed Virgin Mary in Patristic Thought,* tr. Thomas Buffer (San Francisco: Ignatius Press, 1991), p. 109.

what the Church had always believed about the Immaculate Conception of the Blessed Virgin Mary:

> We declare, pronounce and define that the doctrine which holds that the most Blessed Virgin Mary, in the first instant of her conception, by a singular grace and privilege granted by Almighty God, in view of the merits of Jesus Christ, the Savior of the human race, was preserved free from all stain of original sin, is a doctrine revealed by God and therefore to be believed firmly and constantly by all of the faithful.[5]

By his authority as Vicar of Christ on earth, the Holy Father solemnly proclaimed what had been the constant faith of the Church regarding the preparation of Mary, from the moment of her conception, for her vocation and mission of Mother of God. Preserving the Blessed Virgin Mary from every stain of original or actual sin, God the Father granted to Mary, in anticipation, the grace of the Redemption which her Divine Son would win for us by His Passion, Death and Resurrection. Mary was conceived without any stain of original sin, in order that she might belong totally to Christ and be our model and intercessor in belonging more and more to Christ.

The truth of the Immaculate Conception is a great source of consolation and strength for us in the daily struggle which we have in fighting temptation and turning our lives over to Christ unreservedly. The Blessed Virgin Mary was preserved from the stain of original sin to be the Mother of God and Mother of the Church. By

---

[5] "Declaramus, pronunciamus et definimus, doctrinam, quae tenet, beatissimam Virginem Mariam in primo istanti suae Conceptionis fuisse singulari omnipotentis Dei gratia et privilegio, intuitu meritorum Christi Iesu Salvatoris humani generis, ab omni originalis culpae labe praeservatam immunem, esse a Deo revelatam, atque idcirco ad omnibus fidelibus firmiter constanterque credendam." Pii IX, *Pontificis Maxim Act*, Pars Prima (Romae: Ex Typographia Bonarum Artium 1854), *Litterae Apostolicae de dogmatica definition Immaculatae Conceptionis Virginis Deiparae*, p. 616. English translation: Pope Pius IX, *Apostolic Constitution Defining the Dogma of the Immaculate Heart of Mary Conception Ineffabilis Deus with study questions*, by Most Rev. John R. Sheets, S.J. (Boston: St. Paul Books and Media, nd), p. 21.

her Immaculate Conception, she shows us the great grace which is ours from the moment of Baptism, the grace of the indwelling of the Holy Spirit, wiping away all stain of original sin and making us one with Christ in His victory over sin and everlasting death. Looking upon Mary Immaculate, we are confident that Christ will crush the head of Satan in our lives (cf. *Gn* 3:15). When Christ was dying on the Cross, He gave His Mother to us as Mother of the Church, so that she might always lead us to be one with her at the Foot of the Cross and to share in the grace of Redemption, which comes from Christ crucified alone (cf. *Jn* 19:25–7). Mary teaches us that the grace of Christ alone, coming to us from His pierced Heart on the Cross and now glorious at the right hand of the Father, conquers Satan and his works of sin in our lives. Assumed body and soul into glory by God, she intercedes for the graces we so much need. She is the *Mater Divinae Gratiae*—the Mother of Divine Grace.

Mary, our Mother, preserved from all stain of original sin, understands better than any of us the wiles of Satan and the profound harm and eternal death itself, which comes to us through sin. She witnessed the effects of the sin of our First Parents and of our actual sins in the Suffering and Death of her Divine Son. She, therefore, stands ever ready to point out to us Satan's allurements and deceptions, and to sustain us in times of great trial and temptation by leading us to her Son alive for us in the Church, especially through the Sacraments of Penance and the Holy Eucharist. By drawing close to Mary Immaculate, we come to understand ever better the effects of sin in our lives and upon our world; we come to understand our need to go to her Son for the grace of conversion of life and the transformation of our world. In times of great trial and temptation, we rightly call upon the help of our Mother: Mary Immaculate, help us!

I recall briefly the apparition of the Mother of God, in 1830, to Saint Catherine Labouré of the Daughters of Charity of Saint Vincent de Paul, at their novitiate chapel on the Rue du Bac in Paris. Through the apparition, our Blessed Mother taught us to recall her

Immaculate Conception and, therefore, to turn to her for protection and help. She asked that a medal be made in her honor, with the symbols of the Sacred Heart of Jesus and the Immaculate Heart of Mary, upon which would be inscribed the prayer: "O Mary, conceived without sin, pray for us who have recourse to thee!" How often we have uttered the prayer taught to us by Our Lady of the Miraculous Medal! What miracles of conversion have taken place through the intercession of Our Lady of the Miraculous Medal, our Blessed Mother, invoked in prayer under her title of the Immaculate Conception! I think of the conversion of the fiercely anti-Catholic Alphonse Ratisbonne before the image of Our Lady of the Miraculous Medal in the Church of Saint Andrea delle Fratte in Rome on January 20, 1842.

I recall, too, the apparitions of our Blessed Mother to Saint Bernadette Soubirous, in 1858, near the village of Lourdes in southwestern France. The Virgin Mary identified herself to Bernadette with these words: "I am the Immaculate Conception." The spring of water, to which she directed Bernadette, has remained a sign of the saving grace of Christ which comes to us in the Church, through the intercession of the Mother of God, the grace of Christ which heals us physically and spiritually, and transforms our world.

In his Apostolic Letter *Novo millennio ineunte*, Pope Saint John Paul II described the mission of the Church in our time, underlining its organic unity with the perennial mission of the Church, the mission of Christ down the Christian centuries. Before the great challenge of our time, Pope John Paul II cautioned us that we will not save ourselves and our world by discovering "some magic formula" or by "inventing a new programme."[6] In unmistakable terms, he declared:

---

6 "... formulam veluti 'magicam' ... excogitando 'novo consilio.'" Ioannes Paulus PP. II, Epistula Apostolica *Novo Millennio Ineunte*, "Magni Iubilaei anni MM sub exitum," 6 Ianuarii 2001, *Acta Apostolicae Sedis* 93 (2001), p. 285, no. 29. [Hereafter, *NMI*]. English translation: Pope John Paul II, Apostolic Letter *Novo*

No, we shall not be saved by a formula but by a Person, and the assurance which he gives us: *I am with you*.[7]

He reminded us that the program by which we are to address effectively the great spiritual challenges of our time is, in the end, Jesus Christ alive for us in the Church. He explained:

> The programme already exists: it is the plan found in the Gospel and in the living Tradition, it is the same as ever. Ultimately, it has its center in Christ himself, who is to be known, loved and imitated, so that in him we may live the life of the Trinity, and with him transform history until its fulfillment in the heavenly Jerusalem. This is a program which does not change with shifts of times and cultures, even though it takes account of time and culture for the sake of true dialogue and effective communication.[8]

In short, the program leading to freedom and happiness is, for each of us, holiness of life, in accord with our state in life.

In all of the varied and complex situations of the Church and of our lives as members of the Body of Christ, a single vision directs us: to bring Christ to others with new enthusiasm and new energy. Our situation is not unlike the situation of the first Christians and of the first missionaries to the United States of America; we live in a world which has either never heard of Christ and the Gospel, or has

---

Millennio Ineunte, "At the Close of the Great Jubilee of the Year 2000," 6 January 2001 (Boston: Pauline Books & Media, 2001), p. 39, no. 29. [Hereafter, *NMIE*].

[7] "Nullo modo: servabit nos nulla formula, verum Persona una atque certitudo illa quam nobis Ipsa infundit: *Ego vobiscum sum!*" *NMI*, p. 285, no. 29. English translation: *NMIE*, p. 39, no. 29.

[8] "Iam enim praesto est consilium seu 'programma': illud nempe quod de Evangelio derivatur semper vivaque Traditione. Tandem in Christo ipso deprehenditur istud, qui sane cognoscendus est, diligendus atque imitandus, ut vita in eo trinitaria ducatur et cum eo historia ipsa transfiguretur ad suam usque in Hierosolymis caelestibus consummationem. Institutum enim hoc, variantibus quidem temporibus ipsis atque culturae formis, non mutatur quamvis rationem quidem habeat temporis et culturae, ut verum instituat diverbium efficacemque communicationem." *NMI*, pp. 285–6, no. 29. English translation: *NMIE*, pp. 39–40, no. 29.

forgotten Christ and His Gospel. Regarding the grave evils which beset the world in our day, Pope Benedict XVI declared that they are all signs of "the tyranny of mammon which perverts mankind" and that they result from "a fatal misunderstanding of freedom which actually undermines man's freedom and ultimately destroys it."[9] They are manifestations, to be sure, of a way of living, to use the words of Pope Saint John Paul II, "as if God did not exist."[10]

In the United States of America, the de-christianization of the society is manifested, above all, in a culture of death, a culture in which life itself is feared. Contrary to the law inscribed upon the human heart by the Creator, the culture of death picks and chooses whose human life will be safeguarded and fostered, according to who has the power to enact laws which take away the right to life of the unborn, or of those whose lives have become burdened through advanced years, grave illness or special needs. Catholics, finding themselves living in a culture of death, are called to witness to the truth of the inviolable dignity of every human life, expressed, above all, in the unconditional love of Christ for all His brothers and sisters, especially the least brethren (cf. *Mt* 25:31–46).

If Catholics are to bring Christ to the world, they must first know Christ and love Christ. They must strive daily for holiness of life. The great challenge which confronts the whole Church confronts, in particular, the Church in the first cell of Her life, the family. It is the

---

[9] "…dittatura di mammona che perverte l'uomo … un fatale fraintendimento della libertà, in cui proprio la libertà dell'uomo viene minata e alla fine annullata del tutto." Benedictus PP., Allocutio "Omina Nativitatis novique Anni Curiae Romanae significantur," 20 Decembris 2010, *Acta Apostolicae Sedis* 103 (2011), p. 36. English translation: Pope Benedict XVI, "Address of His Holiness Benedict XVI on the Occasion of Christmas Greetings to the Roman Curia," 20 December 2010, *L'Osservatore Romano Weekly Edition in English*, 22–9 December 2010, p. 13.

[10] "… etsi Deus non daretur." Ioannes Paulus PP. II, Adhortatio Apostolica *Christifideles Laici*, "De vocatione et missione Laicorum in Ecclesia et in mundo," 30 Decembris 1988, *Acta Apostolicae Sedis* 81 (1989), p. 454, no. 34. English translation: Pope John Paul II, Post-Synodal Apostolic Exhortation *Christifideles Laici*, "On the Vocation and the Mission of the Lay Faithful in the Church and in the World," 30 December 1988 (Vatican City State: Libreria Editrice Vaticana, nd), p. 95, no. 34.

challenge which Pope John Paul II described in his Apostolic Letter "At the Close of the Great Jubilee of the Year 2000," "*Novo millennio ineunte*," as the "*high standard of ordinary Christian living*."[11]

If we are to bring Christ to the world, our lives must be centered upon the Holy Eucharist, in which Christ makes ever present for us His saving Passion, Death and Resurrection. We must have a strong devotion to the Blessed Virgin Mary, Mary Immaculate, who always draws us to Christ in the Blessed Sacrament, with the maternal counsel: "Do whatever He tells you" (*Jn* 2:5). Pope Saint John Paul II also reminded us that it is through Mary that we come to know and love Christ and become His heralds and agents in the world:

> I would like to rekindle this Eucharistic "amazement" by the present Encyclical Letter, in continuity with the Jubilee heritage which I have left to the Church in the Apostolic Letter *Novo Millennio Ineunte* and its Marian crowning, *Rosarium Virginis Mariae*. To contemplate the face of Christ, and to contemplate it with Mary, is the "program" which I have set before the Church at the dawn of the third millennium, summoning her to put out into the deep on the sea of history with the enthusiasm of the New Evangelization.[12]

The Immaculate Heart of Mary unveils for the Christian the qualities of the heart which longs to rest in the glorious pierced Heart of Jesus and draws all its energy from that divine Source.

---

[11] "… '*superiorem modum*' *ordinariae vitae christianae*." *NMI*, 288, n. 31. English translation: *NMIE*, p. 43, no. 31.

[12] "Illum cupimus eucharisticum 'stuporem' his Litteris Encyclicis rursus excitare, tamquam iubilarem hereditatem quam Epistula Apostolica *Novo Millennio ineunte* Ecclesiae commendare voluimus et cum Mariali eius consummatione in documento *Rosarium Virginis Mariae*. Vultum Christi contemplari, quin immo eum cum Maria contueri, est propositum seu 'programma' quod illucescente tertio Millennio Ecclesiae significavimus, cum eam simul hortaremur ut in altum historiae mare cum novae evangelizationis fervore procederet." Ioannis Pauli PP. II, Litterae Encyclicae *Ecclesia de Eucharistia*, "de Eucharistia eiusque necessitudine cum Ecclesia," 17 Aprilis 2003, *Acta Apostolicae Sedis* 95 (2003), pp. 436–7, no. 6. English translation: Pope John Paul II, Encyclical Letter *Ecclesia de Eucharistia* "On the Eucharist and Its Relationship to the Church (Vatican City: Libreria Editrice Vaticana, 2003), p.8, no. 6.

Pope Saint John Paul II urged us to pray the Rosary as a means of gazing, with Mary, upon the Face of Christ. In his words, the Rosary "serves as an excellent introduction and a faithful echo of the Liturgy, enabling people to participate fully and interiorly in it and to reap its fruits in their daily lives."[13] Pope John Paul II saw the practice of keeping company with Mary in her contemplation of the great mystery of the Redemptive Incarnation as a most powerful tool for the work of establishing a civilization of love through the New Evangelization. He wrote:

> But the most important reason for strongly encouraging the practice of the Rosary is that it represents a most effective means of fostering among the faithful that commitment to the contemplation of the Christian mystery which I proposed in the Apostolic Letter *Novo millennio ineunte*, as a genuine "training in holiness": "What is needed is a Christian life distinguished above all in the art of prayer."[14]

Reflecting upon the mission of the Church to transform the culture of death into a civilization of love, by the example and through the intercession of Mary Immaculate, we are deeply conscious of the particular love which Mary Immaculate has shown to her children of America through her apparitions, beginning on the day of the Feast of the Immaculate Conception in 1531. As Pope John Paul II

---

[13] "haec oratio non modo se Liturgiae Sacrae non opponit sed *illi etiam tamquam fulcrum deservit*, quandoquidem introducit eam atque repetit dum plena interior participatione permittit ut ea vivatur eiusque percipiantur cotidiana in vita fructus." Ioannis Pauli PP. II, Epistula Apostolica *Rosarium Virginis Mariae*, "de Mariali Rosario," 16 Octobris 2002, *Acta Apostolicae Sedis* 95 (2003), p. 8, no. 4 [Hereafter: *RVM*]. English translation: Pope John Paul II, Apostolic Letter *Rosarium Virginis Mariae* "On the Most Holy Rosary" (Vatican City State: Libreria Editrice Vaticana, 2002), p. 8, no. 4 [Hereafter: *RVME*].

[14] "Attamen multo gravior causa cur Rosarii consuetudo vehementer inculcetur inde exsistit quod efficacissimum exhibet instrumentum ad iuvandum illud *officium contemplandi christianum mysterium* intra fidelium communitatem, quod ipsi Nos in Apostolica Epistula *Novo millennio ineunte* exhibuimus tamquam 'sanctitatis paedagogiam': 'Indiget [...] affectu christiano qui cum primis *arte precationis* praecellit.'" *RVM*, p. 8, no. 5. English translation: *RVME*, pp. 8–9, no. 5.

reminded us, Our Lady of Guadalupe played an altogether special role in the First Evangelization of America, as she will in the New Evangelization of America. In his Post-synodal Apostolic Exhortation *Ecclesia in America*, he wrote:

> With the passage of time, pastors and faithful alike have grown increasingly conscious of the role of the Virgin Mary in the evangelization of America. In the prayer composed for the Special Assembly for America of the Synod of Bishops, Holy Mary of Guadalupe is invoked as "Patroness of all America and Star of the First and New Evangelization." In view of this, I welcome with joy the proposal of the Synod Fathers that the feast of Our Lady of Guadalupe, Mother and Evangelizer of America, be celebrated throughout the continent on December 12. It is my heartfelt hope that she, whose intercession was responsible for strengthening the faith of the first disciples (cf. *Jn* 2:11), will by her maternal intercession guide the Church in America, obtaining the outpouring of the Holy Spirit, as she once did for the early Church (cf. *Acts* 1:14), so that the new evangelization may yield a splendid flowering of Christian life.[15]

---

[15] "A lo largo del tiempo ha ido creciendo cada vez más en los Pastores y fieles la conciencia del papel desarrollado por la Virgen en la evangelización del Continente. En la oración compuesta para la Asamblea Especial del Sínodo de los Obispos para América, María Santísima de Guadalupe es invocada como 'Patrona de toda América y Estrella de la primera y de la nueva evangelización.' En este sentido, acojo gozoso la propuesta de los Padres sinodales de que el día 12 de diciembre se celebre en todo el Continente la fiesta de Nuestra Señora de Guadalupe, Madre y Evangelizadora de América. Abrigo en mi corazón la firme esperanza de que ella, a cuya intercesión se debe el fortalecimiento de la fe de los primeros discípulos (cf. Jn 2, 11), guíe con su intercesión maternal a la Iglesia en este Continente, alcanzándole la efusión del Espíritu Santo como en la Iglesia naciente (cf. Hch 1, 14), para que la nueva evangelización produzca un espléndido florecimiento de vida cristiana." Ioannis Pauli PP. II, Adhortatio Apostolica Postsinodalis *Ecclesia in America*, "sobre el encuentro con Jesucristo vivo, camino para la conversión, la comunión y la solidaridad en América" 22 Januarii 1999, *Acta Apostolicae Sedis* 91 (1999), p. 747–8, no. 11. English translation: Pope John Paul II, Post-Synodal Apostolic Exhortation *Ecclesia in America* "On the Encounter with the Living Jesus Christ: The Way to Conversion, Communion, and Solidarity in America," (Washington, D.C.: United States Catholic Conference, 1999), p. 21, no. 11.

The apparitions of Our Lady of Guadalupe are, among all of the apparitions of the Mother of God, most exceptional. Mary Immaculate immediately identifies herself for her messenger, Saint Juan Diego, and makes clear from the first of her four apparitions to him her desire to have a chapel built in which she might manifest the all-merciful love of God to pilgrims, the all-merciful love of God most perfectly manifested in God the Son Incarnate in her womb. In a most miraculous way, God left her image on the mantle of Saint Juan Diego, so that she continues in our day to appeal to all of her children of America and of far beyond, in order to draw them to Christ and His transforming love.

We celebrate the Feast of Our Lady of Guadalupe on December 12th, the day which marks both her last appearance to Saint Juan Diego, with the miracle of the roses and of the sacred image, and her appearance to Juan Bernardino, the dying uncle of Juan Diego. Our Lady of Guadalupe invites us anew, as she has faithfully done, since her appearances from December 9th to 12th in 1531, to know the mystery of God's mercy and love in our lives by coming to know and love her Divine Son. Her words to Juan Diego, at her first appearance, on December 9th, at that time the feast of the Immaculate Conception in the Spanish Empire, are surely her words to us today:

> Know, know for sure, my dearest, littlest, and youngest son, that I am the perfect and ever Virgin Holy Mary, Mother of the God of truth through Whom everything lives…. I want very much to have a little house built here for me, in which I will show Him, I will exalt Him and make Him manifest. I will give Him to the people in all my personal love, in my compassion, in my help, in my protection: because I am truly your merciful Mother, yours and all the people who live united in this land and of all the other

people of different ancestries, my lovers, who love me, those who seek me, those who trust in me.[16]

In her maternal love, Our Lady of Guadalupe wants, most of all, to show us how much God loves us in Jesus Christ, God the Son Incarnate in her immaculate womb. She draws our hearts, which are frequently beset by fear and doubt and sin, to her Immaculate Heart, so that we, with her, may place our hearts into the glorious pierced Heart of Jesus, the only source of our joy and peace, of our healing and strength to carry out the New Evangelization by which our culture will become a civilization of love.

Mary Immaculate, who brought together into one the Spanish and the Native American peoples in the 16th century, will not fail to hear our prayers for unity and peace in our homes, in our local communities, in our nation and among all peoples. She who was the instrument by which Our Lord brought an end to the oppressive racism and the cruel practice of human sacrifice at the time of the First Evangelization of the American continent will also be the instrument by which God brings an end to the many forms of injustice, above all the deliberate killing of the innocent and defenseless unborn, in our time of the New Evangelization. In the beautiful mestiza complexion of the Virgin of Guadalupe, uniting the beauty of both the European and Native American races, we find a constant sign of hope that, with the help of God's grace, all peoples can live in peace with each other, respecting and fostering the life and faith of every citizen, without exception or exclusion. Before the many and most serious challenges which we face in advancing the New Evangelization, especially in living the Gospel of Life in the midst of a culture of death, Our Lady of Guadalupe looks upon us with maternal love and invites us to seek, through her intercession, the grace of conversion of life and

---

[16] *Nican Mopohua. Original Account of Guadalupe*, in *A Handbook on Guadalupe*, by the Franciscan Friars of the Immaculate (New Bedford, MA: Academy of the Immaculate, 1996), p. 194.

the transformation of our culture. Remember her words at the first apparition to Juan Diego: "I am truly your merciful Mother."

Remember also her words to him at the fourth apparition:

Am I not here, I, Who am your Mother? Are you not under my shadow and protection? Am I am not the source of your joy? Are you not in the hollow of my mantle, In the crossing of my arms? Do you have need of anything else? Let nothing afflict you, disturb you.[17]

With the Mother of God, we have all that we need, for she guides us to Christ Who alone is our Salvation. In every trial and suffering, she will lovingly bring us to Christ, our sure anchor of hope. She will lead us to place all our confidence in Him and so never to give way to discouragement in the work of transforming our culture into a civilization of love.

In a very special way, our Blessed Mother teaches us how immeasurably God loves us, treasures every human life, without exception or boundary. She draws us to Jesus Christ, her Divine Son, so that, through our union of heart with His Sacred Heart, we may know directly in our lives, especially through the Sacraments of Penance and the Holy Eucharist, the love of God and become, with Mary Immaculate, bearers of God's love to all our brothers and sisters, especially the most vulnerable and those in most need.

The writing of Jonathan Fleischmann, a husband and father, gives witness to his deep knowledge and ardent love of the Immaculate Virgin Mary. Clearly, he has understood most profoundly the importance of devotion to the Blessed Virgin Mary, which, by its very nature, grows always greater. The maximalism of our devotion to the Immaculate Virgin, Mother of God, is demanded by the great Mystery of Faith, the mystery of the Redemptive Incarnation, in which we participate every day of our lives and, most fully and

---

[17] Ibid., p. 200.

powerfully, through our participation in the Eucharistic Sacrifice and our reception of its incomparable fruit: the Body, Blood, Soul and Divinity of Christ.

With careful and thorough documentation and reasoning, Jonathan Fleischmann aptly shows that it is indeed true that "we can never say enough" of the Blessed Virgin Mary and that, in staying close to her, we are also protected from error and heresy. Jonathan Fleischmann uses both *a priori* and *a posteriori* arguments, in accord with the thought of Blessed John Duns Scotus, to show that it is no mere poetic expression but a sober truth that we can never praise highly enough the Blessed Virgin Mary. In the course of the book, he provides a rich selection from the writings of canonized saints from every period of the life of the Church to illustrate their witness to the truth that one cannot praise highly enough the Immaculate Virgin.

It is my hope and prayer that, through the study of *Marian Maximalism*, the Blessed Virgin Mary will draw you ever closer to her Heart, totally one with the Heart of Jesus, and, therefore, ever closer to the Heart of her Divine Son, Jesus Christ. May *Marian Maximalism* inspire its readers to an ever greater Marian devotion, and through devoted love of Mary, to an ever deeper knowledge of her Divine Son, to worship of Him alone "in spirit and in truth" (*Jn* 4:23–4), and to serving Him with an undivided heart.

Raymond Leo Cardinal BURKE

September 8, 2015

Feast of the Nativity of the Blessed Virgin Mary

Si auctoritati Ecclesiae vel auctoritate Scripturae non repugnat, videtur probabile quod exellentius est tribuere Mariae.

~ Bl. John Duns Scotus ~

"If it is not contrary to the authority of the Church or Sacred Scripture, it seems probable that what is more excellent should be ascribed to Mary."

CHAPTER ONE

INTRODUCTION

I would like to begin this monograph with a "disclaimer" of sorts. I am not a theologian. I am not a member of the clergy. Nor am I trained in philosophy in the modern sense of the term, though I have the title "doctor of philosophy," and my discipline would probably have been called "philosophy" in the time of Aristotle. I am a layman. My formal expertise is in the fields of applied physics, mathematical logic, and pedagogy. I am a professor of engineering. I have published and refereed technical articles on the subjects of micromechanics (which involves the application of Newtonian mechanics at the microscopic scale) and formal intuitionistic-constructive logic (which has applications in the field of theoretical computer science). I am also an associate member of the Mission of the Immaculate Mediatrix, and I have devoted my life to the service of Our Lady, Coredemptrix, Mediatrix of all graces, and Advocate. In the interest of full disclosure, I declare that I am a "Marian Maximalist."

The reader may reasonably object: Whatever the merits of my credentials in my own fields of expertise, they do not seem to qualify me to write about theology, much less the *quaestiones disputatae* of Mariology. I would reply that the separation of the lesser sciences from the greatest "science"—theology—is in fact a relatively modern phenomenon. Bl. Raymond Lull (d. 1315) was perhaps the greatest formal logician of his time. He is considered the father of modern computation theory (theoretical computer science), and he was a

pioneer of the mathematical theory of combinatorics (the organization of information in structures such as "graphs" and "trees"). He
was also a Third Order Franciscan, a novelist, a poet, a mystic, a
theologian, and a martyr. He was beatified by Bl. Pope Pius IX in
1857. In his own time, Bl. Raymond Lull was given the title *Doctor
Illuminatus.* If Bl. John Duns Scotus (d. 1308), the *Doctor Subtilis*
and contemporary of Bl. Raymond Lull, was correct in maintaining
that the paradigm of *all creation*, both spiritual and material, is the
God-Man Jesus Christ—and therefore by association the Virgin-
Mother Mary as well, who in the words of Bl. Pope Pius IX was
predestined with Christ by *one and the same decree* of the Eternal
Father before the creation of the world—then the experience of God
and His Mother permeates all creation, and laypersons such as myself
would be living a lie if we attempted to separate our Faith from our
work—be it intellectual, physical, technical or artistic.

The point of this monograph is to survey instances of Marian
Maximalism among the saints of the Catholic Church, and to apply
sound reasoning and logic to see if Marian Maximalism, as represented by these saints, really presents the danger of heresy of which it
is suspected by the self-proclaimed "Marian Minimalists." The scope
of such a survey (which is extremely vast—as we will see), combined
with the relatively small size of this monograph, necessarily implies
that our survey is *far* from encyclopedic. However, an attempt has
been made to give a representative sampling of Marian Maximalism
within the Catholic Church across both space and time, and to draw
sound conclusions from these examples. Put simply, if somewhat
loosely, my thesis is that a "Marian heretic" *cannot exist*, because such
would be a contradiction in terms, since *if* one is truly Marian, then
one *cannot* be a heretic.

I attempt to prove my thesis in a variety of ways, including (1)
a priori arguments based on the intrinsic relationships between true
and false statements (e.g., employing notions of logical consistency
and performative contradiction); (2) *a posteriori* arguments based on

Sacred Scripture and the Sacred Tradition of the Catholic Church; and (3) the *personal witness* of the saints themselves. These three methods of proof are in many ways analogous to the methods employed in (classical) mathematics, the empirical sciences (e.g., physics), and jurisprudence, respectively. Taken individually, each of these methods of proof is *incomplete* (as was "formally" proven in the case of classical mathematics by Kurt Gödel in 1931). This incompleteness is all the more apparent when these methods of proof are applied individually (to the exclusion of the others) to theology and philosophy, because Sophia (Wisdom) must encompass *all* Truth.[1] Employed simultaneously, however, (with mutual interdependence) these three methods of proof make a *very strong case* for Marian Maximalism, as I endeavor to show. Nevertheless, more is required. As Bl. John Henry Newman insightfully pointed out, any "proof" depends ultimately on the *assent* of the individual, and this is no less true of the so-called "exact" empirical sciences—or even the so-called "*a priori*" science of mathematics—than it is true of theology. Thus, ultimately, and without committing ourselves to the error of Fideism, we must say with St. Anselm (echoing St. Augustine): "I believe in order to understand."

The three "proof paradigms" just mentioned are perhaps nowhere so effectively employed together as in the method of argumentation attributed to Bl. John Duns Scotus and his disciples, classically expressed by the syllogism: *potuit, decuit, ergo fecit*. Somewhat incomprehensibly, however, Scotus' mode of argument has been attacked by modern philosophers, such as Kant and Heidegger, who accuse him of practicing "onto-theology," and by modern theologians (both "conservative" and "liberal"), who accuse him of being the father of "voluntarism," and who call his famous syllogism the principle of "convenience." What is incomprehensible in this attack is that, if Scotus' method of proof is invalid, then so are the methods of modern mathematics, science, and jurisprudence, since Scotus' method

---

[1] Cf. *Jer* 31:22.

encompasses all of these methods taken individually, and still more! Perhaps the most "careful" of all scholastic philosophers, Bl. John Duns Scotus is not called the "Subtle Doctor" for nothing. Nor is it a mere coincidence that the *Subtle Doctor* is also the *Marian Doctor par excellence.*

One recurring theme in this monograph is that Marian Maximalism provides a key to true doctrinal security. That is, Marian Maximalism allows us to face and answer with confidence and *safety* some of the thorniest problems of grace and merit that have historically caused division within the Church (leading to nearly all Protestant denominations). This is not the self-referential or pharisaical sort of *false* "exaggerated doctrinal security" or "hoarding of grace" that has been criticized by Pope Francis. Rather, it is the *true* security of a child resting in the arms of his or her mother, who nourishes, teaches, gently chastises, corrects, and guides her child with a tenderness that only a mother can give. Thus, as we defend the Marian Maximalism of saints against various critiques that have been leveled by theologians and philosophers of the last several centuries, we also show that those who repudiate Marian Maximalism (the so-called Marian Minimalists)—far from remaining "moderate" or choosing the "Catholic middle way," as they claim—in fact invariably fall to one or another extreme of heresy (such as monotheletism or Nestorianism). We argue that it is the Womb of Mary herself, or Marian Maximalism, which provides the authentic "middle ground"—the *Virgin Earth* as the Fathers of the Church called Mary—of Catholicism, which cannot be characterized as a "shade of gray" between two extremes of black and white, any more than truth can be characterized as a composite of opposing lies. The true "Catholic middle way" is the way of maximalism-perfection, not of minimalism-mediocrity. This is the "narrow gate that leadeth to life" spoken of by Jesus, which Pope Francis has characterized as "nearness" and "encounter" with Christ.[2] The most intimate encounter with Jesus Christ ever

---

[2] *Mt* 7:14.

experienced by a creature was experienced by His Blessed Mother, as she carried Him for nine months under the mantle of her Virginal Womb. It is for this reason that Mary is the *Destroyer of All Heresies*.

The doctrinal security of Marian Maximalism must never be abused, however, as a sort of "license to speculate" on matters of Catholic doctrine. Such abuse presupposes spiritual pride, and pride is the very *antithesis* of what it means to be truly Marian. The saints with one voice proclaim that it is Mary's *humility* more than any other virtue which defines her greatness. We have only to take her at her own word: "My soul doth magnify the Lord. And my spirit hath rejoiced in God my Savior. Because he hath regarded the humility of his handmaid."[3] While writing this monograph, I have attempted at all times to guard myself from the vice of spiritual pride, since such a vice is unworthy of the Woman I wish to exalt. Nevertheless, I dare not claim to be free of this vice. If, in attempting to prove my thesis, I inadvertently justify the suspicions of the Marian Minimalists by showing *myself* to be just such a "Marian heretic" who I claim cannot exist, then I am ready to own my own errors, and I submit to the final authority and judgment of the Magisterium of the Catholic Church on any *quaestiones disputatae*. However, *if* I am a heretic, then I maintain that I am only a heretic in so far as I am *not* truly Marian, and no one can convince me otherwise.

---

[3] *Lk* 1:46–8.

CHAPTER TWO

Miso-Gyny

There exists in the Catholic Church today, and in most Christian churches, and indeed in the whole world, a persistent miso-Gyny: a strong irritation with, dislike of, or outright hatred for the Woman. This is odd, considering the witness of countless saints who have emphasized time and again the central and *indispensable* place that the Mother of God has in the salvific economy, not merely passively—as the necessary bearer of Jesus Christ—but actively: both in the objective order of redemption as Coredemptrix with Christ at the Foot of the Cross, and in the subjective order of redemption as Mediatrix of all graces to humankind, now and until the Parousia.

To a man who likes women, this miso-Gyny seems totally inexplicable. How can anyone hate, dislike, or even mildly suspect the *Woman par excellence*, when women in general (in my experience) are such excellent creatures? Indeed, every woman is an image—more or less perfect as the case may be—of this Woman "whom God loved before the world was made, this Dream Woman before women were."[4] For this very reason, miso-Gyny leads to misogyny, and misogyny leads to miso-Gyny, and herein lies the answer to our puzzle, since the world has never been free from misogyny since the Woman became the enemy of the old serpent; and never was this more true than in our own present culture, despite false optimism and claims

---

[4] Ven. Fulton J. Sheen, *The World's First Love*, McGraw-Hill Book Company, Inc., New York, NY (1952).

to the contrary. In the words of Pope Benedict XVI (then Cardinal Joseph Ratzinger):

> It is, I believe, no coincidence, given our Western, masculine mentality, that we have increasingly separated Christ from his Mother, without grasping that Mary's motherhood might have some significance for theology and faith. This attitude characterizes our whole approach to the Church. We treat the Church almost like some technological device that we plan and make with enormous cleverness and expenditure of energy. Then we are surprised when we experience the truth of what Saint Louis-Marie Grignon de Montfort once remarked, paraphrasing the words of the prophet Haggai, when he said, "You do much, but nothing comes of it!"[5] When making becomes autonomous, the things we cannot make but that are alive and need time to mature can no longer survive.[6]

To witness this miso-Gyny, one need only note the repeated statements made by countless theologians who, even in the context of praising the Blessed Virgin Mother of God, never miss an opportunity to mention how many Catholic faithful throughout the ages of the Church, through a misunderstanding of Marian devotion, excessive Marian piety, and misplaced zeal, have given her too much honor, too many dignities and titles, and too much praise, even to the point of becoming "innocent" ("pious") heretics. It is striking, however, that when the aforementioned theologians make these claims, seemingly with an expectation that the reader will nod his or her head in sage agreement, there are never any citations, any references, or any examples given of these nebulous "hosts" of Marian heretics so ominously alluded to. This is strange, since, if in good faith, these authors want to prevent others from falling

---

[5] *Hag* 1:6.
[6] Pope Benedict XVI (then Cardinal Joseph Ratzinger), "My Word Shall Not Return to Me Empty!" in *Mary—the Church at the Source,* Ignatius Press, San Francisco, CA (2005): p. 16.

into the "trap" of excessive Marian devotion, one would think they would be only too willing to provide examples of the ones who have gone astray: the heretics of *Marian Maximalism*, or perhaps *Marian Excessivism*. Where are they? Who are they? Do these Marian heretics really exist? In the following monograph, we will attempt to answer these questions.

First of all, the precise meaning of "too much praise" needs to be clarified. It is not a phrase that can simply be left to intuition. For example, one could ask the following question: Were the Nestorians guilty of giving Christ *too much* praise when they denied that the nature of the Divine Logos could be united to a merely human nature? On one level, their claim may seem very "respectful" of the Divine Logos. However, considering the fact that in the Person of Christ, who is the *Word Made Flesh*, the nature of the Divine Logos *was* united to the human nature of Jesus Christ, the Nestorian claim is in fact a great insult to Christ, since it denies Him His truly exalted *Theandric Being*. Indeed, the Nestorian heresy is typical of all heresies in the sense that it starts out as *Marian Minimalism*, by denying Mary her true title as the *Mother of God*, but immediately leads to (or simultaneously implies) *minimalism with respect to Christ*, by denying the God-Man His divinity.

Second, the precise meaning of "Mary" needs to be clarified. If revisionist feminist theologians claim that what Christians have called "Mary" for the last two thousand years is really only the goddess Artemis "domesticated" to fit a male-dominated worldview, they are certainly not giving Mary too much praise. Rather, they are annihilating the very personhood of Mary in favor of a pagan ideal, which has nothing to do with Christianity and denies the Blessed Virgin Mother of God even her most basic dignity as a *real, corporal woman*. In point of fact, while revisionist feminist theologians typically refer to God as "the Goddess," they typically shun the name of "Mary" with an almost superstitious fear. If they must refer to a created woman as opposed to "the Goddess," then they tend to prefer Eve or the mythical character "Lilith" to the Blessed Virgin Mary, since the former two are more representative of their "liberated" sexual ideal.[7] However, if some revisionist feminist theologian has chosen, or at any point does choose, to give their "Goddess" the name "Mary,"[8] then I contend that, though they are certainly heretics (and rather silly ones), they cannot be called "Marian heretics" in any true sense of the term, since they have no idea of who "Mary" is. They are merely using the name "Mary" without any true reference to Mary, the historical woman of Nazareth, the wife of Joseph, and the Mother of Jesus.

Is this the sort of Marian heretic the Marian Minimalists are afraid of? Is it really true that a "pious" and "simple" Catholic might accidentally mistake the Blessed Virgin Mary for the goddess Artemis?[9] Is it really possible that some Catholic saints have—as some modern theologians have claimed—at least come *close* to making this mistake? Certainly, the saints speak with one voice in praise of the Virgin Mary. Let us consider the words of the saints themselves.

---

[7] Cf. Donna Steichen, *Ungodly Rage: The Hidden Face of Catholic Feminism*, Ignatius Press, San Francisco, CA (1991).

[8] This was, in fact, done by the Collyridian sect in fourth century Arabia, though this example seems to be exceptional. According to St. Epiphanius of Salamis, the Collyridians fused pagan and Christian ideas to such an extent that it is highly doubtful that their "Mary-Goddess" worship began as any kind of truly Marian devotion that developed into exaggeration, but rather as a simple appropriation of the name of Mary for essentially pagan beliefs and practices.

[9] Marco Merlini argues that all Christian devotion to Mary—and the Orthodox devotion to Mary as the *Panagia*, or All-Holy One, in particular—"illustrates well the direct derivation of the Christian Madonna from the ambivalent ancient goddesses who were mistresses of life and death, givers of the correct rules and punishers of the undisciplined." Moreover, he purports to give evidence of "the direct derivation of both the pagan and the Christian goddesses [sic] from the female Neolithic Old European and Minoan prototypes characterized by the quality of the coexistence of seeming contradictory features such as those associated with the very basic foundations of human existence: life-giver, death-wielder, and regeneratrix," Marco Merlini, "The Pagan Artemis in the Virgin Mary Salutation at Great Lavra, Mount Athos," *Journal of Archaeomythology*, 7 (2011): pp. 106–80.

CHAPTER THREE

TESTIMONY OF THE SAINTS

St. Josemaría Escrivá (d. 1975), founder of Opus Dei, said:

> *Felix culpa*, sings the Church: O happy fault because it has obtained for us such a great Redeemer. O happy fault, we can also add, which has merited us to receive Our Lady as Mother. Now we no longer have anything to fear, nothing must alarm us, because Our Lady, who is crowned Queen of heaven and earth, is the omnipotent intercessor before God. Jesus cannot deny anything to Mary, nor to us, children of His very own Mother.[10]

Bl. James Alberione (d. 1971), founder of the Society of St. Paul and the Daughters of St. Paul, said:

> Let us consider why Mary is not remembered in the Gospels during the glorious episodes of her Son (i.e., the transfiguration, the triumphal entry into Jerusalem, etc.), but her presence is recalled on Calvary. She knew her office and her mission: she accomplished these most faithfully, even to the very end, by cooperating with the Son as Coredemptrix. She prepared the Host for sacrifice; and now, behold her offering and immolating it on Calvary. [...] Mary felt in her Heart, with her voluntary presence, the sorrows of Jesus

---

[10] St. Josemaría Escrivá, as quoted by Fr. Stefano Manelli, F.I., "Marian Coredemption in the Hagiography of the 20th Century" in *Mary at the Foot of the Cross: Acts of the International Symposium on Marian Coredemption*, Academy of the Immaculate, New Bedford, MA (2001): p. 222.

in the Crucifixion, the Agony, the Death; she suffered beyond words, and with profound charity she offered the Blood of Jesus and her own pangs in payment to the heavenly Father.[11]

St. Maximilian Maria Kolbe (d. 1941), founder of the City of the Immaculate and Martyr of Charity at Auschwitz, said:

[Mary] is the One closest to God, while we are closest to Her, and, consequently, through Her to God Himself. God has given us this white ladder, and He desires that we may come to Him by climbing it, or rather that She, after having embraced us tightly to Her motherly bosom, may carry us to God. [...] In the womb of the Immaculate the soul is reborn in the form of Jesus Christ [...]. She must nourish the soul with the milk of Her grace, lovingly care for it, and educate it, just as She nourished, cared for, and educated Jesus. On Her lap the soul must learn how to know and love Jesus. It must draw love for Him from Her Heart, or even love Him with Her Heart, and become like unto Him by means of love. [...] She alone must instruct each one of us in every moment; She must lead us, transform us into Herself, in such wise that it is no longer we who live, but She in us, just as Jesus lives in Her and the Father in the Son. Let us allow Her to do with us and by means of us whatever She desires and surely She will accomplish miracles of grace: we will become saints and great saints.[12]

St. Teresa Benedicta of the Cross (d. 1942)—Edith Stein—philosopher, Jewish convert, and sacrificial victim, who was born on the Day of Atonement (*Yom Kippur*) and who, like Mary, followed the Spotless Lamb Jesus Christ to the slaughter, said:

---

[11] Bl. James Alberione, as quoted by ibid.: pp. 224–5.
[12] St. Maximilian Maria Kolbe, SK 461, SK 1295, SK 556. All citations from the writings of St. Maximilian Kolbe are abbreviated SK and are taken from *Scritti di Massimiliano Kolbe*, Roma (1997).

Mary stands at the crucial point of human history and especially at the crucial point of the history of woman; in her, motherhood was transfigured and physical maternity surmounted. Just as the goal of all human education is presented to us in a concrete, vital, and personal way through Christ, so also the goal of all women's education is presented to us through Mary. The most significant evidence of the eternal meaning and value to be found in sexual differentiation lies in the fact that the new Eve stands beside the new Adam on the threshold between the Old and the New Covenants. […] And thereby, as co-redeemer by the side of the Redeemer, she emerges from the natural order. Both mother and Son spring from the human race, and both embody human nature; yet, both are free from that relationship which makes possible the fulfillment of life's meaning only in union with and through another person. Union with God replaces this relationship in both; in Christ through the hypostatic union, in Mary through the surrender of her whole being to the Lord's service. Are they both separated so much from the rest of humankind that we can no longer hold them as models? In no way is this true. They have lived for the sake of humanity, not only to effect our redemption through their power, but also to set an example of how we should live in order to participate ourselves in the redemption.[13]

Bl. Edward Poppe (d. 1924), a "priest on fire" according to Pope St. John Paul II, and a zealous promoter of the *Eucharistic Crusade* for young people, said:

Mary will cover you with Her shadow, and you will remain calm and confident. She will start the journey with you and lead you by secret shortcuts. You will not be spared suffering, but She will make you hungry for it, as if for an essential food. Ah, Mary!

---

[13] St. Edith Stein, "Problems of Women's Education," in *The Collected Works of Edith Stein, Volume Two: Essays on Woman*, Second Edition, Revised, translated by Freda Mary Oben, Ph.D., ICS Publications, Washington, DC (1996): pp. 198–9.

Mary! Her name will be like honey and balm on your lips. Mary! Mary! Ave Maria! Who can resist it? Tell me, who will be lost with the Ave Maria?[14]

St. John Bosco (d. 1888), "Father and Teacher of Youth,"[15] founder of the Salesian Society, and co-founder (with St. Maria Domenica Mazzarello) of the Institute of the Daughters of Mary Help of Christians for the care and education of poor girls, said:

> O Mary, powerful Virgin, Thou art the mighty and glorious protector of the Church; Thou art the marvelous "Help of Christians"; Thou art terrible as an army in battle array; Thou alone hast destroyed every heresy in the whole world. In the midst of our struggles, our anguish, and our distress, defend us from the power of the enemy and at the hour of death, receive our souls into Paradise. Amen.[16]

To learn what the saints who lived before the 18th century said about the Virgin Mary, we need hardly look further than to that almost limitless source of Marian dogma, doctrine, and praxis, *The Glories of Mary*, by St. Alphonsus Maria de Liguori (d. 1787), *Doctor Most Zealous* of the Church.[17] There we read:

---

[14] Bl. Edward Poppe, as quoted by Dom Antoine Marie, O.S.B., *Spiritual Newsletter of the Abbey of Saint-Joseph de Clairval* (May 13, 2001).

[15] St. John Bosco is the father of the pedagogical method known as the "Salesian Preventive System of Education," which is the model of most modern systems of pedagogy based on the availability or presence of the teacher as mentor and guide, in opposition to methods of education based on fear, control, and punishment.

[16] St. John Bosco, as quoted in *The Raccolta: Prayers and Devotions Enriched with Indulgences*, Benziger Brothers, New York, NY (1957): #414.

[17] It should be noted that several significant Mariological works ascribed to well-known saints, at the time St. Alphonsus de Liguori wrote *The Glories of Mary*, are now ascribed to other authors. In particular, the works, *De Excellentia Virginis Mariae* and *De Conceptione Sanctae Mariae*, previously ascribed to St. Anselm of Canterbury, are now ascribed to Fr. Eadmer of Canterbury; and the work, *Speculum Beatae Mariae Virginis*, previously ascribed to St. Bonaventure of Bagnoregio, is now ascribed to Fr. Conrad Holzinger of Saxony. It should also be noted, however, that when St. Alphonsus Liguori makes any of the views of these holy writers his own, those views thereby gain the authority of both a saint and Doctor of the Church.

Hence the divine Mother, on account of the great merit that she acquired by this great sacrifice which she made to God for the salvation of the world, was justly called by St. Augustine "the repairer of the human race"; by St. Epiphanius, "the redeemer of captives"; by St. Anselm, "the repairer of a lost world"; by St. Germanus, "our liberator from our calamities"; by St. Ambrose, "the Mother of all the faithful"; by St. Augustine, "the Mother of the living"; and by St. Andrew of Crete, "the Mother of life." For Arnold of Chartres says, "The wills of Christ and of Mary were then united, so that both offered the same holocaust; she thereby producing with him the one effect, the salvation of the world." At the death of Jesus Mary united her will to that of her Son; so much so, that both offered one and the same sacrifice; and therefore the holy abbot says that both the Son and the Mother effected human redemption, and obtained salvation for men—Jesus by satisfying for our sins, Mary by obtaining the application of this satisfaction to us. Hence Denis the Carthusian also asserts "that the divine Mother can be called the savior of the world, since by the pain that she endured in commiserating with her Son (willingly sacrificed by her to divine justice) she merited that through her prayers the merits of the Passion of the Redeemer should be communicated to men." Mary, then, having by the merit of her sorrows, and by sacrificing her Son, become the Mother of all the redeemed, it is right to believe that through her hands, divine graces, and the means to obtain eternal life, which are the fruits of the merits of Jesus Christ, are given to men. To this it is that St. Bernard refers when he says, that "when God was about to redeem the human race, he deposited the whole price in Mary's hands."[18]

Note that in this single quotation St. Alphonsus Liguori references the following saints and holy writers (in historical

---

[18] St. Alphonsus Maria de Liguori, *The Glories of Mary*, translated from the Italian by Rev. Eugene Grimm, C.Ss.R., Redemptorist Fathers, Brooklyn, NY (1931): pp. 401–2. Subsequent citations are abbreviated GOM.

order): St. Ambrose (d. 397), St. Epiphanius (of Salamis, d. 403), St. Augustine (of Hippo, d. 430), St. Andrew of Crete (d. 720 or 740), St. Germanus (of Constantinople, d. 733 or 740), St. Anselm (of Canterbury, d. 1109), St. Bernard (of Clairvaux, d. 1153), his disciple and friend Arnold of Chartres (d. after 1156), and Denis (or Denys, or Dionysius) the Carthusian (d. 1471). In doing so, St. Alphonsus Liguori makes every one of the theological points typically contained in the writings of so-called "modern" supporters of Mary's role as Coredemptrix, and he goes further than many of them, quoting Denis the Carthusian to say "that the divine Mother can be called the *savior* of the world," on account of "the pain that she endured in commiserating with her Son (willingly sacrificed *by her* to divine justice)," so that "both offered *one and the same sacrifice*," and "both the Son and the mother *effected human redemption*"! Moreover, Mary's role as Coredemptrix in the *objective* redemption of human-kind, accomplished at the Foot of the Cross by commiserating with her Son and sacrificing Him to the Father, is explicitly linked to her role as Mediatrix of all graces in the *subjective* redemption of each human person, since "she *merited* that through her prayers the merits of the Passion of the Redeemer should be communicated to men." This is not a "slip of the pen"! Indeed, St. Alphonsus Liguori had much to say about Mary's role as Mediatrix (or Mediatress) between God and humankind:

> It is well known with what unanimity theologians and holy Fathers give Mary this title of mediatress, on account of her hav-ing obtained salvation for all, by her powerful intercession and her merit "of congruity," thereby procuring the great benefit of redemption for the lost world. I say by her merit of congruity, for Jesus Christ alone is our mediator by way of justice and by merit, "de condigno," as the scholastics say, he having offered his merits to the Eternal Father, who accepted them for our salvation. Mary, on the other hand, is a mediatress of grace, by way of simple

intercession and merit of congruity, she having offered to God, as theologians say, with St. Bonaventure, her merits, for the salvation of all men; and God, as a favor, accepted them with the merits of Jesus Christ. [...] And the holy Church wishes us to understand this, when she honors the divine Mother by applying the following verses of Ecclesiasticus to her: *In me is all grace of the way and the truth.* [...] St. Basil of Seleucia declares that she received this plentitude that she might thus be a worthy mediatress between men and God: "Hail full of grace, mediatress between God and men, and by whom heaven and earth are brought together and united." "Otherwise," says St. Laurence Justinian, "had not the Blessed Virgin been full of divine grace, how could she have become the ladder to heaven [the 'white ladder' of St. Maximilian Kolbe], the advocate of the world, and the most true mediatress between men and God?"[19]

Indeed, not only is the Blessed Virgin Mary the one "by whom heaven and earth are brought together and united" (in the words of St. Basil of Seleucia) and "the ladder to heaven," St. John Damascene (d. 749), *Father and Doctor* of the Church, tells us that the Blessed Virgin Mary *is heaven itself*[20]—and even *better* than the first heaven—from the moment that she was conceived in the womb of her mother, Anne:

> O blessed loins of Joachim, whence the all-pure seed was poured out! O glorious womb of Anna, in which the most holy fetus [Mary] grew and was formed, silently increasing! O womb [of Anne] in which was conceived the living heaven [Mary], wider than the wideness of the heavens. [...] This heaven is clearly much more divine and awesome than the first. Indeed he who created

---

[19] GOM: pp. 325–7.

[20] Cf. Jonathan A. Fleischmann, "Heaven is a Woman" (Parts 1–4), *Missio Immaculatae International*, 8:6; 9:3; 4; 6 (2012–2013): pp. 6–8; pp. 4–6; pp. 10–12; pp. 10–12.

the sun in the first heaven would himself be born of this second heaven, as the Sun of Justice. [...] She is all beautiful, all near to God. For she, surpassing the cherubim, exalted beyond the seraphim, is placed near to God.[21]

Note that here St. John Damascene implicitly affirms Mary's Immaculate Conception. St. Proclus of Constantinople (d. 446 or 447), the friend and disciple of St. John Chrysostom, also calls Mary "heaven," adding that she is the *only bridge* for God to mankind, thus affirming her singular role as Mediatrix:

> [Mary is] handmaid and mother, virgin and heaven, the only bridge for God to mankind; the awesome loom of the divine economy upon which the robe of union was ineffably woven. The loom-worker was the Holy Spirit; the wool-worker the over-shadowing power from on high. The wool was the ancient fleece of Adam; the interlocking thread the spotless flesh of the Virgin. The weaver's shuttle was propelled by the immeasurable grace of him who wore the robe; the artisan was the Word who entered in through her sense of hearing.[22]

St. Irenaeus of Lyons (d. 202), who heard the words of Jesus Christ repeated from St. Polycarp of Smyrna, the disciple of St. John the Apostle himself, had this to say about Mary's role as Advocate, both of Eve and of the whole human race:

> By disobeying, [Eve] became the cause of death for herself and for the whole human race. In the same way, Mary, though she also

---

[21] St. John Damascene, *Homily on the Nativity* 2; 3; 9; as quoted by Fr. Luigi Gambero, S.M., *Mary and the Fathers of the Church: The Blessed Virgin Mary in Patristic Thought*, Ignatius Press, San Francisco, CA (1999): pp. 402–3. Subsequent citations are abbreviated MFC.

[22] St. Proclus of Constantinople, *Homily 1*, as quoted by Nicholas Constas (Ed.), Proclus of Constantinople and the Cult of the Virgin in *Late Antiquity: Homilies 1–5, Texts and Translations* (Vigiliae Christianae, Supplements, 66), Brill Academic Publishers, Leiden (2003): pp. 136–7.

had a husband, was still a virgin, and by obeying, she became the cause of salvation for herself and for the whole human race [...]. The knot of Eve's disobedience was untied by Mary's obedience. What Eve bound through her unbelief, Mary loosed by her faith. [...] And while the former was seduced into disobeying God, the latter was persuaded to obey God, so that the Virgin Mary became the advocate of the virgin Eve. And just as the human race was bound to death because of a virgin, so it was set free from death by a Virgin, since the disobedience of one virgin was counterbalanced by a Virgin's obedience.[23]

As early as the *first century* (possibly contemporary with the Gospel of St. John), we read of the *power* and *grandeur* of the Virgin Mother, as well as her kindness and thanksgiving, in the so-called *Odes of Solomon* (c. 80–210):

The Spirit spread his wings over the Virgin's womb.
She conceived and gave birth.
And she became a virginal mother by great mercy.
She conceived and gave birth to a son without pain,
and there was a purpose for this.
She did not ask for a midwife to aid her,
because God saw to her delivery.
Like a human being, she gave birth according to the will of God.
Manifestly she gave birth.
With great power she acquired him.
With thanksgiving she loved him.
With kindness she guarded him.
With grandeur she manifested him. Alleluia![24]

---

[23] St. Irenaeus of Lyons, *Adversus Haereses*, 3:22; 5:19. MFC: p. 54.
[24] From the Odes of Solomon, as quoted in the *Little Office of the Blessed Virgin Mary*, compiled and edited by John E. Rotelle, O.S.A., Catholic Book Publishing Corp., NJ (1988): pp. 117–8 (Friday Evening Prayer).

We could quote many, many more saints, whom we must omit only because of space. Indeed, it appears that to sum up the thinking of the saints, we have only to invoke the traditional Marian "maximality principle" *de Maria numquam satis*, echoed by St. Maria Faustina Kowalska, who said very simply: "Nothing is too much when it comes to honoring the Immaculate Virgin."[25]

---

[25] St. Maria Faustina Kowalska, as quoted by Fr. Donald Calloway, M.I.C., *Purest of All Lilies*, Marian Press, Stockbridge, MA (2010).

CHAPTER FOUR

MARIAN HERETICS?

At this point, however, we must ask ourselves two questions: Are these saints Marian heretics? And if they are not Marian heretics, is it possible to be a Marian heretic by giving her too much praise? A significant number of Catholic authors (nominally both "conservative" and "liberal") have recently claimed that some of the saints we have quoted were at least very close to being "unwitting" ("pious") Marian heretics. These claims, however, aside from being breathtakingly bold—considering they are being said about saints and Doctors of the Church—do not stand up to close scrutiny.

Consider the claim that St. Maximilian Maria Kolbe opened the door to feminist theology by his reflections on the relationship of the Blessed Virgin Mary to the Blessed Trinity: a relationship which, as St. Alphonsus Maria de Liguori quoted Fr. Suarez to say, "belongs in a certain way to the order of hypostatic union."[26] St. Bonaventure of Bagnoregio (d. 1274), the *Seraphic Doctor* of the Church, discussed the Holy Spirit in terms of a "conception," both in reference to His procession within the Trinity and in reference to His mission.[27] St. Maximilian followed St. Bonaventure's lead (though he may not have been aware that he was doing so) and called the Holy Spirit the Uncreated Immaculate Conception. "Hence the Holy Spirit is an uncreated conception, an eternal one; he is the prototype of every

---

[26] Fr. Francisco Suarez, *De Incar.* P. 2, d. 1, s. 2. GOM: p. 364.
[27] St. Bonaventure, *I Sent.* d. 10, a. 2, q. 1; *III Sent* d. 4, a. 1, q. 1.

sort of human conception in the universe. [...] [He] is a most holy conception, infinitely holy, immaculate."[28] In view of the revelation given to St. Bernadette Soubirous at Lourdes, the Blessed Virgin Mary is the Created Immaculate Conception. St. Maximilian Kolbe reflected that, in virtue of Mary's relationship with the Holy Spirit, most evident at the moment of the Incarnation of the Son of God In her Immaculate womb, the Blessed Virgin Mary is, in fact, both the Spouse of the Holy Spirit and the Holy Spirit *quasi-incarnate.*[29] This is certainly a profound and striking insight! Consider, however, whether this insight is in any way conducive to revisionist feminist theology.

Feminist theology, far from promoting *femininity*, relies on a revolutionary disjunction between womanhood and motherhood, a unity at the very core of femininity, and a further rejection of the complementarity of the male and female genders altogether: the so-called ideal of "androgyny." However, it is precisely the unity of womanhood and motherhood that is most perfectly manifested in the virginal maternity of Mary, Mother of God and Spouse of the Holy Spirit. The term *quasi-incarnate* used by St. Maximilian is a profound and precise expression of the intimacy of the spousal union between the Blessed Virgin Mary and God, especially in the Person of the Holy Spirit, which far excels the spousal union of husband and wife, in which we already know that, in the words of Christ, "they are not two, but one flesh." Mary is not the wife of the Holy Spirit; she is the true wife of St. Joseph, and St. Joseph is her true husband. The words "husband" and "wife" necessarily denote the complementarity of the sexes proper to natural marriage. In the words of Fr. Peter Damian Fehlner:

> Indeed, spousal love is truly realized in marriage, but not perfectly. The exemplar is that of the love of the divine persons, in which

---

[28] SK 1318.
[29] SK 1286.

the Immaculate Virgin shares in a way such as also to be an exemplar for every other form of spousal love. [...] Parallelwise, those who do not take the virginal marriage of Mary and Joseph as the exemplar for both marriage and the virginal state end in misunderstanding all states of human life, married and virginal, clerical and lay.[30]

The unique spousal union between the Blessed Virgin Mary and the Holy Spirit bears the most perfect fruit: the God-Man Jesus Christ. "This uncreated Immaculate Conception [the Holy Spirit] conceives divine life immaculately in the soul of Mary, his Immaculate Conception. The virginal womb of her body, too, is reserved for him who conceives there in time—everything material comes about according to time—the divine life of the God-Man."[31] Clearly then, the dignity of the Blessed Virgin as Spouse of the Holy Spirit and the Holy Spirit *quasi-incarnate*, as with every Marian dignity, hinges on the divine Maternity. Thus, Fr. Manfred Hauke observes the following very negative attitude toward the Blessed Virgin Mary in the writings of one prominent feminist:

> In her 1973 critique, Daly has been inspired once again by Simone de Beauvoir, who had pointed out the contrast between the ancient goddesses and Mary as early as 1949; [...] Daly now sharpens this critique and puts it in a wider systematic context: Mary is "a remnant of the ancient image of the Mother Goddess, enchained and subordinated in Christianity, as the 'Mother of God.'" [...] Mary is "a pale derivative symbol disguising the conquered Goddess," a "flaunting of the tamed Goddess." Her role as servant in the Incarnation of God amounts to nothing other than a "rape." [...] On Mary's being the *Mother of God*—which is,

---

[30] Fr. Peter Damian Fehlner, F.I., *St. Maximilian Ma. Kolbe, Martyr of Charity—Pneumatologist*, Academy of the Immaculate, New Bedford, MA (2004): pp. 174–5. Subsequent citations are abbreviated PDF.
[31] SK 1318.

after all, central to the whole of Mariology—Daly simply refrains from making any definite commentary, even about its function as an isolated symbolic image. The reason for this is understandable: "being a mother" always implies an inherent relation to a child. That, however, is obviously not compatible with Daly's feminist ideal of autonomy.[32]

The same Catholic authors who have accused him of catering to the revisionist feminist theologians have also criticized St. Maximilian Kolbe, along with St. Francis of Assisi (d. 1226) and St. Bernard of Clairvaux (d. 1153), for contributing to a "feminization" of the Trinity and of the Church.[33] However, the idea that the intimate and indeed inexpressible union between the Blessed Virgin Mary and the Holy Trinity would in any way "feminize" the Trinity is ridiculous. First and foremost, in the words of Fr. Peter Damian Fehlner:

> *Per se* divine persons are not differentiated via male or female gender. [...] There is no such thing as a tri-personal divine nature masculine rather than feminine, or feminine rather than masculine. The divine persons as persons are designated with the male pronoun, not in reference to what is called the empirical data of sexual differentiation, but in reference to their real distinction from Mary: *She*, and in the case of the Son, because born New Adam or male, of the Virgin Mary, who thereby is exemplar of the Church as new Eve and virgin bride of Christ. [...] This is what St. Maximilian is saying, this is what St. Francis also affirmed, and it is this which underlies the so-called Franciscan thesis of Scotus

---

[32] Fr. Manfred Hauke, *God or Goddess?*, translated by Dr. David Kipp, Ignatius Press, San Francisco, CA (1995): pp. 182–4.

[33] Cf. Leon Podles, *The Church Impotent: The Feminization of Christianity*, Spence Publishing Company, Dallas, TX (1999). For a definitive refutation of this and other errors regarding St. Maximilian Kolbe and (1) "Creation, Creator and Gender," (2) "Mary Immaculate, the Blessed Trinity and Gender," and (3) "Divine Maternity, the Incarnation of the Word and Gender," cf. PDF: pp. 155–177.

and his metaphysics of person in the Trinity, in the hypostatic order (which includes the Virgin Mother) and in the Church.[34]

The theology of St. Maximilian Kolbe is firmly grounded in the Franciscan theology of Bl. John Duns Scotus (d. 1308), which takes as a point of departure the so-called Joint Primacy of Jesus and Mary (the Franciscan or Scotistic thesis).[35] This Joint Primacy was mentioned by Bl. Pope Pius IX in his declaration of the dogma of the Immaculate Conception, when he said that "from the very beginning, and before time began, the eternal Father [...], by one and the same decree, had established the origin of Mary and the Incarnation of Divine Wisdom."[36] That is, before Adam and Eve were made, the first models of man and woman (and in fact all created things) were Jesus and Mary in the mind of God. Thus, Jesus and Mary are the original and perfect prototypes of Man and Woman. Again in the words of Fr. Peter Damian Fehlner:

Hence, the correct way of speaking theologically, is determined not by biological priorities, but by the mysteries of salvation, in which the recognition or denial of the central place of the first born daughter of the Father and spouse of the Holy Spirit in revealing the person of Father and Spirit, because Mother of the Son, is the crucial and operative question. Obviously, the approach of St. Maximilian is fully Catholic. Can the same be said for those, who whether conservative or liberal, fail to root their theology in the full mystery of Christ, a mystery including the divine Maternity, and in the *signa divinae voluntatis?* [...] In any case, it is important to note that feminism is a consequence, not of stressing the Marian mystery at the center of our theology (and the scotistic thesis especially sustaining this truth of faith), but of

---

[34] PDF: pp. 170–2.
[35] Cf. Fr. Maximilian Mary Dean, F.I., *A Primer on the Absolute Primacy of Christ*, Academy of the Immaculate, New Bedford, MA (2006).
[36] Bl. Pope Pius IX, *Ineffabilis Deus*, Apostolic Constitution (December 8, 1854).

a denial that Woman as such is essentially defined by Maternity: not *abstractly*, but *concretely* as the Immaculate Conception whose only reason to exist is to conceive and give birth virginally to the Son of God. For the sake of her qua Immaculate Mother of God all the rest of creation was made. [...] That is why St. Maximilian (and before him St. Francis and St. Bernard) in setting Marian spirituality at the heart of male conformity to Christ crucified, viz., the spirituality of spousal love, far from being responsible for the feminization of the Church, offer the only key to an authentic realization of what masculine and feminine are about, both in the community and in each member of the community.[37]

Thus, in Mary, we find the true original prototype and the perfect realization of Woman, essentially defined by Maternity (which is to say, *fecundity*). In a singular way, however, Mary's maternal fecundity was attained through her virginal purity. The juxtaposition of Virginal Purity and Maternal Fecundity in the Perfect Woman strikes a deathblow to the ideal of selfish autonomy in all its forms, from radical feminism to homosexuality, and a host of other prevalent secularist mindsets, all of which abhor motherhood in the natural sense as incompatible with "personal freedom," and all of which abhor virginity as incompatible with "sexual fulfillment." Moreover, St. Maximilian Kolbe (and St. Bernard and St. Francis) cannot have "feminized" the Church, because the Church has always been feminine, and indeed essentially *Marian*, as Bl. Pope Paul VI affirms:

When the liturgy turns its gaze either to the primitive Church or to the Church of our own days it always finds Mary. [...] And since the liturgy is worship that requires [a] way of living consistent with it, it asks that devotion to the Blessed Virgin should become a concrete and deeply-felt love for the Church, as is wonderfully expressed in the prayer after Communion in the Mass

---

[37] PDF: pp. 175–6.

of September: "… that as we recall the sufferings shared by the Blessed Virgin Mary, we may with the Church fulfill in ourselves what is lacking in the sufferings of Christ."[38]

True feminism—that is, a *truly felt* desire to raise all womankind to a higher dignity than has, in fact, been afforded them throughout much of history—is *radically dependent* on the Blessed Virgin-Mother Mary. This fact has been recognized within the Church from the time of the Fathers. As St. Proclus of Constantinople observed:

Thanks to her, all women are blessed. It is not possible that woman should remain under her curse; to the contrary, she now has a reason to surpass even the glory of the angels. Eve has been healed […]. Today, a list of women is admired: [Sarah, Rebekah, Leah, Deborah, etc.]; Elizabeth is called blessed for having carried the Forerunner, who leapt for joy in her womb, and for having given witness to grace; Mary is venerated, because she became the Mother, the cloud, the bridal chamber, and the ark of the Lord.[39]

And as Pope St. John Paul II confirmed:

Attentive consideration of the figure of Mary, as she is presented to us in Sacred Scripture as the Church reads it in faith, is still more necessary in view of the disparagement she sometimes receives from certain feminist currents. In some cases, the Virgin of Nazareth has been presented as the symbol of the female personality imprisoned in a narrow, confining domesticity. On the contrary, Mary is the model of the full development of woman's vocation. Despite the objective limits imposed by her special condition, she exercised a vast influence on the destiny of humanity and the transformation of society. Moreover, Marian doctrine can shed light on the multiple ways in which the life of grace promotes

---

[38] Bl. Pope Paul VI, *Marialis Cultus*, Apostolic Exhortation (February 2, 1974): 11.
[39] St. Proclus of Constantinople, *Homily* 5:3. MFC: p. 256.

woman's spiritual beauty. In view of the shameful exploitation that sometimes makes woman an object without dignity, destined for the satisfaction of base passions, Mary reaffirms the sublime meaning of feminine beauty, a gift and reflection of God's beauty.[40]

---

[40] Pope St. John Paul II, *General Audience* (November 29, 1995).

CHAPTER FIVE

Appeal to Vatican II

Some modern theologians make one last attempt at justifying their criticism of the dreaded Marian Maximalism by appealing to Vatican II. This, however, cannot be taken seriously by anyone who has taken the trouble to read the eighth chapter of *Lumen Gentium*, where it is stated:

> Committing herself whole-heartedly and impeded by no sin to God's saving will, [Mary] devoted herself totally, as a handmaid of the Lord, to the person and work of her Son, under and with him, serving the mystery of redemption, by the grace of Almighty God. Rightly, therefore, the Fathers see Mary not merely as passively engaged by God, but as freely cooperating in the work of man's salvation through faith and obedience. For, as St. Irenaeus says, she "being obedient, became the cause of salvation for herself and for the whole human race." […] This union of the mother with the Son in the work of salvation is made manifest from the time of Christ's virginal conception up to his death […]. Thus the Blessed Virgin advanced in her pilgrimage of faith, and faithfully persevered in her union with her Son unto the cross, where she stood, in keeping with the divine plan, enduring with her only begotten Son the intensity of his suffering, associating herself with his sacrifice in her mother's heart, and lovingly consenting to the immolation of this victim which was born of her. Finally, she was

given by the same Christ Jesus dying on the cross as a mother to his disciple, with these words: "Woman, behold thy son" (*Jn* 19:26–7).[41]

These words of Vatican II clearly echo the words of the saints already quoted (in no uncertain terms). Furthermore, even if the Council Fathers did not define any new Marian dogmas, they also stated clearly that they had no intention of closing the book on future Marian dogmas, or of restricting any Marian devotions:

> Wherefore this sacred synod, while expounding the doctrine on the Church, in which the divine Redeemer brings about our salvation, intends to set forth painstakingly both the role of the Blessed Virgin in the mystery of the Incarnate Word and the Mystical Body, and the duties of the redeemed towards the Mother of God, who is mother of Christ and mother of men, and most of all those who believe. It does not, however, intend to give a complete doctrine on Mary, nor does it wish to decide those questions which the work of theologians has not yet fully clarified. Those opinions therefore may be lawfully retained which are propounded in Catholic schools concerning her, who occupies a place in the Church which is the highest after Christ and also closest to us.[42]

This is especially true regarding Mary's cooperation with her Son Jesus in the work of salvation, as Pope St. John Paul II confirmed when he said:

> During the Council's sessions, many Fathers wished further to enrich Marian doctrine with other statements on Mary's role in the work of salvation. The particular context in which Vatican II's Mariological debate took place did not allow these wishes, although substantial and widespread, to be accepted. But the

---

[41] *Lumen Gentium* Chapter 8, Dogmatic Constitution on the Church (November 21, 1964): LG 56–8.

[42] LG 54.

Council's entire discussion of Mary remains vigorous and balanced. The topics themselves, *though not fully defined, received significant attention* [emphasis added] in the overall treatment.[43]

The Marian doctrine expressed succinctly in Chapter 8 of *Lumen Gentium* was in fact greatly influenced by the Franciscan school of Mariology. This school of Mariology, which is based on the scholastic theology of Bl. John Duns Scotus, had previously been suppressed by certain Neo-Thomistic currents early in the twentieth century, despite the fact that the Franciscan (Scotistic) thesis of the Absolute Joint Primacy of Jesus and Mary was given explicit papal endorsement in *Ineffabilis Deus* in 1854, when Bl. Pope Pius IX solemnly defined the dogma of Mary's Immaculate Conception. The original schema for *Lumen Gentium*, Chapter 8, was authored by the Franciscan theologian Fr. Carl Balić,[44] who was a *bona fide* Marian Maximalist; and despite the fact that the final text was the result of various compromises following a famous debate between the "Marian Maximalists" and the "Marian Minimalists" during the Council,[45] the substance of the original schema was preserved. Indeed, a careful comparison of the key texts of *Lumen Gentium* Chapter 8 regarding the joint predestination of Jesus and Mary and their cooperation in the work of salvation with the famous compendium of Franciscan

---

[43] Pope St. John Paul II, *General Audience* (December 13, 1995).

[44] According to Fr. Michael O'Carroll: "[Balić] served on the advisory committee on *Munificentissimus Deus* [in 1950, when Ven. Pope Pius XII solemnly defined the dogma of Mary's Assumption]. His contribution to Vatican II was capital. He drafted the first schema [on Mary], collaborated with Msgr. G. Philips on the second, issued various documents and assessments of reactions, and was consulted on the final draft which was to be accepted by the Fathers." Fr. Michael O'Carroll, C.S.Sp., *Theotokos: A Theological Encyclopedia of the Blessed Virgin Mary*, Wipf and Stock Publishers, Eugene, OR (2000): p. 68.

[45] For an insightful discussion of the context of the Vatican II debate on Mary and its repercussions, cf. Pope Benedict XVI (then Cardinal Joseph Ratzinger), "Thoughts on the Place of Marian Doctrine and Piety in Faith and Theology as a Whole" in *Mary—the Church at the Source*, Ignatius Press, San Francisco, CA (2005): pp. 19–36.

Marian Maximalism: *The Mystical City of God*, by Ven. Mother Mary of Agreda (d. 1665), shows *remarkable* correspondence.[46]

The influence of the Franciscan-Scotistic school of Mariology on Vatican II includes the insights of the saint who is perhaps the most maximal of Marian Maximalists (and most feared by Marian Minimalists): St. Maximilian Maria Kolbe. Bl. Pope Paul VI explicitly defended St. Maximilian Kolbe's Marian Maximalism in his beatification homily, when he said:

> Let no hesitation restrain our admiration and commitment to all that our new Blessed has left us as a heritage and an example, as if we too were distrustful of such an exaltation of Mary in view of two other theological movements, the Christological and ecclesiological, which seem to compete today with the Mariological. On the contrary, there is no competition, for in Father Kolbe's Mariology, Christ holds not only the first place but the only necessary and sufficient place in the economy of salvation. His love of the Church and its salvational mission was never forgotten either in his doctrinal outlook or in his apostolic aim. On the contrary, it is precisely from our Lady's complementary, subordinate role in regard to Christ's universal, saving design for man that she derives all of her prerogatives and greatness. [...] Therefore our Blessed is not to be reproved, nor the Church with him, because of their enthusiasm for the formal religious veneration of the Mother of God. This veneration with its rites and practices will never fully achieve the level it merits, nor the benefits it can bring precisely because of the mystery that unites her to Christ, and which finds fascinating documentation in the New Testament. The result will never be "Mariolatry," just as the sun will never be darkened by the moon; nor will the mission of salvation specifically entrusted to the ministry of the Church ever be distorted if the latter honors

---

[46] Cf. Fr. Enrique Llamas, O.C.D., *Mother Agreda and the Mariology of Vatican II*, Academy of the Immaculate, New Bedford, MA (2006): p. 45, 92.

in Mary an exceptional Daughter and Spiritual Mother. The characteristic aspect, if you like, and the original quality of Blessed Kolbe's devotion, of his "hyperdulia" to Mary, is the importance he attributes to it with regard to the present needs of the Church, the efficacy of her prophecy about the glory of the Lord and the vindication of the humble, the power of her intercession, the splendor of her exemplariness, the presence of her maternal charity. The Council confirmed us in these certainties, and now from heaven Father Kolbe is teaching us and helping us to meditate upon them and live them. This Marian profile of our new Blessed places him among the great saints and seers who have understood, venerated and sung the mystery of Mary.[47]

We note in particular Bl. Pope Paul VI's claim that our exaltation of Mary according to the example of the *Marian Maximalism*, or "hyperdulia," left to us as a heritage by St. Maximilian Kolbe *will never be* "Mariolatry." This confirms the words of the Master General of the Order of Preachers (the Dominicans), Fr. Aniceto Fernandez, at the Second Vatican Council:

When has a Catholic theologian or preacher ever, in the past or present, taught that Mary is equal to Her Son? Can one reasonably fear that in the future Catholic theologians and preachers will have the temerity to teach something so absurd? Why, therefore, should one advise them to cast off such an excess, when they are already so far from it? [...] Such recommendations not only do nothing in favor of Ecumenism, but rather greatly obstruct it.[48]

---

[47] Bl. Pope Paul VI, *Homily for the Beatification of Father Maximilian Maria Kolbe* (October 17, 1971).

[48] Fr. Aniceto Fernandez, O.P., as quoted by Fr. Alessandro M. Apollonio, F.I., "Mary Coredemptress: Mother of Unity—A probing glance at the hidden face of Vatican Council II" in *Mary at the Foot of the Cross—III: Mater Unitatis. Acts of the Third International Symposium on Marian Coredemption*, Academy of the Immaculate, New Bedford, MA (2003): pp. 349–50.

CHAPTER SIX

TRANSUBSTANTIATION
INTO THE IMMACULATE

We have already considered St. Maximilian Kolbe's use of the term *quasi-incarnate* to express, as far as human language permits, the inexpressible intimacy of the spousal union between the Blessed Virgin Mary and the Holy Spirit. We have also seen that, far from being heretical, this assertion directly combats radical feminism, and is perfectly in line with previous insights of Fr. Suarez and St. Bonaventure. Another term used by St. Maximilian Kolbe to express his *hyperdulia* for the Immaculate Virgin Mary is *transubstantiation*.[49]

Kolbe uses the expression *transubstantiation into the Immaculate* to describe the desired effect of total consecration to the Blessed Virgin Mary. The use of the same term that describes the complete substantial transformation of bread and wine into the Body and Blood of Christ to describe our complete substantial offering of ourselves to Mary is not by chance. Nor should it surprise us, since we commonly use the term "consecration" for both as well. In the case of the consecration of the Eucharist, nothing of the substances of the original bread and wine remain, but only the Body and Blood of Christ. In the case of the consecration of ourselves to Mary, we can say with St. Paul, "I no longer live, but Christ [living in Mary]

---

[49] SK 508.

lives in me."[50] In Kolbe's thought, it is only through transubstantiation of ourselves into Mary that we can attain transubstantiation of ourselves into Christ. This hinges on the Franciscan thesis, because God created the world for Mary, and Mary for Christ.[51] To quote the classical Aristotelian axiom: "What is first in intention is last in execution." Christ was the first in the mind of God before the creation of the world. The thought of Christ was "followed" immediately in the mind of God by the thought of the Blessed Virgin Mary, who was predestined by God's eternal decree to be the Mother of Christ. In the return of all created things to God the Father,[52] "the equal and contrary reaction," says St. Maximilian Kolbe, "proceeds inversely from that of creation." In creation, the Saint goes on to say, the action of God "proceeds from the Father through the Son and the Spirit, while in the return, by means of the Spirit, the Son becomes incarnate in [the Blessed Virgin Mary's] womb and through Him love returns to the Father."[53] So it was that Mary came before Christ in time, and so it is that we must be transubstantiated into Mary in order to be transubstantiated into Christ.

Just as Kolbe's Marian Maximalism or *hyperdulia* led him to call the Blessed Virgin Mary the Holy Spirit *quasi-incarnate* in order to supersede the ordinary term "union," his Marian Maximalism led him to say that we must be *transubstantiated into the Immaculate* in order to supersede the ordinary term of "consecration" (even "total consecration") to the Blessed Virgin Mary. To say less would be too little. To say enough about Mary would be impossible. How does one say more than what can possibly be said?[54] In St. Maximilian Kolbe's own words:

---

[50] *Gal* 2:20.

[51] St. Bernard of Clairvaux says that "for this Blessed Virgin, who was to be his Mother, God created the whole world": "Propter hanc totus mundus factus est," In *Salve Reg.* s. 3. GOM: pp. 367–8.

[52] Cf. *Jn* 1:1; 16:28.

[53] SK 1318.

[54] St. Bernardine of Siena says that "the greatness and dignity of this Blessed Virgin are such that God alone does, and can, comprehend it": "Tanta fuit perfectio

She is God's. She belongs to God in a perfect way to the extent that she is as if a part of the most Holy Trinity, although she is a finite creature. Moreover she is not only a "handmaid," a "daughter," a "property," a "possession," etc., but also the Mother of God! Here one is seized with giddiness… she is almost above God, as a mother is above her sons who must respect her. The Immaculate is a Spouse of the Holy Spirit in an unspeakable way… She has the same Son as the heavenly Father has. What an ineffable family! We belong to her, to the Immaculate. We are hers without limits, most perfectly hers; we are, as it were, herself. Through our mediation she loves the good God. With our poor heart she loves her divine Son. We become the mediators through whom the Immaculate loves Jesus. And Jesus, considering us her property and, as it were, a part of his beloved Mother, loves her in us and through us. What a lovely mystery![55]

Has St. Maximilian Kolbe finally gone too far when he claims that Mary "belongs to God in a perfect way to the extent that she is as if a part of the most Holy Trinity"? If so, he is not alone. We have already quoted the Jesuit Fr. Francisco Suarez (d. 1617), who said that "the dignity of Mother of God […] belongs in a certain way to the order of hypostatic union; for it intrinsically appertains to it; and has a necessary conjunction with it."[56] St. Bernardine of Siena (d. 1444) concurs that "to become the Mother of God, the Blessed Virgin had to be raised to a sort of equality with the divine Persons by an almost infinity of graces."[57] St. Peter Damian (d. 1072), Doctor of the Church, says: "Let every creature be silent and tremble,

Virginis, ut soli Deo cognoscenda reservetur," *Pro Fest. V. M.* s. 4, a. 3, c. 1. GOM: p. 363.

[55] SK 508.

[56] Fr. Francisco Suarez: "Dignitas matris est altioris ordinis; pertinet enim quodammodo ad ordinem unionis hypostaticae; illam enim intrinsice respicit, et cum illa necessariam conjunctionem habet," *De Incar.* P. 2, d. 1, s. 2. GOM: p. 364.

[57] St. Bernardine of Siena: "Quod femina conciperet et pareret Deum, oportuit eam elevari ad quamdam aequalitatem divinam, per quamdam infinitatem gratiarum," *Pro Fest. V. M.* s. 5, c. 12. GOM: p. 365.

and scarcely dare glance at the immensity of so great a dignity. God dwells in the Blessed Virgin, with whom he has the identity of one nature."[58] St. Alphonsus Liguori explains:

> And as children are, morally speaking, regarded one with their parents, so that their properties and honors are in common, it follows, says St. Peter Damian, that God, who dwells in creatures in different ways, dwelt in Mary in an especial way, and was singularly identified with her, making himself one and the same thing with her.[59]

Fr. Peter Damian Fehlner reflects on St. Maximilian Kolbe's claim that Mary is "quasi-part of the Trinity" as follows:

> In this universe of discourse the term *quasi-part of the Trinity* may be pondered with considerable profit. [...] Our Lady is not, emphatically is not in Kolbean language, a fourth or numerical addition to the Trinity, but a participant in the divine nature (as St. Peter uses this very terminology: 2 *Pet* 1:4) in a way absolutely unique: remaining a "pure creature," viz., a finite person,[60] she could not be more like, more within, closer and in no way distant from the three divine Persons as persons in their circumincessory life than in fact she is in virtue of the Immaculate Conception: "without compare in her love of God more than in all other saints."[61] In

---

[58] St. Peter Damian: "Hic taceat, et contremiscat omnis creatura, et vix audeat aspicere tantae dignitatis [et dignationis] immensitatem. ['Dominus tecum (Luc. 1),' inquit archangelus. Habitat in angelis Deus, sed non cum angelis, quia cum illis eiusdem non est essentiae.] Habitat Deus in Virgine, [habitat cum illa,] cum qua unius naturae habet identitatem," In *Nat. B. V. M.*, s. 1. GOM: p. 365. St. Peter Damian follows this striking statement with a beautiful Marian maximal principle: "This is the finest gold with which the throne is clothed, because God puts on the Virgin and in the Virgin He is put on in a way that could not possibly be better": "Hoc est ergo aurum fulvum nimis, quo thronus est vestitus, quia tali modo Deus Virginem induit et in Virgine indutus est, ut meliori non posset," In *Nat. B. V. M.*, s. 1, viz., *Sermo* 44: Migne Patrologia Latina (PL) 144, 738D.

[59] GOM: p. 365.

[60] SK 1305; 1320.

[61] SK 1305.

the words of St. Francis in his antiphon for the *Officium Passionis,* Mary is absolutely unique; or of St. Bonaventure, an order unto herself: other creatures may be compared and related to her; she, however, in relation to them is incomparable, which is to say in Scotistic terminology she enjoys with her Son an absolute primacy in the divine counsels of creation because by the grace of the Immaculate Conception she is daughter and handmaid of the Father, thus capable of being Mother of the Son and Coredemptrix, or still more succinctly, a "quasi-part" of the Trinity, as it were within the circle of triune love as spouse of the Holy Spirit, making it possible therefore for all her children to be so also. Hence, according to St. Maximilian, paraphrased in the terminology of the Seraphic Doctor, of all the creatures *prope Deum*, Mary in virtue of the Immaculate Conception is *propinquissima* incomparably and so absolutely, associated with Christ in the order of his absolute primacy and so capable of being His Mother in the strictest sense.[62]

When St. Maximilian claims that Mary "is almost above God, as a mother is above her sons who must respect her," he is simply invoking the traditional biblical typology of the Old Testament, when Solomon, who is a type of Christ, received his mother Bathsheba, who is a type of the Virgin-Mother. Solomon arose to meet her, bowed before her, and set up a throne for her at his right hand: "And she said to him: I desire one small petition of thee, do not put me to confusion. And the king said to her: My mother, ask: for I must not turn away thy face."[63] In the same way, St. Maximilian claims, the God-Man Jesus bows before His Mother with the respect and obedience of a true son, and He will not deny even her smallest petition. St. Maximilian is not alone in making such a claim:

---

[62] PDF: pp. 51–2.
[63] *1 Kings* 2:20.

"At the command of Mary, all obey, even God."[64] St. Bernardine fears not to utter this sentence; meaning, indeed, to say that God grants the prayers of Mary as if they were commands. And hence St. Anselm [or more probably Fr. Eadmer] addressing Mary says: "Our Lord, O most holy Virgin, has exalted thee to such a degree that by his favor all things that are possible to him should be possible to thee."[65] "For thy protection is omnipotent, O Mary,"[66] says Cosmas of Jerusalem. "Yes, Mary is omnipotent," repeats Richard of St. Laurence; "for the queen by every law enjoys the same privileges as the king. And as," he adds, "the power of the son and that of the mother is the same, a mother is made omnipotent by an omnipotent son."[67] "And thus," says St. Antoninus, "God has placed the whole Church, not only under the patronage, but even under the dominion of Mary."[68]

It was St. Paul himself who first pointed out the connection between our own transubstantiation into Christ and the transubstantiation of the Eucharistic bread and wine into the Body and Blood of Christ, when he said: "Now you are the Body of Christ, and individually members thereof. And God has appointed in the church, first apostles, second prophets, third teachers, then miracles, then gifts of healings, helps, administrations, various kinds of tongues," and "Because there is one bread, we who are many are one body, for we all partake of the one bread."[69] To the early Christian

---

[64] St. Bernardine of Siena: "Imperio Virginis omnia famulantur, etiam Deus," *Pro Fest. V. M.*, s. 5, c. 6. GOM: p. 181.

[65] Fr. Eadmer of Canterbury (previously ascribed to St. Anselm of Canterbury): "Te, Domina, Deus sic exaltavit, et omnia tibi secum possibilia esse donavit," *De Excell. Virg.*, c. 12. GOM: p. 181.

[66] St. Cosmas of Jerusalem (also known as Cosmas of Maiuma or Cosmas the Poet): "Omnipotens auxilium tuum, O Maria!," *Hymn 6*. GOM: p. 181.

[67] Fr. Richard of Saint-Laurent: "Eisdem privilegiis secundum leges gaudent Rex et Regina. Cum autem eadem sit potestas Matris et Filii ab omnipotente Filio omnipotens Mater est effecta," *De Laud. B. M. V.*, l. 4. GOM: p. 181.

[68] St. Antoninus of Florence: "Sub protectione ejus et dominio," P. 4, t. 15, c. 20, #2. GOM: p. 181.

[69] *1 Cor* 12:27–8; 10:17.

community, St. Paul's references to the Body of Christ must have brought the Eucharist immediately to mind, as it should to any Catholic today. But St. Paul tells us that the Body of Christ is the Church. And St. Francis tells us that the Church is Mary: the *Virgo Ecclesia Facta*—the Virgin-Made-Church.[70] Thus, when we use the expression *transubstantiation into the Immaculate* to refer to our consecration to Mary, we are also referring to our membership in the Church. In the words of Fr. Peter Damian Fehlner:

> The use of the term "transubstantiation" to describe the ultimate perfection of the union of love between divine and human will known as the Immaculate Conception recalls *a parte rei* the connection between the mystery of Mary on the one hand (and derivatively any type of Mariology, whether "Christo" or "Ecclesio" typical) and that of the Eucharist, whether in reference to the Head of the Church or in reference to the members of the Body of Christ perfectly incorporated into that Body.[71]

It follows that it is *only* by means of being transubstantiated into Mary, the *created Immaculate Conception*, that we can be united to God as she is uniquely united to God, being *transubstantiated with her into the uncreated Immaculate Conception*, the Holy Spirit. In virtue of this transubstantiation, we are possessed by the Immaculate, and we are thereby formed into a single community or Church sharing her personality: "radiant [...] without stain or wrinkle or any other blemish."[72] In the words of St. Maximilian Kolbe, "we become the mediators through whom the Immaculate loves Jesus. And Jesus, considering us her property and, as it were, a part of His beloved

---

[70] The title "Virgo Ecclesia Facta," or Virgin-Made-Church, is applied to the Blessed Virgin Mary by St. Francis of Assisi in his Salute to the Blessed Virgin Mary. Cf. Fr. Johannes Schneider, O.F.M., *Virgo Ecclesia Facta: The Presence of Mary in the Crucifix of San Damiano and in the Office of the Passion of St. Francis of Assisi*, Academy of the Immaculate, New Bedford, MA (2004): p. 70.

[71] PDF: p. 150.

[72] *Eph* 5:27.

Mother, loves her in us and through us." This co-mediation with the Blessed Virgin Mary and Jesus is precisely what defines our membership in the Church, as expressed by the Second Vatican Council. Fr. Peter Damian Fehlner expounds:

> The transubstantative action whereby the Eucharistic sacrifice and presence [are] realized, a sacrifice and presence directed to the perfect communion of the members of the Church and so to the realization of a Church *sine macula et sine ruga* (*Eph* 5:27), is by the will of God linked to the mediation of the Mother of God and to the virginal maternity of the preeminent member of the Church, the Immaculate Virgin. That link is not only *per Mariam* in the sense that without devotion to her and without her mediation we will not be properly and/or sufficiently disposed to be fully incorporated or transformed into Christ as members of His Body, but also *in Maria*, in the sense that when our participation in the mystery of the Eucharist as Sacrifice and Sacrament is all that it should be, then the communion of the members with the Head and with each other is Marian in mode. What St. Bonaventure calls the Marian mode of the Incarnation and Redemption, applied to the Church as its realization, might be called the Marian personality of the Church, or the triumph of the Immaculate Heart, effectively the transubstantiation of all the members of the Church into the Immaculate so as to share in the Spirit of the Father and the Son, to be one as they are one (cf. *Jn* 17), a transformation in this life consummated in the Eucharist.[73]

The transubstantiation of the elements of bread and wine into the Body and Blood of Jesus presupposes the mystery of the Incarnation and the unique maternal role of the Virgin Mary in that mystery, because, she, the created Immaculate Conception, is the Spouse of the Holy Spirit, the uncreated Immaculate Conception—in Eucharistic

---

[73] PDF: pp. 150–1.

terms a union which involves a kind of transubstantiation. So, too, the transformation of the members of the mystical body who eat of the Body and drink of the Blood of the Savior presupposes the transubstantiation of our spiritual Mother into the Holy Spirit, and so shares aspects of the mystery of the Immaculate Conception described as a kind of transubstantiation. The invocation or *epiklesis* of the Holy Spirit and Mary in the canon of the Mass is the liturgical expression of what St. Maximilian has is mind when he refers to our transubstantiation into Mary and so into the Holy Spirit. In this, once again, St. Maximilian Kolbe is not introducing "new" theology. Over 1,400 years earlier, St. Fulgentius Ruspensis (d. 535) said:

> When could holy Church ask more fittingly for the coming of the Holy Spirit (*Epiklesis*) than for the consecration of the Sacrifice, since she knows that her Head was born according to the flesh by this same Holy Spirit? For Mary was told by the word of an angel: the Holy Spirit shall come upon thee and the power of the Most High shall overshadow thee.[74]

From the earliest centuries, the Fathers of the Church have linked the mystery of the Incarnation (enfleshment) of the God-Man Jesus at the Annunciation to the mystery of the transubstantiation of bread and wine into the Body and Blood of the God-Man Jesus Christ in the Eucharist. In both of these mysteries, the three central protagonists are (1) Jesus, (2) the Holy Spirit, and (3) Mary. By the eternal and unchangeable will of the Heavenly Father, both mysteries are accomplished in the same way. That is, both mysteries are by one and the same decree of the Eternal Father *essentially* dependent on the unique maternal role of the Blessed Virgin Mary, the created Immaculate Conception, as well as on the power of the Holy Spirit her Spouse, the uncreated Immaculate Conception. In the words of St. John Damascene:

---

[74] St. Fulgentius Ruspensis, *Ad Monimum* 1, 2, 6, as quoted by Robert Moynihan, "The Glory of Jesus," *Inside the Vatican*, 13:9 (2005): p. 9.

Since we know that the Word has formed for Himself a body from His pure and immaculate Virgin Mother, is it therefore not conceivable that He can form for Himself a body from bread and blood from wine? "How shall this be," said the holy Virgin, "since I do not know man?" The archangel answered: "The Holy Spirit…" If you ask the manner (of consecration), it shall suffice for you to know that it is done by the Holy Spirit, in the same way as the Lord has formed for Himself flesh of the blood of the holy Mother of God.[75]

The Eucharist is no mere "symbol." Rather, as the true Body and true Blood of our Lord and Savior Jesus Christ, it is the concrete extension and prolongation of the Incarnation of Jesus Christ in time and space. In the words of Pope Leo XIII:

The Eucharist, according to the testimony of the holy Fathers, must be regarded as a certain continuation and expansion of the incarnation. For by it the substance of the incarnate Word is united with individual men; and the supreme Sacrifice of Calvary is in an admirable manner renewed.[76]

Just as the Eucharist is no mere "symbol," so the historical event that it prolongs and extends—that is, the Incarnation of Jesus Christ—is no merely "symbolic" event, but the concrete realization of God's eternal plan to be united in the most intimate way possible with humanity by becoming a God-Man. This historical event, foreseen in eternity but realized in the fullness of time, occurred in the womb of a particular and unique woman: the Blessed Virgin Mary. If the transubstantiation of the Eucharistic elements of bread and wine into the Body and Blood of Jesus comes about as St. John Damascene tells us "in the same way as the Lord has formed for Himself flesh of the blood of the holy Mother of God," by the power of the Holy Spirit,

---

[75] St. John Damascene, *De Fide Orthodoxa* 4, 13, as quoted by ibid.: pp. 8–9.
[76] Pope Leo XIII, *Mirae Caritatis* (May 28, 1902), as quoted by ibid.: p. 8.

then our own transubstantiation into the Mystical Body of Christ must come about in the same way. That is, we must be transubstantiated into the Body of Christ "of the blood of the holy Mother of God," the created Immaculate Conception, by the power of the Holy Spirit her Spouse, the uncreated Immaculate Conception.

As Bl. Pope Paul VI said, the reason we can never venerate Mary at the level she merits is because of "the mystery that unites her to Christ." According to the theology of Bl. John Duns Scotus, God created the universe only on condition of the fact that He would become man in the Incarnation. Thus, the Incarnation of Jesus was decreed in eternity. Since the very fact of the Incarnation of Jesus is bound to the existence of the Virgin in whom He would be conceived, Mary, the Mother of God, was present in God's plan *before* God created the first man, Adam, and the first woman, Eve; before the creation of the world, and indeed even before the fall of the angels, and before the existence of sin. That is why Mary is the only created being whose existence actually belongs to the order of the hypostatic union (which is the interior life of God), because she was uniquely present in God's thought in eternity, and in this way she was with Him before He had created any other thing. That is why the Catholic Church uses this reading from Proverbs in the Liturgy of the Hours for Mary's feast days:

> The Lord begot me, the firstborn of his ways, the forerunner of his prodigies of long ago; From of old I was poured forth, at the first, before the earth. When there were no depths I was brought forth, when there were no foundations or springs of water; Before the mountains were settled into place, before the hills, I was brought forth; While as yet the earth and the fields were not made, nor the first clods of the world. When he established the heavens I was there, when he marked out the vault over the face of the deep; When he made firm the skies above, when he fixed fast the foundations of the earth; When he set for the sea its limit, so that the

waters should not transgress his command; Then was I beside him as his craftsman, and I was his delight day by day, playing before him all the while, playing on the surface of his earth.[77]

The Church recognizes both Jesus *and* Mary as the one who is speaking in this passage of Proverbs, as confirmed by Bl. Pope Pius IX:

> And hence the very words with which the Sacred Scriptures speak of Uncreated Wisdom and set forth his eternal origin, the Church, both in its ecclesiastical offices and in its liturgy, has been wont to apply likewise to the origin of the Blessed Virgin, inasmuch as God, by one and the same decree, had established the origin of Mary and the Incarnation of Divine Wisdom.[78]

---

[77] *Prov* 8:22–31.

[78] Bl. Pope Pius IX, *Ineffabilis Deus*, Apostolic Constitution (December 8, 1854).

CHAPTER SEVEN

A MARIAN MAXIMAL PRINCIPLE

We have witnessed in the writings of the saints the *hyperdulia* or maximality of praise with which they acclaim the Blessed Virgin Mary. Still, a question remains: Is this hyperdulia merely the "language of emotional love" or "pious devotional language"? Is it truly justifiable to use a principle of Marian Maximalism as a basis for Mariological reflection, or even to define such a principle dogmatically (which was essentially done, for example, in the dogma of Mary's Immaculate Conception)? Let us seek an answer to this question by considering an analogy with what many consider to be the most objective (and even *a priori*) of sciences: mathematics.

St. Maximilian Kolbe, a true son of St. Francis, used analogy with the physical world to gain insight into the spiritual world, and in doing so he was perfectly justified, as St. Thomas Aquinas says:

> For, according to its manner of knowing in the present life, the intellect depends on the sense for the origin of knowledge; and so those things that do not fall under the senses cannot be grasped by the human intellect except in so far as the knowledge of them is gathered from sensible things.[79]

---

[79] St. Thomas Aquinas, *Summa Contra Gentiles, Book One: God*, translated, with an introduction and notes, by Anton C. Pegis, F.R.S.C., University of Notre Dame Press, Notre Dame, IN (1975): p. 64.

Indeed, the use of analogy to attempt to understand the actions of God is the basis of all scholastic theology, both Thomistic and Scotistic. When St. Maximilian Kolbe refers to "the equal and contrary reaction" in the return of all created things to God the Father, he is employing an analogy with Newtonian mechanics,[80] specifically the proposition known as Newton's third law: "For every action force there is an equal-and-opposite reaction force." Thus, we may visualize the image being employed by St. Maximilian Kolbe as two "bodies" in equilibrium, which meet at a single point of contact at the "center" of salvation history. The two contacting bodies represent heaven and earth; the Uncreated and created orders; God and His creation. The contact point is the Immaculate Conception: the Vertex of Love, the Immaculate Virgin Mary.[81] In the words of St. Maximilian Kolbe:

> In the union of the Holy Spirit with her, not only does love bind these two beings, but the first of them [the Holy Spirit] is all the love of the Most Holy Trinity, while the second [the Blessed Virgin Mary] is all the love of creation, and thus in that union heaven is joined to earth, the whole heaven with the whole earth, the whole of Uncreated Love with the whole of created love: this is *the vertex of love.*[82]

Just as Kolbe used physics in the created order to find an analogy with the Uncreated order, so we may use mathematics. In the fields of mathematical logic and set theory, which essentially study properties of general and unique existence among sets of numbers on the real line or points in geometric space, the use of maximal principles is ubiquitous. This concept extends to all fields in mathematics. For

---

[80] St. Maximilian Kolbe liked physics. He once consulted with one of his physics professors on how he could build "ballistic missiles" that could drop packets of Marian publications on cities around the world more quickly than they could be delivered by regular mail.

[81] Cf. Figure 1 in Jonathan A. Fleischmann, "The Vertex of Love," *Homiletic & Pastoral Review* (October 8, 2012).

[82] SK 1318.

example, there is the "Hausdorff maximal principle" in set theory (which is equivalent to the so-called "axiom of choice"), the "greatest fixed point" or "least fixed point" in complexity theory, the "limit point" in topology, and the well-known "limit" in calculus. An interesting property of the mathematical theory of sets is that, even when a unique maximal element or set can be defined in a given well-defined subset of the mathematical universe of sets, it is always possible to prove that a larger and mathematically incomparable element or set exists, by a process called *diagonalization* due to Georg Cantor (d. 1918). This process is the basis of the modern mathematical theory of infinite sets (leading to infinite cardinal and ordinal numbers), and it was used by Kurt Gödel in 1931 to show that mathematical logic cannot prove its own consistency (the argument is similar to the classical "liar's paradox"). Thus was destroyed the (somewhat naïve) program of the positivist philosophical school of the early twentieth century.

Now, it is a fact that mathematical logic is very limited when applied outside the field of mathematics. However, I would maintain that there is a clear analogy between maximal principles in the fields of mathematical logic and set theory and the created order in the following sense. If there is a unique member of the created order that is indeed greater than any other member—and we know this member is the Blessed Virgin Mary—this fact cannot *in any way* limit the greatness of God, who "diagonalizes" out of every set we can construct due to His essential transcendence. Indeed, in St. Anselm's famous (so-called "ontological") proof of God's existence, he uses precisely this property of God's essential transcendence to show that God's existence is a logical necessity, in an argument that in many ways prefigured the diagonalization arguments used by Cantor and Gödel. Since it has great bearing on what we wish to say about the Blessed Virgin Mary, let us consider St. Anselm's proof in more detail.

St. Anselm's proof hinges on the fact that God is "that than which nothing greater can be thought."[83] While St. Anselm's argument has been criticized by many since the time it was written (c. 1077), including St. Thomas Aquinas and Immanuel Kant, in modern times it is almost always represented in the form in which it was reformulated by Gottfried Wilhelm Leibniz (d. 1716), which invokes the modal logic of "necessity" and "possibility."[84] Recently, however, St. Anselm's argument has received renewed attention in its *original* form, and it is believed that it is essentially a *diagonalization* argument rather than an argument based on modal logic that actually lies at the heart of his proof.[85] This interpretation of St. Anselm's argument is supported by the fact that St. Anselm does not use the modalities of necessity or possibility to argue for God's existence in his *Proslogion*, but only introduces this terminology in his *Responsio* to the critiques made by Gaunilo in *Pro Insipiente*.[86]

We will soon argue that it is *logically impossible* to give the Blessed Virgin Mary too much praise. As we have already indicated, central to this argument is the fact that God's transcendence is absolute, which results in His "diagonalization" out of any definable

---

[83] St. Anselm of Canterbury: "aliquid quo nihil maius cogitari potest," *Proslogion*, 2.

[84] The reformulation of St. Anselm's argument in terms of the modalities of necessary and possible existence due to Leibniz (using possible world semantics) was formalized using modern symbolic modal logic by Kurt Gödel (d. 1978), who believed the argument to be valid, though such a modal treatment may not be what St. Anselm himself intended. For a version of the modal argument that corrects some serious flaws in Gödel's version, cf. C. Anthony Anderson, "Some Emendations of Gödel's Ontological Proof," *Faith and Philosophy*, 7 (1990): pp. 291–303.

[85] Cf. Ian Logan, *Reading Anselm's Proslogion: The History of Anselm's Argument and its Significance Today* (Ashgate New Critical Thinking in Religion, Theology, and Biblical Studies), Ashgate Publishing Company, Burlington, VT (2009). Subsequent citations are abbreviated RAP.

[86] In *Pro Insipiente* ("On Behalf of the Fool"), St. Anselm's contemporary Gaunilo attempts to use the same logical argument used by St. Anselm in his *Proslogion* to prove the actual existence of an imaginary island, and hence to prove by *reductio ad absurdum* that the logic of St. Anselm's argument is fallacious. St. Anselm replied to the critiques of *Pro Insipiente* in his *Responsio*. It was St. Anselm's wish that all publications of his *Proslogion* should include both Gaunilo's *Pro Insipiente* and his *Responsio*.

(i.e., expressible) set or category. This absolute transcendence of God is also the crux of the "diagonalization argument" inherent in *any* version of St. Anselm's "ontological" proof, even when the proof is expressed in terms of the modalities of contingent and necessary existence. This conclusion is supported by the following analysis of Fr. Peter Damian Fehlner:

> What is the primary point of the demonstration of God in the Augustinian-Anselmian-Bonaventurian-Scotistic tradition? Not another existent, but the clear differentiation between contingent and necessary existence by recognizing the difference between finite (created, effectible) being or essence and infinite, non-effectible, uncreated essence. When we encounter the HOLY NAME [JESUS—I AM WHO AM, who saves you], we have a direct, even if now by faith, perception of that difference, and why: the eternal generation of the Son from the Father, revealed in His temporal generation, virginally, by the VIRGIN. The love of that NAME includes a knowledge transcending even the most perfect, natural knowledge; this because, like Mary, we keep in our hearts (memory) all that has been said about Him, pondering and loving. It is in this Trinitarian context that we begin to grasp the reality of the person as formally distinct from nature: *existentia incommunicabilis naturae intellectualis*, above all in the three divine Persons, the difference between personal and non-personal being and the link between the so-called "ontological" proof and the proof of God's existence from conscience ([as can be found, for example, in St. Bonaventure's] *Itinerarium* and [in the Grammar of Assent of Bl. John Henry] Newman).[87]

As an example of such a "diagonalization argument" used by St. Anselm, consider his proof of the following claim in the *Responsio*:

---

[87] Fr. Peter Damian Fehlner, F.I., *The Triple Way or The Kindling of Love by St. Bonaventure of Bagnoregio, Doctor Seraphicus*, Academy of the Immaculate, New Bedford, MA (2012): p. 216. Subsequent citations are abbreviated TTW.

"something than which a greater cannot be thought, which exists by such certain logic and truth, cannot be thought not to exist." If we let X = "something than which a greater cannot be thought," then Ian Logan explains:

> If one tries to think that X does not exist, then a contradiction arises between what is thought and the active process of thinking it; what Coreth called "a contradiction in performance." It is obvious that there is a sense in which X can be thought not to exist, but thinking in this way is of no significance. It is simply employing the concept without content, or, if one uses the concept with content, it is knowingly to postulate a contradiction. Anselm has made explicit this "contradiction in performance" by means of an analysis of the act of thinking about God, and not simply by an analysis of the concept of God.[88]

This notion of a "contradiction in performance," or *performative contradiction*, which Ian Logan claims is central to St. Anselm's "ontological" proof, is essentially the same as the so-called "diagonalization argument" used by Kurt Gödel in his proofs of the "incompleteness theorems" for mathematical logic.[89] Thus, while much maligned

---

[88] RAP: p. 121.

[89] To prove his incompleteness theorems, Gödel constructs a purely mathematical sentence (a statement regarding arithmetic) in such a way that the sentence essentially says "I am not provable." To be precise, the rules of formal logic are "encoded" into mathematical operations in such a way that our understanding of the meaning of this sentence and the rules of mathematical logic result in our understanding that this is what the sentence "says," because of the way in which the sentence was constructed, even though this "Gödel sentence" itself is just a very long and complicated (but otherwise unmysterious) mathematical assertion regarding the arithmetic of prime numbers. Thus, the first incompleteness theorem states that there exist formal, mathematical sentences regarding arithmetic (expressed in any given formal system) that are true but cannot be proven. This is because, if mathematical logic is sound (that is, consistent), then it cannot prove the Gödel sentence, because that would be a performative contradiction. This also implies that the Gödel sentence itself is true (based on our understanding of its meaning), because the sentence itself "says" that it is not provable. From this it follows (somewhat nontrivially) that mathematical logic cannot prove its own consistency, which is Gödel's second incompleteness theorem. Cf. Torkel Franzén,

by history, St. Anselm's use of a "maximal principle" as a basis for theological reflection may indeed turn out to be logically valid.[90]

Given this fact, it is very interesting to note that St. Anselm, the *Marian Doctor*, also formulated a similar maximal principle for the Blessed Virgin Mary, who "shines with a purity greater than which none can be imagined, except for God's."[91] Indeed, the same maximal principle is found in *Lumen Gentium*, where we read that Mary "occupies a place in the Church which is the highest after Christ." Far from being either dangerous or merely devotional, such a maximal principle is both precise and objective. Moreover, just as St. Anselm successfully used a maximal principle for God to argue for the logical necessity of God's existence, I believe that such a maximal principle can be successfully used as a basis for Mariological reflection. Bl. John Duns Scotus, the *Subtle Doctor*, used just such a Marian maximal principle in his famous (and successful) argument in favor of Mary's Immaculate Conception.

Gödel's Theorem: An Incomplete Guide to Its Use and Abuse, A K Peters, Wellesley, MA (2005).

[90] This was the opinion of Bl. John Duns Scotus, who formulated the so-called *coloratio Anselmi*, or "nuanced" version of St. Anselm's "ontological" argument, in which Duns Scotus explicitly defends St. Anselm's argument against the critique (made by St. Thomas Aquinas) of the logical error of passing from the modality of possibility (*posse*) to the modality of actuality (*esse*). This was also the opinion of Bl. John Henry Newman, who likewise defended both the arguments of St. Anselm and Bl. John Duns Scotus against the critiques of Immanuel Kant. In the words of Fr. Peter Damian Fehlner: "Duns Scotus is often accused today of being a practitioner of 'onto-theology,' an attempt to base our natural knowledge of God not on factual, extra-mental reality, but primarily on an idea which, during the high Middle Ages, was called a proof of existence based on an invalid illation by the critics of St. Anselm [...]. There are various, often complex, replies which can be made to this objection. But a very simple one is this: the critics overlook the importance of the so-called 'anthropological' or phenomenological proof first associated with the name of St. Augustine, quite clearly present in the analyses of St. Bonaventure, and the central proof developed, at least implicitly, by Card. [Bl. John Henry] Newman in modern times, in rebuttal to the position of Kant and his rejection of the 'ontological' proof." TTW: p. 217.

[91] St. Anselm of Canterbury, *De Conceptu Virginali et de Originali Peccato*, 18.

His principle is this: in speaking of Mary, "one should attribute to her whatever is objectively most 'excellent,' provided that it be not contrary to the authority of the Church and of Scripture."[92]

In this, as in everything, Bl. John Duns Scotus is a true son of St. Francis and a worthy intellectual disciple of St. Bonaventure, the *Seraphic Doctor*, who said: "No one can be too devout to Mary."[93] The distinctive Marian Maximalism of the *Seraphic Father* St. Francis himself is attested in his biography written by St. Bonaventure. There we read that not only did St. Francis surround Mary with love beyond what can be spoken or thought, but he also worked to inflame his friars with the same love for the Mother of Jesus, who made the Lord of Glory our Brother:[94]

> Francis surrounded the Mother of the Lord Jesus Christ with an ineffable [*indicibili*: inexpressible or unspeakable] love, because the Mother of Jesus made the Lord of Majesty our Brother, and through her we have obtained mercy. Confiding in her especially after Jesus, [Francis] made her Advocate of himself and of his [friars], and in her honor he devotedly fasted from the feast of the Apostles Peter and Paul to the feast of the Assumption [from June 29 to August 15]. [Francis] was bound by an inseparable bond of love to the angelic spirits burning with wonderful love rising in praise to God and inflaming the souls of the elect. Thus, to deepen the [friars'] devotion [to the Virgin Mother of God, the Queen of Angels] he insisted on their fasting and praying continually for forty days after the Assumption of the glorious Virgin [from August 15 to September 29, the feast of St. Michael the Archangel].[95]

---

[92] Fr. Ruggero Rosini, O.F.M., *Mariology of Blessed John Duns Scotus*, translated by Fr. Peter Damian Fehlner, F.I., Academy of the Immaculate, New Bedford, MA (2008): p. 73. Subsequent citations are abbreviated JDS.

[93] St. Bonaventure: "Mariae nullus nimis potest esse devotus," *III Sent.*, d. 3, p. 1, a. 1, q. 1 ad 4.

[94] Cf. *Ps* 24.

[95] St. Bonaventure: "Matrem Domini Jesu Christi indicibili complectebatur [Franciscus] amore, eo quod [Mater Jesu] Dominum majestatis fratrem nobis

Indeed, the Marian maximal principle of the entire Franciscan school is well represented in a work previously ascribed to St. Bonaventure, the *Speculum Beatae Mariae Virginis*, written by his contemporary Fr. Conrad of Saxony (d. 1279), which is one of the first Franciscan works to expressly cite St. Francis' use of the Marian title "Spouse of the Holy Spirit."[96] There we read that "to be the Mother of God is the greatest grace that can be conferred on a creature. It is such that God could make a greater world, a greater heaven, but that he cannot exalt a creature more than by making her his Mother."[97] Thus, in the words of St. Bonaventure, since "[the Blessed Virgin] is above all orders [hierarchies], she constitutes in herself an order."[98]

St. Albert the Great (d. 1280), the *Universal Doctor*, expresses the same Marian maximal principle when he says that "to be the Mother of God is the highest dignity after that of being God" and

---

effecerit, et per eam simus misericordiam simus consecuti. In ipsa post Christum praecipue fidens, eam sui ac suorum advocatam constituit et ad honorem ipsius a festo Apostolorum Petri et Pauli usque ad festum Assumptionis [Matris] devotissime ieiunabat [a die 29 Junii ad diem 15 Augusti]. Angelicis spiritibus ardentibus igne mirifico ad excedendum in Deum et electorum animas inflammandas inseparabalis erat amoris vinculo copulatus et ob devotionem ipsorum ab Assumptione Virginis gloriosae et ob devotionem ipsorum quadraginta diebus ieiunans orationi iugiter insistebat [a die 15 Augusti ad diem 29 Septembris]." *Legenda Maior Sancti Francisci*, ch. 9, par. 3, in *S. Bonaventurae Opera Omnia*, Ad Claras Aquas 1898, vol. VIII, p. 530 b.

[96] The title "Spouse of the Holy Spirit" is applied to the Blessed Virgin Mary by St. Francis of Assisi in the Antiphon "Sancta Maria Virgo" for his *Office of the Passion*. Cf. Fr. Johannes Schneider, O.F.M., *Virgo Ecclesia Facta: The Presence of Mary in the Crucifix of San Damiano and in the Office of the Passion of St. Francis of Assisi*, Academy of the Immaculate, New Bedford, MA (2004): p. 105.

[97] Fr. Conrad of Saxony (previously ascribed to St. Bonaventure): "Quid mirabilius quam esse Dei Matrem? ipsa est qua majorem Deus facere non posset: majorem mundum posset facere Deus, majus coelum; majorem matrem quam matrem Dei non posset facere," *Spec. B. M. V.*, lect. 9, 10. GOM: p. 367. Fr. Conrad of Saxony's use of "possible world semantics" to state the quintessential Franciscan Marian maximal principle may vindicate the use of modern, symbolic modal logic (which is based on possible world semantics—a special case of so-called Kripke semantics) in formalizations of maximal principles such as this one and the one used in St. Anselm's "ontological" argument in the *Proslogion*, provided we keep in mind with Fr. Peter Damian Fehlner that "without the 'anthropological' argument from conscience [e.g., that of Bl. John Henry Newman], the 'ontological' argument has no clear, primary setting outside mental constructs." TTW: p. 220.

[98] St. Bonaventure, *II Sent.*, d. 9, q. 7. TTW: p. 85.

"Mary could not have been more closely united to God without becoming God."[99] St. Thomas Aquinas (d. 1274), the *Angelic Doctor*, says the same thing as his mentor St. Albert the Great, only replacing the word "dignity" with "grace" (and clearly inspiring the wording of *Lumen Gentium*):

> The Blessed Virgin Mary was the nearest possible to Christ; for from her it was that he received his human nature, and therefore she must have obtained a greater plenitude of grace from him than all others.[100]

To summarize all of the Marian maximal principles so far, we may borrow the language of St. Anselm to say that, by God's eternal decree, *Mary has a glory greater than which none can be imagined, except for God's.* The glory of Mary includes her purity (St. Anselm), her "place" (*Lumen Gentium*), her dignity (St. Albert the Great), her union with God (St. Albert the Great, St. Peter Damian, St. Alphonsus Liguori), her grace (St. Thomas Aquinas), her intercessory power on behalf of sinners, her humility, compassion, wisdom, strength, beauty, and indeed whatever is objectively most "excellent" (Bl. John Duns Scotus). The formulation of our Marian maximal principle is almost exactly that of St. Lawrence of Brindisi (d. 1619), the *Apostolic Doctor*, who said as he contemplated St. John's vision of the Woman clothed with the sun:

> How was it possible for the Virgin not to shine with sun-like splendor when she carried Christ, the Sun of infinite light, in her virginal womb? If God enclosed the sun in an immense crystal vase, would not that vase seem to be clothed with the very sun?

---

[99] St. Albert the Great: "Immediate post esse Deum, est esse Matrem Dei"; "Magis Deo conjungi, nisi fieret Deus, non potuit," *Super Miss. r.*, ad 3, q. 140. GOM: p. 365.

[100] St. Thomas Aquinas: "Beata autem Virgo Maria propinquissima Christo fuit, quia ex ea accepit humanam naturam; et ideo prae caeteris majorem debuit a Christo gratiae plenitudinem obtinere," *Summa Theologiæ* III, Q. 27, Art. 5. GOM: p. 364.

In this way the sun clothes and adorns with its brilliant rays the pure substance of heaven, which it surrounds and engulfs. Just as the sun, glowing within the crystal on every side with its light, so the heavenly Virgin is clothed with Christ, the Sun of justice and glory. This divine vision signifies that, as bride and mother, the most holy Virgin shares in the glory of Christ and God to so high a degree that no greater sharing or participation can be thought of.[101]

How does one apply such a Marian maximal principle? It would seem that Mary's glories are limitless, and indeed, as far as words can express, they are. Central to Mary's *subsisting relation to God* (which by definition is her *very identity as a person*)[102] is the Divine Maternity, ordained by the Father in eternity, by which God has made Mary *one and the same thing with Himself* (according to St. Peter Damian and St. Alphonsus Liguori), a *quasi-part of the Trinity* (according to St. Maximilian Kolbe), included her in the *hypostatic order* (according to Fr. Suarez), and made her an *order unto herself* (according to St. Bonaventure). Yet, paradoxically, despite the infinite exaltation of Mary by God, Mary is not God, because Mary is created. As St. Maximilian Kolbe reminds us:

Who are you, O Immaculate Conception? Not God, for God has no beginning. Not Adam, made from the dust of the earth. Not Eve, drawn from Adam's body. Nor is she the Incarnate Word who already existed from all eternity and who was conceived, but is not really a "conception." Prior to their conception the children of Eve do not exist, hence they can more properly be called "conceptions"; and yet you, O Mary, differ from them too, because they

---

[101] St. Lawrence of Brindisi, *Mariale*, S. 3, "On the Inestimable Treasures of the Virgin Mother of God," as quoted by Stanley Gahan, O.F.M. Cap., "'The Woman Clothed with the Sun' According to St. Lawrence of Brindisi," *The American Ecclesiastical Review*, The Catholic University of America Press, Washington, DC (1962): pp. 395–402. Subsequent citations are abbreviated WOM.

[102] Cf. St. Thomas Aquinas, *ST* I, Q. 29, Art. 4.

are conceptions contaminated by original sin, whereas you are the one and only Immaculate Conception.[103]

Those who think that Mary is worshiped as God by the saints and Doctors of the Catholic Church probably understand quite correctly the place that is given *Mary* by these saints and Doctors of the Catholic Church, but they fail to understand the unspeakable transcendence of *God Himself*.[104] St. Thomas Aquinas says in regard to the Blessed Virgin's dignity as Mother of God: "Which dignity is in a certain manner infinite, inasmuch as God is an infinite good; in this respect, then, she could not have been made greater."[105] Thus, it is a case of two infinities: the Mother of God and God Himself. Both infinities are incommensurate with all else that exists, but they are still incommensurate with each other—though, at the same time, as intimately close as a mother is to her son. It is precisely for this reason that our knowledge of God (as finite creatures) actually *depends* on our knowledge of Mary. Reflecting on St. Anselm's Marian maximal principle, Fr. Peter Damian Fehlner says:

> With this we catch a glimpse of the intimate link between dogmatic metaphysics centering on the Trinity (infinity of God) and the Incarnation (cf. ch. 6, *Itinerarium*) and the mystery of Mary (Immaculate Conception), and of why metaphysics must

---

[103] SK 1318.

[104] Consider, for example, the "ontological" proof of God's existence due to the Islamic philosopher Mulla Sadra (d. 1640), which is based on the idea that observable or knowable existence is a singular reality that is graded in intensity on a scale of perfection, and that scale must have a limit point—which is a point of greatest intensity of perfection—and God is that point, and therefore God exists. However, this puts God in a place that more properly belongs to the Blessed Virgin Mary, since she is, in fact, the maximal element on a scale of perfection inside the set of knowable existence. God Himself transcends such a set (or in other words, God "diagonalizes" out of such a set), because, as St. John Damascene teaches us, God is essentially unknowable. Cf. St. John Damascene, *An Exposition of the Orthodox Faith:* Bk. 1, Ch. 1.

[105] St. Thomas Aquinas: "Beata Virgo ex hoc quod est Mater Dei, habet quondam dignitatem infinitam ex bono infinito, quod est Deus: et ex hac parte, non potest aliquid fieri melius," *ST* I, Q. 25, Art. 6. GOM: p. 366.

be Marian to be fully genuine. It is no accident that the subtle Doctor par excellence (Bl. John Duns Scotus) is also the Marian Doctor [with St. Anselm], and that this link should be reflected in the "alliance" of the two hearts. The relation may also be expressed in terms reflecting *The Triple Way* [of St. Bonaventure]: there is no fruition of the greatness (infinite goodness) of God, except via the purity of the Immaculate Heart. Only the pure of heart shall see God (*Mt* 5:8). That is why they, and only they, are blessed. With this, we see the importance of purity for the memory as heart of the first way known as the purgative way since the fall of Adam, because purity is only possible via purgation. But even had Adam not sinned, we clearly see in the memory or heart of Mary that perfect purity which is the starting point of a holy and blessed life, one concluding in being the Mother of God.[106]

Furthermore, St. John Damascene teaches us that there are truths which, even if *knowable*, are still *essentially unspeakable*, because they transcend our finite language (the theological "equivalent" of Gödel's incompleteness theorem):

> It is necessary, therefore, that one who wishes to speak or to hear of God should understand clearly that alike in the doctrine of Deity and in that of the Incarnation, neither are all things unutterable nor all utterable; neither all unknowable nor all knowable. But the knowable belongs to one order, and the utterable to another; just as it is one thing to speak and another thing to know. Many of the things relating to God, therefore, that are dimly understood cannot be put into fitting terms, but on things above us we cannot do else than express ourselves according to our limited capacity.[107]

---

[106] TTW: p. 213.

[107] St. John Damascene, *An Exposition of the Orthodox Faith*, Translated by E.W. Watson and L. Pullan, from Nicene and Post-Nicene Fathers, Second Series, Vol. 9, edited by Philip Schaff and Henry Wace, Christian Literature Publishing Co., Buffalo, NY (1899): Bk. 1, Ch. 2.

The glories of God and the glories of Mary, both infinite by God's design (albeit incommensurate) belong in varying degrees to the categories of unspeakable and unknowable truth. God's glory is essentially unknowable (to us as finite creatures), because, as St. Anselm argues, not only is God "that than which a greater cannot be thought," but He is also *greater* than that which can be thought."[108] It follows, then, that God's glory is unutterable as well. However, while perhaps knowable in essence (because she is a finite creature), Mary's glory is nevertheless essentially unutterable. This can be proven from our Marian maximal principle as follows: Suppose we utter any statement regarding Mary's glory (e.g., "Mary is …"). Then we could utter a greater statement (e.g., "Mary is greater than …"). Since such a statement is utterable, it follows that Mary's glory would still be less than God's. But then Mary's glory could be imagined to be greater, and still less than God's, which contradicts the principle that *Mary has a glory greater than which none can be imagined, except for God's*. Therefore, *Mary's glory must be unutterable*. It does not follow, however, that because Mary's glory and God's glory are both unutterable, they are therefore equal! Nevertheless, because Mary's glory is truly unutterable, it is impossible to concretely limit her glory in any way, beyond saying precisely that she is "not God," without making her glory less than what it actually is (which is what God made it, and what He wanted it to be from eternity). Hence, with perfect accuracy and objectivity (and no pious exaggeration!), we may proclaim the concise Marian maximal principle with all the saints in glory: *De Maria numquam satis*—About Mary we can never say enough!

---

[108] St. Anselm argues thus: "Therefore, O Lord, not only are you that than which a greater cannot be thought, but you are also greater than that which can be thought. For, since such a thing can be imagined to be, if you are not this selfsame thing, then it is possible to imagine something greater than you; That cannot happen": "Ergo, Domine, non solum es quo maius cogitari nequit, sed es quiddam maius quam cogitari possit. Quoniam namque valet cogitari esse aliquid huiusmodi: si tu non es hoc ipsum, potest cogitari aliquid maius te; quod fieri nequit," *Proslogion*, 15.

Indeed, the friend and disciple of St. Anselm of Canterbury, Fr. Eadmer of Canterbury (d. after 1126), said precisely this:

O Mary, what can we say? With what organ of speech or with what joy of heart could we express how much we owe you? Yes, Lady, whatever we may have understood or conceived in our minds or spoken with our mouths, it is insignificant and as nothing compared with what we owe you in fairness. For you were preordained in the mind of God, before every other creature, the most chaste among all women, so that you might give birth to God as true man, born of your flesh, and so that, having become the glorious Queen of heaven, you might rule over all things … and prepare for a fallen world the entry into recovery and the prize of eternal life.[109]

These words of Fr. Eadmer echo those of St. Proclus of Constantinople, who said:

O man, run through all creation with your thought, and see if there exists anything comparable to or greater than the holy Virgin, Mother of God. Circle the whole world, explore all the oceans, survey the air, question the skies, consider all the unseen powers, and see if there exists any other similar wonder in the whole creation […]. Count, then, the portents, and wonder at the superiority of the Virgin: she alone, in a way beyond words, received into her bridal chamber him before whom all creation kneels with fear and trembling.[110]

In this context, it is surprising and sad to note that in his otherwise excellent book, *Mary in the Middle Ages*, Fr. Luigi Gambero refers several times to Fr. Eadmer's "tendency to exaggerate" (he makes

---

[109] Fr. Eadmer of Canterbury, *De Conceptione Sanctae Mariae*, as quoted by Fr. Luigi Gambero, S.M., *Mary in the Middle Ages*, Ignatius Press, San Francisco, CA (2005): p. 123. Subsequent citations are abbreviated MMA.

[110] St. Proclus of Constantinople, *Homily* 5:2. MFC: p. 251.

similar unfortunate comments regarding the Marian Maximalism of St. Bernardine of Siena, Bernardine de Bustis, and others),[111] for example when Fr. Eadmer says in praise to Mary: "Just as your Son is the Savior of the whole world, so you [Mary] are the one who reconciles the whole world [to God]."[112] Is this truly an exaggeration? We have already heard St. Alphonsus Liguori say precisely the same thing![113] Moreover, is it fair to say (as Fr. Gambero does) that "Eadmer offers thoughts and arguments that come close to appearing naïve," for example when "it seems that he wants to put a monopoly over divine mercy into the Virgin's hands"?[114] If so, then Fr. Eadmer shares this naïveté with St. Maximilian Kolbe, who also asserts that "God has entrusted the entire order of mercy to [Mary]."[115]

---

[111] Cf. MMA: p. 121; p. 292; p. 321. About Fr. Eadmer of Canterbury, Fr. Gambero says: "In keeping with the tendency to exaggerate that we have already mentioned, Eadmer goes so far as to say that, in danger, it seems more useful to call upon Mary than upon her divine Son." MMA: p. 121. Perhaps Fr. Gambero is unaware of the following vision of Br. Leo: "The Franciscan Chronicles relate that a certain Brother Leo saw in a vision two ladders the one red, the other white. On the upper end of the red ladder, stood Jesus and on the other stood His holy Mother. The brother saw that some tried to climb the red ladder; but scarcely had they mounted some rungs when they fell back, they tried again but with no better success. Then they were advised to try the white ladder and to their surprise they succeeded for the Blessed Virgin stretched out her hand and with her aid they reached heaven." GOM: p. 246. About St. Bernardine of Siena, Fr. Gambero says: "It cannot be ignored that some of Bernardine's statements about the Virgin can sound exaggerated, or downright strange and unacceptable," and he later notes that "Hilda Graef considers Bernardine of Siena precisely a representative of the kind of so-called 'Mariolatry' she thinks provoked the Protestant reaction in the next century." MMA: p. 292. Hilda Graef would have benefited from the homily given by Bl. Pope Paul VI for the beatification of St. Maximilian Kolbe, when he said of the Marian Maximalism represented by the Saint: "The result will never be 'Mariolatry,' just as the sun will never be darkened by the moon."

[112] Fr. Eadmer of Canterbury, *De Excellentia Virginis Mariae*, 12. MMA: p. 121.

[113] Cf. GOM: pp. 401–2.

[114] MMA: p. 120.

[115] Of course, as we have already noted, many theologians think that St. Maximilian Kolbe was naïve, precisely for this reason. In the words of Fr. Peter Damian Fehlner: "For example [Ignazio] Calabuig, [Riflessioni conclusive: "San Massimiliano Maria Kolbe nel suo tempo e oggi," in *Miles Immaculatae* 38 (2002)] pp. 1037–8, classifies the well known view of St. Bernard concerning Christ's reservation of the economy of justice to himself and entrusting that of mercy to His Mother, a conviction of St. Maximilian as well—cf. SK 1248—as an example of decadent Mariology, 'false, misleading, smacking of maximalism.' What Calabuig seems not

Given his own obvious Marian devotion, Fr. Luigi Gambero may be playing the "devil's advocate." However, for the sake of argument, let us briefly consider his claim that Fr. Eadmer had "a way of speaking that would not survive the scrutiny of pure reason," though he adds that, "within a context of mystical experience, it is possible to understand and justify" such a way of speaking because "that alone is able to let us penetrate more deeply the incomprehensible depths of divine mysteries."[116] While we do not doubt Fr. Gambero's good intentions toward both Fr. Eadmer and the divine mysteries, we must respectfully disagree with *both* of these claims.

First, it is simply not true that Fr. Eadmer's Marian Maximalism does "not survive the scrutiny of pure reason" (as it is not true of the Marian Maximalism of Bl. John Duns Scotus, or St. Alphonsus Liguori, or St. Maximilian Kolbe), since his principle was precisely "that everything worthy that God wanted for someone other than himself, he wanted for [Mary]."[117] We have already argued that such a Marian maximal principle is both precise and objective in terms of logic, and we have also shown that it is fully Catholic in terms of tradition (the testimony of the saints). Therefore, the Marian Maximalism of Fr. Eadmer is eminently *reasonable*.[118]

Second, can it be true that "a way of speaking that would not survive the scrutiny of pure reason" is "able to let us penetrate more deeply the incomprehensible depths of divine mysteries"? Pope

---

to have realized is that in denying this, his own exegesis of Scripture is prejudiced in the direction of the Lutheran *solus*. In entrusting mercy to His Mother Jesus does not cease to be merciful. Mary's virginal maternity: divine and spiritual, becomes rather the revelation of the paternity of God and his justice as merciful. [...] This is also crystal clear in the Bible from beginning to end. Perhaps it is the theology of Calabuig which is 'decadent.' One should be cautious about the future of current academic fads." PDF: p. 25, footnote 37.

[116] MMA: p. 121.

[117] Fr. Eadmer of Canterbury, *De Conceptione Sanctae Mariae*. MMA: p. 119.

[118] The fact that both of Fr. Eadmer's (probable) Mariological works *De Excellentia Virginis Mariae* and *De Conceptione Sanctae Mariae* were for centuries attributed to St. Anselm confirms their quality, since St. Anselm is the Father of Scholasticism. Given this fact, in all fairness, perhaps Fr. Eadmer should share with St. Anselm (and Bl. John Duns Scotus) the title of "Marian Doctor"!

Benedict XVI didn't think so, when in his Regensburg lecture of 2006 he said "not to act in accordance with reason is contrary to God's nature."[119] The divine mysteries do transcend both our finite language and our finite understanding, but Catholic mysticism cannot entail a contradiction, and that which does not entail a contradiction does indeed survive the scrutiny of pure reason. Moreover, as St. John Damascene teaches us, there is a marked difference between a fact being knowable and its being expressible, and simply because a fact is inexpressible in a human language (either formal or natural) it certainly does not follow that it is unreasonable (indeed, this is true even in the comparatively mundane subject of mathematical logic, to say nothing of theology or mysticism). It is true that pure reason is limited, since, by itself, it can only affirm logical consistency (non-contradiction), which is formally a negative concept (i.e., the impossibility of deriving a contradiction), and as such cannot be expected to penetrate the divine mysteries, because God's truth (which is Himself) is *supremely positive*. However, the unprovability or inexpressibility of a fact, even when this unprovability or inexpressibility is *intrinsic* (as for example in the case of the consistency of mathematics), is not the same thing as the *derivability of a contradiction*, which is formally a positive concept (i.e., the existence of a proof that leads to a conjunction of some sentence and its absolute negation). The latter concept, Pope Benedict XVI tells us, being eminently contrary to reason, is contrary to God's nature, and therefore cannot be accepted as a way of knowing God, mystically or otherwise.

As we have seen, there is nothing contrary to reason in a Marian maximal principle. On the contrary, the notion of a "maximal element" within the set of knowable existence (the created Woman Mary, whose glory is both inexpressible and infinite precisely as a logical consequence of her maximality), together with the notion of

---

[119] Pope Benedict XVI, *Lecture of the Holy Father, Meeting with the Representatives of Science at the University of Regensburg* (September 12, 2006).

"diagonalization" as the crux of St. Anselm's "ontological" argument (which depends on the revelation of God's Holy Name: Jesus, the Son of Mary—I AM WHO AM, who saves you), provide us with an objective, rational basis for a fully integrated theology, which, by the immutable will of the Eternal Father, necessarily includes Christology, Mariology, and Ecclesiology.

CHAPTER EIGHT

POTUIT, DECUIT, ERGO FECIT

The "mode of argument" used by Bl. John Duns Scotus to defend Mary's Immaculate Conception during the famous disputation at the University of Paris (c. 1307) can be summarized as follows: First, Scotus argued that *God was able—potuit—*to grant Mary the grace of her Immaculate Conception. That is, he argued that Mary's Immaculate Conception is *consistent* with all that we know of Who God Is: I AM WHO AM; who is Good;[120] who is Love;[121] who is the Way, the Truth, and the Life;[122] who is just in all His ways, and holy in all His works;[123] who is compassionate and merciful, slow to anger and abounding in kindness;[124] who has suffered, died, and risen from the dead in order to save you. This also entails logical consistency, since, though God is omnipotent, He *cannot* will a contradiction. This puts no (true) limits on God's omnipotence, because God is truth, and, as C. S. Lewis argued (essentially quoting St. Augustine and St. Thomas Aquinas), just as a circle cannot be a square, God cannot be other than Who He Is! However, *potuit* cannot be reduced to *logical* consistency alone, since that is only one small part of Who God Is (as God has revealed Himself to us). Second, Scotus argued that *it was fitting—decuit—*that God *had* granted Mary the grace of her

---

[120] Cf. *Ps* 34:8; 100:5; 118:1.
[121] Cf. *1 Jn* 4:8.
[122] *Jn* 14:6.
[123] Cf. *Ps* 145.
[124] Cf. *Ps* 86:15; 103:8; 145:8.

Immaculate Conception, since Bl. John Duns Scotus' own Marian maximal principle was that "one should attribute to her, whatever is objectively most 'excellent,' provided that it be not contrary to the authority of the Church and of Scripture."[125] Only after having *definitely established* these two assertions did Bl. John Duns Scotus feel justified to conclude that God did indeed grant Mary the grace of her Immaculate Conception. That is, *He did it—fecit.* Thus, Bl. John Duns Scotus' mode of argument runs as follows: *potuit, decuit, ergo fecit—God was able, it was fitting, therefore He did it.*

In the words of Fr. Ruggero Rosini:

Does the famous syllogism: "potuit, decuit, ergo fecit," originate with Scotus or with the scotists? As formulated it originates with his disciples; but its substance is from Scotus. In its structure it expresses an argument of "fittingness," which is misunderstood by some.[126] Certainly, we cannot *a priori* know the mind of God; we can, however, know it *a posteriori*. For this reason, according to Scotus, God is *a priori* perfectly free to choose among all women the one who will be His Mother. But once chosen, therefore *a posteriori*, He is not perfectly free toward her. In relation to her He contracts certain duties, as every child does toward his mother (the fourth commandment "Honor…" also applies here). Here emerges the argument of Scotus: the maximum dishonor for a creature consists in the contraction of original sin, from which comes the greatest offense to God, by reason of which "no one perfectly satisfies for anyone, unless He can prevent the offense, if possible" (*Elementa*, 48). And this offense Christ could prevent ("*potuit*," Scotus insists, *Elementa*, 28. 213. 216), preserving that

---

[125] Bl. John Duns Scotus: "if it is not contrary to the authority of the Church or Sacred Scripture, it seems probable that what is more excellent should be ascribed to Mary": "si auctoritati Ecclesiae vel auctoritate Scripturae non repugnat, videtur probabile quod exellentius est tribuere Mariae," *Ordinatio*, III, d. 3, q. 1, n. 10. Cf. JDS: p. 73.

[126] Cf. R. Laurentin, *La question mariale*, Paris 1963, p. 123, Eng. Version: *The Question of Mary*, Techny Il. 1967.

person precisely from original sin (*Elementa*, 24). And logically, were there a creature [to] whom Christ "must" concede such a privilege, this would be His Mother: "this (exemption) was fitting precisely for Christ's Mother" (*Elementa*, 211). "Therefore… He did it." For this reason, "if Christ is the most perfect Mediator," He is such because "He has prevented all offense in His Mother" (*Elementa*, 48).[127]

A similar mode of argument was used by Fr. Eadmer of Canterbury centuries earlier, also to argue in favor of Mary's Immaculate Conception. Fr. Eadmer ended his argument (which was based on an analogy with the chestnut) with the following words: "[God] certainly could do it, and he wanted to do it. Therefore, if he wanted to do it, he did it."[128] Unfortunately, as with much of the rest of the Marian Maximalism of Fr. Eadmer and Bl. John Duns Scotus, this mode of argument has been the subject of much misunderstanding and suspicion among later theologians. For example, Fr. Gambero says of Fr. Eadmer's argument:

> We note how much progress was being made by the argument of fittingness, which will receive its classic formulation in three terms: *potuit, decuit, ergo fecit*. A few centuries later, this saying would be made famous by the Franciscan Duns Scotus, who would apply it to the mystery of the Immaculate Conception. Eadmer anticipates him almost to the letter, when he writes: "Potuit plane et voluit; si igitur voluit, fecit." On the other hand, this very same principle, the so-called principle of "convenience," will also lead to unchecked, exaggerated, and arbitrary statements about the greatness and dignity of the Mother of God. The Christian people, moved by inappropriate zeal and poorly understood Marian devotion, sometimes fails to eliminate such excesses.[129]

---

[127] JDS: p. 76, footnote 16.
[128] MMA: p. 119.
[129] Ibid.

Is it fair to call this mode of argument a principle of "convenience"? And does it really lead to "arbitrary statements about the greatness and dignity of the Mother of God"? As we have already argued, there is nothing imprecise or ambiguous about a Marian Maximal principle. Consider, for example, the following statement made by Bl. Pope Pius IX in *Ineffabilis Deus*: "[Mary] approaches as near to God Himself as it is possible for a created being."[130] This statement could not be more precise. It directly implies the following maximal principle regarding Mary: "For any essential property X, if it is possible for a created being to have the property X, and if it is objectively better to have the property X than not to have the property X, then Mary has the property X." This maximal principle is exactly parallel to the corresponding maximal principle used by St. Anselm regarding God: "For any essential property X, if it is objectively better to have the property X than not to have the property X, then God has the property X."[131] Both of these maximal principles are wonderfully precise starting points for theological discussion! Indeed, they are so precise that they can be expressed in the language of symbolic logic and easily shown to be logically consistent (given a consistent and appropriate definition of "essential property").[132]

---

[130] Bl. Pope Pius IX, *Ineffabilis Deus*, Apostolic Constitution (December 8, 1854).

[131] This version of St. Anselm's maximal principle is based on the *coloratio Anselmi* or "coloration" of St. Anselm's argument due to Bl. John Duns Scotus. In *A Treatise on God as First Principle*, 4.9–4.11, Bl. John Duns Scotus defines a "pure perfection" as "something which is better in everything than what is not it." Then he proves: "Every pure perfection is predicated of the supreme nature as being present necessarily and in the highest degree." In the course of his proof, Bl. John Duns Scotus clarifies: "Take 'better than what is not it' as referring to anything which is both positive and incompatible [and hence] entails the idea of not being this thing. [...] Briefly, then, one may say that a pure perfection is whatever is absolutely and without qualification better than anything incompatible with it." This added insight regarding the compatibility of "positive properties" in the definition of a "pure perfection" is essential to the logical consistency of all modern formalizations of St. Anselm's "ontological" argument using symbolic modal logic, such as the one proposed by Kurt Gödel. Cf. C. Anthony Anderson, "Some Emendations of Gödel's Ontological Proof," *Faith and Philosophy*, 7 (1990): pp. 291–303.

[132] The axioms used by Kurt Gödel to formalize (Leibniz's version of) St. Anselm's "ontological" proof, though logically consistent, contain certain "flaws" that lead

Logical consistency, however, being *a priori*, is only one small part of *truth*.[133] It remains the task of the theologian to determine, as for example in the case of the Marian maximal principle, (1) exactly what essential properties are possible for a created being (*potuit*), and (2) what essential properties are objectively better to have than not to have (*decuit*). Answering these questions may not be a simple task, but that fact does not make the maximal principles themselves imprecise or arbitrary. It is precisely for this reason that Bl. John Duns Scotus goes through so much trouble to verify both the *potuit* and *decuit* of his theological assertions, and why these together form the "extra-logical" (that is, *non a priori*) crux of his arguments.

Remarkably, Bl. John Duns Scotus has been accused of being the father of *voluntarism*, which is closely related to *nominalism*, and consequently is the forerunner of philosophers such as Kant and Hegel, and indeed of modernism in general.[134] Voluntarism

---

to a so-called "modal collapse," which entails a conflation of necessity and actuality in the modal universe. That is, Gödel's axioms entail that everything that happens must happen "necessarily" in a formal sense. What this says precisely about God, voluntarism, and predestination is subject to interpretation. Even so, this "modal collapse" can be avoided in a variety of ways, since it depends both on the choice of axioms as well as on the choice of the underlying system of modal predicate logic. Cf. Petr Hájek, "A New Small Emendation of Gödel's Ontological Proof," *Studia Logica*, 71:2 (2002): pp. 149–64.

[133] Moreover, logical consistency is formally a negative concept. That is, a sentence q is logically consistent with a set of sentences T already presumed to be consistent if and only if it is impossible to derive a contradiction from the set T+{q}. Since it is a negative concept, logical consistency cannot be the formal principle of anything, much less truth, which is a positive concept, and which, being God, is the formal principle of everything.

[134] The relationship between nominalism-voluntarism and modernism, as well as its impact on any kind of meaningful ritual (including the Catholic liturgy) is explained by Clemens Cavallin as follows: "Modernity at least in its more ideological versions carries with it a major impetus toward the subjective and hence individualism, the very opposite of the ritual commitment (cf. Taylor 2002, Ferguson 2000: 198). But deeper still, I maintain that nominalism is the basic feature of modernity, which inclines it toward deritualization. Nominalism signifies a stance according to which only the individual has being and the ideal realm in the form of notions and norms is in reality merely made up of more or less arbitrary collections of particulars (conceptual nominalism) and acts of will on the part of individuals (voluntarism). In such a demythologized universe, the action logic of religious rituals becomes absurd, or has to be interpreted as merely expressive actions in order to salvage the rationality of the ritual practitioner."

essentially holds that "God can do whatever He wants." For example, according to voluntarism, God could have made evil good and good evil (as we understand it), or He could have become incarnate as a donkey—as William of Ockham, the *true* father of voluntarism-nominalism, famously (or infamously) said. However, this is a gross misrepresentation of Bl. John Duns Scotus, since it reduces his *argument* of *potuit and decuit* (God was able and it was fitting) to his *conclusion only* (*fecit*—He did it). Why would Bl. John Duns Scotus "waste his time" constructing subtle arguments to prove that "God is able" to do something, or that "it is fitting" that he would do it, if God "can do anything" in the (erroneous) sense of voluntarism? The idea that God could have been evil (or that God could have been a donkey) does not make God omnipotent, but rather makes God a contradiction (either in reference to pure logic *or* in reference to the rest of what God has revealed about Who He Is), *which is not possible*—a truth of which Bl. John Duns Scotus was eminently aware.[135]

On the other (but still wrong) end of the stick, Bl. John Duns Scotus has been accused of being a practitioner of "onto-theology" (along with St. Anselm and most of the Scholastics) by philosophers such as Kant and Heidegger. These philosophers accuse Bl. John Duns Scotus of basing his theological arguments on *a priori* considerations only, rather than on *a posteriori* evidence. However, this is also a gross misrepresentation of Bl. John Duns Scotus, since it ignores his

---

Clemens Cavallin, *Ritualization and Human Interiority*, Museum Tusculanum Press, University of Copenhagen (2013): pp. 114–5.

[135] In the words of Fr. Peter Damian Fehlner: "The Bonaventurian concept of will and love anticipates that of Scotus. Set in this context, the teaching of Scotus clearly appears as a development of St. Bonaventure's profound analysis of our interior, personal life and not an anticipation of Ockham's nominalism-voluntarism." TTW: p. 72, footnote 73. Understood thus in terms of St. Bonaventure's doctrine of free will, and bearing in mind how the Seraphic Doctor's notion of will differs from appetite, the metaphysics of Bl. John Duns Scotus is completely vindicated of the charge of voluntarism: "With his distinction between natural and voluntary actions and how this does not correspond to the distinction between necessary and contingent as two modes of exercising free will, the Seraphic Doctor provides the indispensible basis for the subsequent teaching of Scotus." TTW: pp. 71–2.

argument of *decuit* entirely, and it reduces his argument of *potuit* to logical consistency only, without any reference to the *rest* of God's revelation of Who He Is, which, as we have already explained, is not the way Bl. John Duns Scotus argued at all.[136]

How can Bl. John Duns Scotus be accused of holding diametrically opposed opinions at the same time, when his own writings contain no contradictions? Perhaps it is because Bl. John Duns Scotus found the *true* "middle way" that has been repeatedly endorsed by Pope Francis: That is, the "middle way" between *Pelagianism* on the one hand, which is a form of *a priori* causal determinism in the order of grace,[137] and *Gnosticism* on the other hand, which is related to nominalism.[138] This "middle way" is Marian Maximalism: to place oneself and one's thoughts literally in the *middle*, or in the Virginal womb, of the Blessed Virgin Mary.[139]

This is the key to the Christocentrism of the whole theology of Bl. John Duns Scotus: All arguments of "fittingness" (*decuit*) with regard to the Virgin-Mother Mary *invariably hinge* on her unique closeness to the God-Man Jesus. That is, Mary's fullness of grace "flows" from her divine Maternity. In the words of Fr. Ruggero Rosini:

> Hence, Mary's maternity and grace are the two titles which enter
>
> into the technical argument of fittingness. But in what manner?

---

[136] For example, in *A Treatise on God as First Principle*, 4.2, Bl. John Duns Scotus prays: "O Lord, our God, if you would grant me that favor, I would like to show somehow those perfections which I do not doubt are in your unique and truly first nature. I believe that you are simple, infinite, wise, and endowed with a will. And as I wish to avoid a [vicious] circle in the proofs, I shall begin with certain conclusions about simplicity which can be proved at the outset." Thus, the theological reasoning of Bl. John Duns Scotus contains both *a priori* and *a posteriori* elements, always enlightened by faith (like St. Anselm and St. Augustine) and subject to the authority of the Catholic Church and Sacred Scripture.

[137] Cf. A. Pablo Iannone, *Dictionary of World Philosophy*, Routledge, New York, NY (2001): p. 148 (entry on "Determinism").

[138] Hans Blumenberg defines nominalism as "practical Gnosticism." Cf. Cyril O'Regan, *Gnostic Return in Modernity*, State University of New York Press, Albany, NY (2001): p. 54.

[139] Cf. Jonathan A. Fleischmann, "Transformation in Mary's Womb," *Missio Immaculatae International*, 10:1 (2014): pp. 18–23.

The solution depends upon the conception of the relation between the two titles, seen in relation to Christ and to one another.[140]

In his outline of Mariology *ad mentem Scoti* based on the absolute joint predestination of Jesus and Mary Fr. Peter Damian Fehlner explains that while "the 'primary principle' of Mariology is the virginal divine and spiritual Maternity" in the order of *divine intention*, the mystery of the Immaculate Conception is the primary principle of Mariology in the order of *divine execution*, which is "subordinate to that of the order of intention or predestination."[141] Once again, what is first in intention is last in execution. However, in divine execution, "how much" grace did Mary receive? We have already argued based on our Marian Maximal principle that Mary's glory must be infinite (and hence unspeakable), or else it could not be "greater than which none can be imagined, except for God's." The angel Gabriel addressed Mary: "Hail, *full of grace*."[142] Thus, we know on Scriptural authority that Mary's grace is *maximal*. What does this maximality of grace entail? In the words of Fr. Ruggero Rosini:

> In a certain sense, an exchange of gifts is verified between Christ and Mary: the Son gives divine grace to His Mother; the Mother gives her human nature to the Son. Two "gifts," both perfect in their kind. [...] It is a truth of Faith that Mary transmitted her own nature to the Son in its "totality"; but did Jesus transfuse into His Mother the "totality" of His grace? Can this be maintained, if not in the full sense, at least in a certain sense? In other words, can we believe that that grace which, according to the expression of Scotus, was granted to Christ by God "without measure," was

---

[140] JDS: p. 56.

[141] Fr. Peter Damian M. Fehlner, F.I., "Coredemption and the Assumption in the Franciscan School of Mariology: The 'Franciscan Thesis' as Key" in *Mariological Studies in Honor of Our Lady of Guadalupe—I*, Academy of the Immaculate, New Bedford, MA (2013): p. 224. Subsequent citations are abbreviated OLG.

[142] *Lk* 1:28.

in turn also transmitted from the Son to the Mother "without measure," therefore in its "totality"?[143]

Indeed, the answer to this question posed by Fr. Rosini is *yes*! Bl. John Duns Scotus maintains "that every intelligent being, man or angel, by his very nature has the capacity to receive any degree of grace, even were it an infinite degree. And this infinite receptive capacity he attributes to the divine image existing within these intellectual creatures, including Christ."[144] Thus, if Christ did not transmit His own grace to Mary *in its entirety* according to *His human nature*, then Mary's grace would not be *maximal* according to *her human nature*, which we know, *a posteriori*, was *completely shared* with Jesus on account of the divine Maternity. However, this *complete sharing* of the "fullness" of grace in the created human natures of Jesus and Mary implies no equality of their *persons*, since the person of Mary is created and finite, and the divine Person of Jesus is uncreated and infinite. Moreover, the "fullnesses" of grace in Jesus and Mary, though both infinite in *degree* on account of the "total" transmission of grace from Jesus to Mary, are nevertheless different in nature and in origin, and so remain incommensurate with each other. This is why Jesus remains the one absolute Mediator, "because there cannot be more than one Head in the Church, from whom every grace would flow into her members."[145] Fr. Ruggero Rosini explains:

> Seen in relation to nature, the "fullness" [of grace] in Christ is absolute, while the "fullness" [of grace] in Mary is relative; His is natural, hers is participated. Seen in relation to their origin, the "fullness" of Christ is immediately from God, whereas the "fullness" of Mary is immediately from Christ; therefore, as we shall see further on, Christ presents himself to us as the absolute, natural Mediator; Mary as a relative, moral Mediatrix. From this

---

[143] JDS: p. 59.
[144] JDS: p. 60.
[145] Bl. John Duns Scotus, *Ordinatio*, III, d. 13, q. 4, n. 8. JDS: p. 61.

it is clear that as much as one might possibly desire to accentuate Mary's "fullness" of "participated" grace, one could never even minimally compromise Christ's "natural" fullness. Rather, by exalting the dignity of the Mother, one shall exalt all the more the dignity of the Son! Standing by Scotus' principles, therefore, there are no insoluble difficulties opposed to the "total" transmission of Christ's grace into Mary.[146]

In the words of Fr. Peter Damian Fehlner:

For this reason, the maternal mediation of Mary in relation to the mystical Body of Christ, basis of her unique role in the economy of salvation (soteriological order), in no way lessens the role of the "One Mediator of God and man" in this same order. Rather, her subordinate role or modal qualification of Christ's mediation reveals the perfection of this latter. The mediation of Christ is absolutely one, because first rooted in the grace of the hypostatic union and then given soteriological form through His fullness of grace or holiness in His human nature. That of Mary, however, also involving a fullness of grace resting on the privilege of the Immaculate Conception, is not the fruit of a second "hypostatic union," but of a unique sharing in the fullness of grace of her Son, a fullness upon which the Son has made the holiness of all His mystical members depend. On this depends all cooperation with the Savior in the work of salvation, the importance of merit, and meritorious satisfaction *de condigno* on the part of Christ: absolutely, and on the part of Mary: relatively. For Scotus, Christ as Head of the Church represents a kind of summit of creation, because of which He infuses the Spirit of light and love into the minds and hearts of His members ever through His Mother who, in belonging to the order of the hypostatic union, shares uniquely in the fullness of grace or of the Holy Spirit. This approach nicely

---

[146] JDS: p. 62.

corresponds to that found in Galatians 4:4–7, and [is] so important for a reading of Vatican II.[147]

This is why one can never compromise Christ by exalting Mary. This is also why exalting Mary can never compromise the Holy Spirit, whose sanctifying role in the Church is realized exclusively, *a posteriori*, through Mary His Spouse, who by God's will is consecrated from eternity Mediatrix of all graces with Christ the perfect Mediator, and through whom *alone* the Church and all things external to God are made intelligible to us by God's mercy. In the words of Fr. Peter Damian Fehlner:

> Sanctification of the members of Christ's body, the Church, is the goal of the mission of the Holy Spirit. But this does not occur [note well—not *cannot*, but *does not*, whence a question not of the *potentia Dei absoluta*, but of the *potentia Dei ordinata*,] except on the supposition of what is rightly called in tradition the "consecration" of the Virgin by God to God as part of that first *signum* of the divine creative will to which all else *extra Deum* is subordinated and from which subordination they derive their intelligibility (Bl. John Duns Scotus). What this first sign is, is first revealed in the Incarnation, and fully effected in the sacrifice of Calvary. Alone among the redeemed and saved is the Virgin Mother actively present in this consecration of the Son of God.[148]

Moreover, we can say that if the very *intelligibility* of all that God has created, including ourselves, depends on the consecration and joint predestination of Jesus and Mary in the will of the Eternal Father, then from our point of view (*a posteriori*) we cannot deny

---

[147] Fr. Peter Damian M. Fehlner, F.I., "Coredemption and the Assumption in the Franciscan School of Mariology: The 'Franciscan Thesis' as Key" in OLG: pp. 166–7.

[148] Fr. Peter Damian M. Fehlner, F.I., "Maria Coredemptrix—Mater Viventium (Gen. 3, 20)" in *Mary at the Foot of the Cross—IV: Mater Viventium (Gen. 3, 20). Acts of the Fourth International Symposium on Marian Coredemption*, Academy of the Immaculate, New Bedford, MA (2004): p. 3.

the *necessity* of the Virgin Mother in God's plan of creation and redemption without trapping ourselves in a kind of "liar's paradox" (a *performative contradiction*), since in so denying we would be forced to deny the intelligibility of our own thoughts. This is why Fr. Peter Damian Fehlner says:

> Often enough the facile and superficial objection is raised: but God could have acted otherwise. But the fact is He did not, because it pleased Him (*decuit*) to create and to save only in the most perfectly possible scenario (*potuit*—rooted in the absolute and joint predestination of Christ and Mary—*Filius et Filia*), therefore he did it this way (*ergo fecit*). So runs the classic mode of theological reflection in the Franciscan-Scotistic-Kolbean school.[149]

---

[149] Ibid., 6.

CHAPTER NINE

GRACE AND MERIT

To see where the Marian Maximalism of Bl. John Duns Scotus can (safely!) take us, let us consider Mary's *merit* as Mediatrix of all graces and as Coredemptrix. At the outset, we should note that merit is intimately related to grace, and, as such it has a (perhaps deserved) reputation of being a "dangerous" subject for theological speculation. In the words of Fr. John Hardon:

> The theology of grace is not simple, as may be seen from the sequence of errors strewn along the path of the Church's history. The complexity of the subject is due as much to its intrinsically mysterious character, since it deals with nothing less than the life of God shared by His creatures, as to our natural proneness to rationalize and explain everything in this-worldly terms. Yet a clear grasp of the basic principles is useful and may at times be indispensable, for directing oneself and others on the road to salvation. It is no coincidence that the great heresies on grace, like Pelagianism and Jansenism, had a profound influence on the morals and spiritual life of those who professed these errors; and that influence is still exerted centuries after the original aberrations arose.[150]

It is also *no coincidence* that both Pelagianism and Jansenism (old and new) are hostile to Marian Maximalism, and especially the

---

[150] Fr. John A. Hardon, S.J., *History and Theology of Grace*, Sapientia Press, Ave Maria, FL (2002): pp. xiii–xiv.

unique grace of Mary's Immaculate Conception: According to the Pelagians, Mary's Immaculate Conception is unnecessary, because they believe that human nature is untainted by original sin. According to the Jansenists, Mary's Immaculate Conception is impossible (a "pious exaggeration"), because they believe that human depravity is absolute and irrevocable after the fall. Thus, when discussing merit and grace, "safety" is found precisely in the arms of Our Mother, the *Destroyer of All Heresies*. A physicist friend of mine has a principle that "God does not trick us." Indeed, it is precisely by giving us His Mother as an example that God has provided us with an infallible "answer key" to the subtle problems of grace and merit. It is *Marian Maximalism* that guides the Barque of St. Peter with a sure rudder to the *true* "Catholic Middle-Ground" between "the two shoals of despairing of man's native powers because of the fall, or ignoring original sin and so exalting human nature that nothing is supposed to be impossible to man."[151]

We have already heard St. Alphonsus Liguori explicitly refer to Mary's merit in both of her roles as Mediatrix of all graces and Coredemptrix, in both the subjective and objective orders of redemption.[152] However, even among Marian Maximalists who support Mary's role as Coredemptrix, it is often believed that in the work of redemption Mary obtained only merit *de congruo*, which is merit obtained on the basis of pure fittingness and ordered toward grace; and Jesus alone obtained merit *de condigno*, which is merit obtained on the basis of justice and ordered toward glory and eternal life. However, while Bl. John Duns Scotus never explicitly discussed merit in relation to Mary, on the basis of his doctrine of merit in general it is indeed possible and even necessary to attribute merit *de condigno* to Mary in the work of redemption, precisely because of her closeness to her divine Son. In the words of Fr. Ruggero Rosini: "As

---

[151] Ibid., 76.
[152] Cf. GOM: pp. 325–7; pp. 401–2.

Christ was able to and in fact did merit *de condigno* for others, but not for Himself, so, too, was this the case with Mary."[153]

According to Bl. John Duns Scotus, "grace is the sole root of merit."[154] However, besides the conditions for *de condigno* merit that are intrinsic to the act (e.g., "goodness, righteousness, conformity with reason, intensity of charity, etc.") and intrinsic to the person performing the act (e.g., the person must be "in the state of pilgrimage" and in the state of sanctifying grace), Bl. John Duns Scotus adds, "I believe that there is one other condition, to be verified as actual in fact, namely, the acceptability of such merit to God: not only in virtue of that common acceptance, whereby God accepts every creature…, but in virtue of a special acceptance, which is the ordaining of this act by the divine will to eternal life, as condign merit worthy of reward."[155]

The fact that merit depends on divine acceptance means essentially that merit, like grace, is *not deterministic* from our point of view as creatures, because merit, like grace, ultimately depends on the divine will—*ergo,* the demise of all forms of causal or natural determinism (Pelagianism). The divine will, however, is not arbitrary, because once chosen, God contracts certain "responsibilities" consistent with Who He Is, such as His "duty" to honor His Mother—*ergo,* the demise of all forms of "theistic" or supernatural determinism (Jansenism and Calvinism), as well as Gnosticism and its "practical" variants (nominalism and voluntarism). This fact is at the heart of the mystery of "why God has preferences,"[156] which is spoken of at some length by St. Thérèse of Lisieux (d. 1897), the *Doctor of the Little Way,* at the beginning of her autobiography:

---

[153] JDS: p. 171.

[154] JDS: p. 173.

[155] Bl. John Duns Scotus, *Ordinatio*, I, d. 17, pars 1, q. 1–2, n. 129. JDS: p. 167, footnote 77.

[156] St. Thérèse of Lisieux, *Story of a Soul*, Third Edition, Translated from the Original Manuscripts by John Clarke, O.C.D., ICS Publications, Washington, DC (1996): p. 13.

Before taking up my pen, I knelt before a statue of Mary (the one that has given so many proofs of the maternal preferences of heaven's Queen for our family), and I begged her to guide my hand that it trace no line displeasing to her. Then opening the Holy Gospels my eyes fell on these words: "And going up a mountain, he called to him men of his *own choosing*, and they came to him" (*Mk* 3:13). This is the mystery of my vocation, my whole life, and especially the mystery of the privileges Jesus showered on my soul. He does not call those who are worthy but those whom He *pleases* or as St. Paul says: "God will have mercy on whom he will have mercy, and he will show pity to whom he will show pity. So then there is question not of him who wills nor of him who runs, but of God showing mercy" (*Rom* 9:15–6).[157]

Fr. Ruggero Rosini explains:

Once it is understood that merit depends upon divine acceptance, merit by its very nature is then intrinsically the same for everyone [that is, the *term* "merit" can be used *univocally* for everyone, though the *degree* of merit is not the same]: Christ, Mary and the just. The difference lies in its extension. Scotus explains this by the fact that merit, not consisting in the personal act alone, is in some way also constituted by the circumstances in which the person accomplishes the meritorious act; hence God, in accepting the act, also accepts the circumstances of the one who performs the meritorious work. [...] We saw that Christ merited for all, Mary included; by virtue of His divine Person He was able to merit in an infinite manner. In Mary, of course, we do not have an infinite person; however, in her case there is a circumstance which intimately links her to the very Person of the Word; and it is her divine Maternity. And if one participates in Christ's perfections according to one's degree of closeness to Him, certainly nobody

---

[157] Ibid.

was nor ever shall be characterized by a more rigorous union with Christ Himself than Mary.[158]

Thus, Christ's merit *de condigno* as our perfect Redeemer and Mary's merit *de condigno* as "our dear Coredemptrix" (in the words of St. Pio of Pietrelcina) are *both infinite in value*, but for different reasons. The value of the merit obtained by Christ by His Passion and Death on the Cross is infinite on account of His infinite Person, because He is God. The value of the merit obtained by Mary by her Compassion at the Foot of the Cross is infinite because of the circumstance that intimately links her to the Person of the Word: her Divine Maternity. Both, according to Bl. John Duns Scotus, depend on divine acceptance. Thus, it is a case of "relative infinities." The merits of Jesus and Mary in the work of the objective Redemption are both infinite in value on account of the divine Person of the God-Man Jesus Christ and the Divine Maternity of the Virgin-Mother Mary, and on account of the acceptance of their work as infinite in value by the will of the Eternal Father in order to accomplish the "most perfect Redemption possible" after such Redemption was occasioned by the fall of our first parents, Adam and Eve. As such, the merits obtained by Jesus and Mary are incommensurate in value with the merit obtained by any other person, but they are also incommensurate with each other, the merit of Jesus Christ being incomparably *greater* than that of Mary, because He is God.

This brings us to a subtle and important point. So far, we have used the term "infinite" in a sense that resembles the mathematical notion of infinity,[159] which is defined *negatively*, viz., in terms of

---

[158] JDS: pp. 173–5.

[159] In the mathematical subject of set theory, a set X is infinite by definition if there exists no bijective relation between X and any finite set F. That is, X is infinite if and only if X is incommensurate with all finite sets F. Similarly, a set Y is infinitely larger than X by definition if there exists an injective relation from X into Y but no bijective relation between X and Y. That is, Y is infinitely larger than X if and only if Y is both larger than X and incommensurate with X. This last definition leads to an infinite hierarchy of infinite sets, called infinite ordinals.

incommensurability, rather than *positively*, viz., in terms of *absolute transcendence*. The former (negative notion) is "infinity in the relative sense: the non measurability of some creature's perfection because it surpasses in value that of all other creatures taken singly and collectively"; the latter (positive notion) is "infinity in the absolute sense: that of being as such proper to the divine nature alone and incapable of participation by the creature, even the created nature assumed hypostatically by a divine Person."[160] In the words of Fr. Peter Damian Fehlner:

> Thus, merit and satisfaction may be described as infinite in value, as in the case of Jesus because they are human acts of a divine Person, but not because they are infinite absolutely. Similarly, one may speak of the manner in which sin offends God as relatively infinite in view of the divine dignity, but not in the absolute sense.[161]

It is on this point that Bl. John Duns Scotus' doctrine of merit *de condigno* differs subtly (but importantly) from the classic formulation due to St. Anselm in *Cur Deus Homo?* (Why did God become Man?), specifically with regard to the infinite satisfaction of the God-Man Jesus Christ for the sins of humankind, from which the classical Thomistic thesis follows: "on the hypothesis that condign satisfaction is required for sin, the Incarnation is absolutely necessary."[162] Fr. Peter Damian Fehlner explains:

> Here the question disputed is not whether the salvation wrought by Jesus is a work of justice [*de condigno*] in the proper sense, but *why* this should have been so [emphasis added]. One party [Thomist] claims this was so, because of the very nature of condign satisfaction for sin: because the offense to God by sin is infinite

---

[160] Fr. Peter Damian M. Fehlner, F.I., "Coredemption and the Assumption in the Franciscan School of Mariology: The 'Franciscan Thesis' as Key" in OLG: p. 201.
[161] Ibid.
[162] Ibid., 194.

[on account of the infinite dignity of the One offended], so condign satisfaction must be infinite in value, and this is only possible
via an Incarnation. God willed condign satisfaction, therefore,
[and] as a *consequence* [emphasis added], willed the Incarnation.
The other party (Scotus) holds that neither sin as offense, nor any
form of reparation for sin per se can be infinite [in the absolute
sense]. Hence, theoretically speaking, God might well have
ordered condign satisfaction without necessarily having ordered
an incarnation. Rather, because he had antecedently decreed the
Incarnation apart from the prevision of sin, therefore in view of
sin, God decreed condign satisfaction of a most perfect kind by
the man-God in order to realize the original recapitulation of all
things by and in that man-God.[163]

The Scotist point of view is obviously motivated by the Scotistic
(or Franciscan) thesis of the absolute joint primacy of Jesus and Mary
by one and the same decree of the Eternal Father before the creation
of the world, as the paradigms and *cause* of creation, *prior* (in an
ontological sense) to any consideration of sin—either that of Adam
and Eve or even that of Lucifer himself. Thus, the Incarnation of
Jesus cannot be *conditioned* by the necessity of divine satisfaction for
the sin of humankind. In the words of Fr. Peter Damian Fehlner:
"Absolute primacy implies that the Incarnation is in the first instance
pure grace, and in no way a necessity, even hypothetical."[164]

This brings us to a second subtle and important point. One
must distinguish between "necessity" *a priori*, viz., from the point
of view of God, and *a posteriori*, viz., from our point view as created
beings. One might call the former "ontological necessity" and the
latter "epistemological necessity." The importance of considering
both kinds of necessity—*a priori* and *a posteriori*—becomes clear in
the formal semantics of symbolic modal logic, or so-called *Kripke*

[163] Ibid., 185–6.
[164] Ibid., 200.

semantics.[165] If the *intelligibility of all creation* (including ourselves), depends on the absolute joint predestination of Jesus and Mary, then we cannot deny the *epistemological necessity* of both the God-Man Jesus and the Virgin-Mother Mary if we wish to avoid a *performative contradiction* in our own act of denial, similar to the *performative contradiction* inherent in the act of denying God's existence according to St. Anselm's "ontological" proof. However, Bl. John Duns Scotus argues that there was no *ontological necessity* that the God-Man Jesus Christ would become Incarnate in order to die for our sins. Rather, according to Bl. John Duns Scotus, the Incarnation of the God-Man Jesus and the Divine Maternity of the Virgin-Mother Mary by one and the same decree of the Eternal Father before the creation of the world, and before any prevision of sin, was, like the act of creation itself, a totally gratuitous act of *Pure Love* on the part of God.

In summary, the central difference between the classical Thomistic and Scotistic understandings of the *infinite satisfaction* rendered by Jesus Christ to the Eternal Father for the sin of humankind (as formulated by St. Anselm in *Cur Deus Homo?*) can be explained as follows, in the words of Fr. Peter Damian Fehlner:

> What Scotus questions [...] is not the use of the term infinite analogically or metaphorically, but whether "non measurability" in this context provides sufficient grounds for concluding that only a divine Person could make adequate satisfaction for sin where such satisfaction by divine decree must be condign. Scotus will point out at this juncture that "non measurability" is a negative concept and does not exclude participation by a creature who is not a divine Person, once we realize that the positive aspect of "relative infinity" or immeasurability of the value of Christ's merit and satisfaction is the divine goodness or sanctity, not the divine infinity, this latter being strictly speaking incapable of

---

[165] Cf. Saul A. Kripke, *Naming and Necessity*, Harvard University Press, Cambridge, MA (1980).

participation by a finite being. This sanctity or fullness of grace, formally present in the human nature of Jesus by reason of the hypostatic union, is also uniquely shared by the Virgin Mother because of her Immaculate Conception.[166]

Ultimately, what is at stake here is the distinction of the human will of Jesus Christ and the divine will of the Eternal Word, which are not identical.[167] According to Bl. John Duns Scotus, divine acceptance is a manifestation of the divine will (free, but not arbitrary), and thus the ordering of the "relative infinities" of Jesus and Mary, which include their glories, graces, and merits, is ultimately a manifestation of *divine Love*. In the words of Fr. Peter Damian Fehlner:

> The human love of Christ, all perfect and sinless: viz., maximal, nonetheless remains formally and objectively finite. To claim otherwise is to confuse the human will of Christ with the divine (monotheletism, ultimately leading to monophysitism and some form of patripassianism or suffering on the part of the divine nature to explain the redemptive sacrifice of Jesus, a position subsequently, effectively embraced by Luther and seemingly by Rahner in our times).[168]

In his Roman conference of 1937, St. Maximilian Kolbe famously defined sanctity with an equation: "S: v = V." The letter "S" stands for sanctity, the lowercase letter "v" stands for the will of a creature, and the uppercase letter "V" stands for the will of God. It must be

---

[166] Fr. Peter Damian M. Fehlner, F.I., "Coredemption and the Assumption in the Franciscan School of Mariology: The 'Franciscan Thesis' as Key" in OLG: pp. 201–2.

[167] The heresy of monotheletism, which claims that the God-Man Jesus Christ and the Eternal Word have only one shared will, was condemned in the Lateran Council of 649, which was summoned by Pope St. Martin I (d. 655) expressly to deal with this heresy. The summoning of this council was one of Pope St. Martin I's first official acts as Pope, and it resulted in his almost immediate exile and eventual martyrdom, since the heresy had the support of the reigning Byzantine emperor Constans II.

[168] Fr. Peter Damian M. Fehlner, F.I., "Coredemption and the Assumption in the Franciscan School of Mariology: The 'Franciscan Thesis' as Key" in OLG: p. 207.

noted that St. Maximilian Kolbe interprets the mathematical symbol for equality "=" in the sense of an "equivalence relation" rather than strict "identity," which is a perfectly valid way of interpreting the symbol, common in the field of mathematical logic.[169] Thus, Mary Immaculate is the perfect image, or icon, of sanctity, because her will, while not *identical* with the divine will in essence, is nevertheless *perfectly* united to the will of God: "v = V." In this context, one might be tempted to distinguish between Mary and Jesus as follows: "Mary—S: v = V" and "Jesus—S: V = V," implying that the will of Jesus is identical in essence to the divine will. But this would be the heresy of monotheletism! Instead, according to Bl. John Duns Scotus (and St. Maximlian Kolbe), *both* Mary and Jesus are the perfect icons of sanctity: "Jesus & Mary—S: v = V," which is why *both* Jesus and Mary obtain merit *de condigno* of relative infinite value in the work of the objective redemption of humankind—as perfect Redeemer and perfect Coredemptrix—on account of the divine acceptance of their works as such because of their *perfect sanctity*: "This sanctity or fullness of grace, formally present in the human nature of Jesus by reason of the hypostatic union, is also uniquely shared by the Virgin Mother because of her Immaculate Conception."

Finally, while Mary merited grace *de condigno* as *Coredemptrix* while still on earth, she also merits grace *de congruo* as *Distributrix of all graces* in Heaven. This is what Pope St. Pius X (d. 1914) asserts when he says: "Mary merits for us *de congruo*, as the theologians say, that which Christ merited for us *de condigno*; therefore she became the principal Distributrix of graces which she received from Him."[170]

---

[169] Syntactically, the symbol for equality "=" must always be interpreted as an equivalence relation (rather than strict identity), since the same thing may have different names. Semantically, the symbol for equality "=" may sometimes be interpreted as strict identity (as for example in the case of classical mathematical logic), but even this is not always possible (as for example in the case of formal modal logic) because of the distinction between *a priori* and *a posteriori* necessity. Cf. Saul A. Kripke, *Naming and Necessity*, Harvard University Press, Cambridge, MA (1980).

[170] Pope St. Pius X, *Ad Diem Illum Laetissimum*, Encyclical Letter (February 2, 1904).

Mary's merit *de congruo* consists, not in the acquisition of new graces, but rather in the application and distribution of the graces already won *de condigno* on Calvary to us wayfarers still on earth, through the intercessory prayers offered on our behalf by our *Mother in Heaven*. Fr. Ruggero Rosini expounds:

> Thus the verb in the present tense in the Pope's phrase "Mary merits ('*promeret*') for us *de congruo*" means that Mary in Heaven continues her office of Distributrix of all graces acquired during her earthly life and, not only her own, but even those of her Son. In short, this text synthesizes in an incredible way all that has been said up to now regarding Mary's mediation. Indeed it declares that while the Mother and the Son concurred in this present life in the work of the objective Redemption—Mary's role always subordinate to that of Christ—all of which is found elsewhere in the same encyclical, now, however, seated on her heavenly throne, the Mother alone according to the disposition of her Son cares for the subjective application of the Redemption itself.[171]

While Mary's *fullness of grace* flows from her divine *Maternity* in virtue of the *Incarnation*, Mary's *fullness of merit* flows from her *Compassion* with her divine Son Jesus on *Calvary*. Once more, in the words of Fr. Ruggero Rosini:

> Here we want to underscore how Mary's merit reaches its maximum degree ("*summe meruit*") precisely in relation to her "compassion" with her Son. On Calvary one and the same sacrifice was wrought in the Passion of Jesus and the Compassion of Mary (her Compassion being always subordinate and dependent upon His Passion); thus there were established two sources of merit having one and the same value. Consequently, the merit of the Mother could not have been other than *de condigno* like that of the Son. It is worth noting the two scotistic expressions regarding Mary:

---

[171] JDS: pp. 187–8.

at the "conception" of her Son she is adorned with the "summit" in the order of grace; at the "death" of the same Son she acquires the "summit" in the order of merit. As the first case does not allow any increase of grace, so the second does not admit of an act whose object is greater in merit; otherwise no "summit" would be involved. From these derive Mary's two claims (old and new) to Motherhood in our regards [172]

Marian Maximalism is the "answer key" that allows us to *safely* and *confidently* answer the subtle questions related to grace and merit which have caused so much division and misunderstanding within the Christian faith through the centuries. Just as the Marian title "Theotókos" and the ascription of Divine Maternity to Mary at the Council of Ephesus safeguarded the divine Personhood of Jesus Christ against the errors of Nestorius,[173] so the Marian title "Coredemptrix" and the ascription of merit *de condigno* to Mary in the work of the objective Redemption on the basis of personal sanctity and divine acceptance safeguards the human nature and will of Jesus Christ against the errors of monophysitism and monotheletism, which lead to the rejection of the possibility of merit for any human being, and consequently despair and abandonment of morality.[174] In the words of Fr. Peter Damian Fehlner:

---

[172] JDS: pp. 177–8.

[173] The heresy of Nestorianism, which claims that the God-Man Jesus Christ and the Eternal Word are separate persons (though Nestorius' own terminology is somewhat ambiguous) was condemned at the First Council of Ephesus in 431. Nestorius claimed that Mary should not be given the title *Theotokos* (Mother or Bearer of God), but only the title *Christotokos* (Mother or Bearer of Christ). The views of Nestorius were strongly opposed by St. Cyril of Alexandria and St. Proclus of Constantinople.

[174] If Jesus has no free human will of His own (monotheletism), then His temptations in the desert (cf. *Mt* 4:1–11) can only be considered "symbolic"; and if the Master's confrontation with and victory over temptation was merely symbolic, then where does that leave the Master's servant when he or she is faced with temptation, except in a state of utter despair and subsequent abandonment to sin? Perhaps this is why Luther advised his disciples to "sin boldly."

Either Mary is Mediatrix of all graces because she is Coredemptrix, or there is no fruitful mediation: magisterial, pastoral, sacramental, charismatic, by anyone in the Church. In rejecting the maternal mediation of Mary in the Church and her invocation (not merely her veneration) in time of trouble and the practice of true devotion to her, the Protestant reformation logically also rejected the mediation of the Church, in particular priestly-sacramental. With this, it becomes clear that the slogan: *Christus solus* is simply a modern western version of the ancient monophysitism and monotheletism: a radical denial of the very possibility of creaturely, free cooperation (merit and good works above all) in the work of redemption, beginning with the divine Maternity and effecting of the Incarnation. The mystery of Mary as Mediatrix, whether affirmed or denied, becomes the center of a controversy over grace and justification, faith and good works, above all over the mission of the Holy Spirit and of life in the Spirit in the realization of the plan of salvation. The reason is this: at the center of the working of the Spirit is the maternal mediation of the Virgin Mother.[175]

Stephen Ray insightfully likens the Marian doctrines of the Catholic Church to the moat around a castle—there to help define and defend the doctrines of Christ.[176]

Pope Benedict XVI (then Cardinal Joseph Ratzinger) goes further:

Conversely: only when it touches Mary and becomes Mariology is Christology itself as radical as the faith of the Church requires. The appearance of a truly Marian awareness serves as the touchstone indicating whether or not the Christological substance is fully

---

[175] Fr. Peter Damian M. Fehlner, "Opening Address" in *Mary at the Foot of the Cross—VII: Coredemptrix, therefore Mediatrix of All Graces. Acts of the Seventh International Symposium on Marian Coredemption*, Academy of the Immaculate, New Bedford, MA (2008): p. 3.

[176] Cf. Stephen Ray, "Mary, the Mother of God," in *The Footprints of God* documentary series, Ignatius Press, Ft. Collins, CO (2003).

present. Nestorianism involves the fabrication of a Christology from which the nativity and the Mother are removed, a Christology without Mariological consequences. Precisely this operation, which surgically removes God so far from man that nativity and maternity—all of corporeality—remain in a different sphere, indicated unambiguously to the Christian consciousness that the discussion no longer concerned the Incarnation (becoming *flesh*), that the center of Christ's mystery was endangered, if not already destroyed. Thus in Mariology Christology was defended. Far from belittling Christology, it signifies the comprehensive triumph of a confession of faith in Christ which has achieved authenticity.[177]

Mariology is indeed the safeguard of Christology, and the key to Pneumatology (the theology of the Person and mission of the Holy Spirit); but more than that, *Christology must become Mariology* (and vice versa, and similarly for Pneumatology) in order to be "as radical as the faith of the Church requires," to ensure that the Catholic Church retains an authentic closeness to the *Incarnate* God-Man Jesus Christ. But Mary is not only a way of doctrinal safety for *Catholics* which, if reduced to a kind of "hoarding" of grace or "exaggerated doctrinal security," could lead to a form of the "inward-directed moralizing ideology" so often criticized by Pope Francis. Rather, Marian Maximalism is the most effective way of reconciliation with our separated Protestant brothers and sisters, including her Anglican[178] and Lutheran[179] children, who (if they are free of misogynist neuroses) cannot resist the attraction of the perfect

---

[177] Pope Benedict XVI (then Cardinal Joseph Ratzinger), *Daughter Zion: Meditations on the Church's Marian Belief,* translated by John M. McDermott, S.J., Ignatius Press, San Francisco, CA (1983): pp. 35–6.

[178] Cf. Dr. Judith Marie Gentle, "Reclaiming England for Our Lady: The Concept of Redemption in the Caroline Divines and in the Anglo-Catholic Theologians" in *Mary at the Foot of the Cross—VIII: Coredemption as Key to a Correct Understanding of Redemption, and Recent Attempts to Redefine Redemption Contrary to the Belief of the Church Acts of the Eighth International Symposium on Marian Coredemption,* Academy of the Immaculate, New Bedford, MA (2008): pp. 259–84.

[179] Cf. Clara M.B. Fleischmann, "The Daughters of Mary: Why We Should Listen," *Missio Immaculatae International,* 10:3 (2014): pp. 34–5.

Mother, who loves them with as much love as she bears her Catholic children, and who would rather die herself than see any one of her children lost.

CHAPTER TEN

TRUE, VIRGINAL WIFE OF JOSEPH

Sadly, it has been suggested that the intimate union of Mary, the created Immaculate Conception, with the Holy Spirit, the uncreated Immaculate Conception, as *Spouse of the Holy Spirit* (cf. St. Francis of Assisi) and consequently *the Holy Spirit quasi-incarnate* (cf. St. Maximilian Kolbe), would necessarily make any semblance of Mary's genuine personality disappear on account of the infinite Personality of the Holy Spirit (i.e., Mary would become a kind of "robot" controlled by the will of the Holy Spirit, with no human will of her own).[180] This is a major fallacy for at least two reasons: First, it implicitly accepts the heresy of "monotheletism," since even the human will of Jesus Christ Himself, who is *truly the Eternal Word incarnate*, is not identical with the will of His divine nature, and so Jesus is not a kind of "robot" controlled by the will of the Eternal Word! Second, it completely ignores the nature of *union in love*—"and the two become as one flesh"[181]—including the loving union between God and man. Pope Benedict XVI assures us that "man can indeed enter into union with God—his primordial aspiration. But this union *is no mere fusion* [emphasis added], a sinking in the nameless ocean of the Divine; it is a unity which creates love, a unity in which both God and man remain themselves and yet become fully one."[182]

---

[180] Cf. Monica Migliorino Miller, "The Gender of the Holy Trinity," *New Oxford Review* (May 2003).

[181] *Mk* 10:8.

[182] Pope Benedict XVI, *Deus Caritas Est*, Encyclical Letter (December 25, 2005).

Mary is *truly* the Spouse of the Holy Spirit as well as the Holy Spirit quasi-incarnate. Nevertheless, according to Bl. John Duns Scotus, Mary remains always the *true, virginal wife of Joseph*, just as Joseph remains the *true, virginal husband of Mary*. In fact, it can even be said that Joseph is the *true, virginal father of Jesus Christ*, since, in the words of Fr. Ruggero Rosini:

> As such Joseph is the co-proprietor with Mary of this "Fruit" which matured in her womb. The Mother herself attests to this when she says, "*Son, why hast Thou done so to us? Behold, in sorrow Thy father and I have been seeking Thee*" (*Lk* 2:48). By calling Joseph "*Thy father,*" Mary indicates that he is something more than a simple "custodian"; she shows that both of them are equally proprietors, both equally co-responsible. It is not without reason that Jesus is called "*the son of Joseph*" (*Jn* 1:45). This is precisely because Joseph does not derive his *rights* over that Child and his *duties* towards Him from some external delegation, or from his good will, but from the matrimony itself. The final end of this marriage, in part, is reserved to God insofar as the conception of the Child goes; whereas the other part, insofar as the consequences of conception go—propriety, responsibility, custody, etc.—belongs to Joseph.[183]

This was also the opinion of Pope St. John Paul II[184] and St. Maximilian Kolbe. In the words of Fr. Joaquín Ferrer Arellano:

> Although singular, unique, and not univocal with fatherhood as this is ordinarily understood and commonly found among men, *the position more common and traditional* among theologians *upholds the truly real fatherhood of Joseph in relation to Jesus, based 1) on his marriage to Mary, the Mother of Jesus, and 2) on the right of the husband over his wife. He, therefore, who is born virginally of*

---

[183] JDS: pp. 112–3.

[184] Cf. Pope St. John Paul II, *Redemptoris Custos*, Apostolic Exhortation (August 15, 1989).

Mary, by reason of his birth, intimately pertains in some manner to Joseph as father. [...] In view of the dignity of Joseph as husband of Mary to whom belongs the fruit of his wife's womb, one is not permitted to overlook, as F. Canals wisely observes, how the *indivisible virginity* of both spouses—not simply that of Mary, but also that of her husband, the son of David—is ordered to the *virginal fatherhood* of Joseph according to the Spirit, in virtue of the obedience of faith to the saving plan of God. This plan includes the *messianic fatherhood* of Joseph as son of David in relation to his virginal Son, constituted Son of David, the messianic King, because He was Son of Joseph.[185]

Just as Mary does not "disappear" next to the relative infinity of the Holy Spirit, her divine Spouse, so also Joseph does not "disappear" next to the relative infinity of Mary, his wife. Indeed, many saints and holy writers believe that Joseph occupies a place in the Church that is uniquely highest after Mary.[186] Thus, by the circumstance of his closeness to the Blessed Virgin Mary, according to the doctrine of merit of Bl. John Duns Scotus, the glories, graces, and merits of Joseph have their own level of relative infinity, infinitely greater than (and therefore incommensurate with) those of any other member of

---

[185] Fr. Joaquín Ferrer Arellano, "The Virginal Marriage of Mary and Joseph according to Bl. John Duns Scotus" in *Blessed John Duns Scotus and His Mariology, Commemoration of the Seventh Centenary of His Death*, Academy of the Immaculate, New Bedford, MA (2009): pp. 385–6.

[186] Cf. Msgr. Arthur Burton Calkins, "The Cultus of the Heart of St. Joseph. An Inquiry into the Status Quaestionis," *Akten des IX Internationalen des hl. Joseph*, 28 Sept. – 2 Oct., 2005, Kevelaer, Germany, vol. 2: pp. 937–51; Edward Healy Thompson, *The Life and Glories of St. Joseph*, Burns & Oates, London (1888). In the words of Fr. Joaquín Ferrer Arellano: "The devotion to the 'Three Hearts' united of Jesus, Mary, and Joseph began in Portugal and Brazil (1733) and flourished especially in Mexico. Around the middle of the 18th century, it was spread in France, Spain and Italy by the Discalced Carmelite Fr. Elias of the Three Hearts. With the approbation of [Pope] Gregory XVI (April 28, 1843), this devotion expanded very much in Europe and America, promoted especially by F. L. Filas, SJ, and by a good number of well-known ecclesiastics." Fr. Joaquín Ferrer Arellano, "Mariology of St. Paul" in *Mary at the Foot of the Cross—IX: Mary: Spouse of the Holy Spirit, Coredemptrix and Mother of the Church. Acts of the Ninth International Symposium on Marian Coredemption*, Academy of the Immaculate, New Bedford, MA (2010): p. 183, footnote 7.

the Church except for Jesus and Mary, and still infinitely less than (and therefore incommensurate with) those of Mary, who occupies a place in the Church that is uniquely highest after Christ.[187] In the words of Fr. Joaquín Ferrer Arellano:

> This association of the two spouses must be understood from the perspective of the inseparability of the Three, in their being and in the work of salvation, according to a certain hierarchical subordination. Mary received her privilege of a fullness of immaculate holiness from Jesus by reason of her preservative redemption, as Scotus knew how to explain so well. This made her capable of being 1) Mother of God, first in her heart and in her mind, and then in her womb (in the flesh formed by the Holy Spirit in her virginal womb with her fully active, maternal cooperation, as we have seen Scotus underscore with such insistence), and 2) Coredemptrix. [...] In turn, through his Spouse [Mary], Joseph received the fullness of grace which we can quite adequately term paternal. This made him capable of a messianic, virginal fatherhood, not according to the flesh, but according to the Spirit in virtue of his unconditional, silent response in faith. In virtue of this, he became co-participant with Mary in constituting the theandric being of the Redeemer. This is the basis of his redemptive work: both objective from Nazareth to Calvary, and subjective in his saving dispensation during history until the Parousia. Hence, Joseph is father and lord of the Family of God which is the Church, prolongation of the Family of Nazareth, summit of the divine plan of salvation of the world.[188]

The reader may wonder what the glories of Joseph have to do with the glories of Mary. Indeed, one may be tempted to suppose

---

[187] LG 54.

[188] Fr. Joaquín Ferrer Arellano, "The Virginal Marriage of Mary and Joseph according to Bl. John Duns Scotus" in *Blessed John Duns Scotus and His Mariology, Commemoration of the Seventh Centenary of His Death*, Academy of the Immaculate, New Bedford, MA (2009): p. 387.

that we simply have "maximalism on our minds" and that we are spewing glories willy-nilly. This, however, would be a great mistake. The importance of including Joseph in any discussion of Marian Maximalism goes far beyond merely providing an example of the hierarchy of relative infinities, or making the point, as we have done, that Joseph does not "disappear" next to the relative infinity of Mary, his wife, just as Mary does not "disappear" next to the relative infinity of the Holy Spirit, her divine Spouse, or Jesus, her divine Son. Nor should the reader suppose that applying a *maximality* of praise to Joseph can in any way *detract* from Mary, any more than applying a maximality of praise to Mary can in any way detract from the Holy Spirit or Jesus. In fact, precisely the opposite is true! The glories of Joseph actually *safeguard* the glories of Mary, just as the glories of Mary safeguard the glories of Jesus. To see that this is true, consider the fact that there would be nothing special about Joseph if there were nothing special about Mary, just as there would be nothing special about Mary if there were nothing special about Jesus. It follows with logical certainty (by contrapositive) that *if* there is something special about Joseph, then there *must* be something special about Mary, and *if* there is something special about Mary, then there *must* be something special about Jesus!

In this way, we see very practically how our devotion to Joseph safeguards both our devotion to Mary and our devotion to Jesus, just as our devotion to Mary safeguards our devotion to Jesus. Joseph fulfills his role as perfect husband and father by protecting both his wife, Mary, and their son, Jesus, just as Mary fulfills her role as perfect wife and mother by protecting their son, Jesus, the virginal fruit of their virginal marriage. In so doing, the Holy Family of Nazareth, Joseph, Mary, and the God-Man Jesus Christ, provide us with an incomparable example of Christian marriage, as the true paradigms for every member of the Christian family: father-husband, mother-wife, and child—the consummation of the love between husband and wife.

Given the intrinsic correspondence between maximal praise and honor given to Mary and maximal praise and honor given to Joseph—indeed, the intrinsic correspondence between maximal praise and honor given to *all three members* of the Earthly Trinity: Jesus, Mary, and Joseph—it comes as no surprise that Joseph was proclaimed the patron and protector of the Church by the same pope who proclaimed the dogma of Mary's Immaculate Conception: Bl. Pope Pius IX.

In the return of all created things to God the Father, it is under the leadership of Joseph, our Patriarch, and in imitation of him that the individual members of the Church must, by the merits gained for us through the Redemptive Sacrifice of Jesus Christ, the Incarnate Word of God, be transubstantiated into Mary, the *Virgo Ecclesia Facta*. It is *only* by being transubstantiated into Mary, the created Immaculate Conception, that we can be united to God as she is uniquely united to God, and be transubstantiated with her into the uncreated Immaculate Conception, the Holy Spirit. In virtue of this transubstantiation, we are possessed by the Immaculate, and we are thereby transformed in her womb into a single community or Church, having the personality of both our parents: our mother, Mary, and our father, Joseph, who is himself a perfect or transparent icon of the Eternal Father in Heaven.

CHAPTER ELEVEN

The Panagia

Before the end of the first millennium, while still virtually unknown in continental Western Europe, the feast of Mary's Immaculate Conception was celebrated in pre-Norman Anglo-Saxon England. Suppressed after the Norman Conquest of 1066, the feast was reintroduced in England by a nephew of St. Anselm of Canterbury, earning for England the title of "Our Lady's Dowry,"[189] and providing the fertile earth for the theological insights of Bl. John Duns Scotus.[190] Though still a novelty in the liturgy of the Western Church at this time, the feast of Mary's Immaculate Conception (called the feast of the Conception of St. Anne, but referring to the same event) had already been celebrated in the Greek liturgy for centuries, and its adoption in the British Isles was probably due to the influence of the well-traveled Irish missionaries who had encountered the feast during their travels in the East.[191] Thus, the Eastern Church shared with the Western Church what has been called a "hermeneutic

---

[189] Cf. Fr. Timothy Finigan, "Belief in and Devotion to the Immaculate Conception in Medieval England" in *Mary at the Foot of the Cross—V: Redemption and Coredemption under the Sign of the Immaculate Conception. Acts of the Fifth International Symposium on Marian Coredemption*, Academy of the Immaculate, New Bedford, MA (2005): pp. 344–59.

[190] Cf. Fr. Gerard Manley Hopkins, S.J., "Duns Scotus's Oxford" in *Poems and Prose of Gerard Manley Hopkins*, selected with an introduction and notes by W. H. Gardner, Penguin Books (1953): p. 40.

[191] John Janaro, "Saint Anselm and the Development of the Doctrine of the Immaculate Conception: Historical and Theological Perspectives," *The Saint Anselm Journal* 3.2 (Spring 2006).

of doxology"[192] regarding the Theotókos, "rooted above all in the ecstatic celebration of Mary as the 'All-Holy' (Panagia) so frequently expressed in the liturgy, hymnography, and homiletics of the Greek Fathers in the second half of the first millennium."[193]

The singularly *maximal* devotion of the Eastern Church to the Mother of God, who is known as *The Panagia—The All-Holy One*, is manifest in the Byzantine liturgy of the Ukrainian Greek Catholic Church,[194] to take just one example. We have only to read (or preferably hear sung) the *Molében* to the Mother of God,[195] which is recited every Wednesday and throughout the month of May, from which the following is only a small excerpt:

> Rejoice, O most pure Virgin; rejoice, O precious Scepter of Christ the King; rejoice, you who mysteriously gave growth to the Vine; rejoice, O Gate of heaven and Bush unconsumed by fire; rejoice, O Light of the whole world; rejoice, Joy of all mankind; rejoice, Salvation of the faithful; rejoice, Helper and Refuge of all Christians, O Sovereign Lady.

> [...]

---

[192] Ibid. The term "doxology" comes from the Greek words "Doxa Soi," which occur so frequently in the Byzantine liturgy. These words can mean both "Glory be to Thee" and "I believe in Thee"—a combination of meanings which seem to represent well the spirituality of the Eastern Church.

[193] Ibid.

[194] The Ukrainian Greek Catholic Church (UGCC), like the Melkite Catholic Church, uses the Byzantine Rite composed in part by St. Basil the Great (d. 379) and St. John Chrysostom (d. 407) and is in full communion with the Roman Catholic Church *sui juris*. With over 4 million members worldwide, the UGCC is the largest Eastern Rite Catholic Church in full communion with the Holy See.

[195] According to Fr. Francis Marsden: "The *Moleben* is shorter than the *Akathist*. Taking about half an hour, it is basically a liturgy of the word with some versicles and then the Gospel, a liturgy of invocation and then more versicles and Litanies. There exist *Moleben* not just to our Lady, but also to different saints and to Christ himself." Fr. Francis Marsden, "Breathing with Both Lungs: Some Reflections on Prayer to Mary from the Ukrainian Greek-Catholic Tradition" in *Mary at the Foot of the Cross—III: Mater Unitatis. Acts of the Third International Symposium on Marian Coredemption*, Academy of the Immaculate, New Bedford, MA (2003): p. 439.

Rejoice, for the whole world praises you; rejoice, O Temple of the Lord; rejoice, O Mountain, wrapped in shadows; rejoice, O Refuge of all; rejoice, O golden Lampstand; rejoice, highly honored Glory of true believers; rejoice, O Mary, Mother of Christ our God; rejoice, O Paradise; rejoice, O divine Table-Refectory; rejoice, O pleasant Shade; rejoice, O Hand of gold; rejoice, O Hope of the living.[196]

A worthy commentary on even half of the Marian titles found in this excerpt would fill volumes, and we will not attempt it here. However, to get an indication of the rich exegesis of these (ancient) Marian titles, we turn to the Mariological treatise of the Byzantine Orthodox saint Mark Eugenicus of Ephesus (d. 1444):

For God has been called a consuming fire, not only toward vileness, but also toward a created nature. Also, his melodious God-inspired witness from Damascus [St. John Damascene], harmonizes with this all-blameless Virgin:

"O divine bridal nymph, a bush unburnt by fire on the mountain and a dewy-aired Chaldean furnace forescribes you clearly; for you received the divine consuming fire in your material belly unburnt!"[197]

Not only is Mary likened to the burning bush on Mount Horeb that was unconsumed by fire, both on account of her perpetual virginity and on account of her "prepurification," which allowed her created nature to remain unconsumed by the divine consuming fire Incarnate in her womb;[198] she is also likened to the furnace in which

---

[196] From the Moleben to the Mother of God, as quoted by ibid.: p. 446.

[197] Mark Eugenicus of Ephesus, as quoted by Rev. Christiaan W. Kappes, *The Immaculate Conception: Why Thomas Aquinas Denied, While John Duns Scotus, Gregory Palamas, and Mark Eugenicus Professed the Absolute Immaculate Existence of Mary*, Academy of the Immaculate, New Bedford, MA (2014): p. 149. Subsequent citations are abbreviated TIC.

[198] Cf. *Ex* 3:2.

the three young men were unburned, along with a fourth "like the Son of God,"[199] because in giving her Immaculate flesh to the God-Man Jesus, she thereby gave a purity (like dew) to His human nature that "allowed" it to be joined to His divine nature without being burnt up.[200]

The notion of the "prepurification" of the Blessed Virgin, or her *prokatharsis*, which led to the Eastern celebration of the feast of Mary's Immaculate Conception (or the feast of the Conception of St. Anne), is common in the writings of the Greek Fathers from the time of St. Gregory Nazianzen (d. 390), who said:

> And in every way He became man, save sin; for He has been conceived from a virgin, after she had been prepurified with respect to soul and body through the Holy Spirit (for it was necessary that His birth be honored, and virginity be honored prior to that); and in every way He was born a man, save sin.[201]

The doctrine of Mary's prepurification was repeated by a monk named Alexander:

> He closed the heavens, and descended, though not cut-off from the heavens, and he dwelt in the space of the holy, glorious, and ever-virgin Mary, after she herself was prepurified with respect to soul and along with her members through the Holy Spirit; the Word became flesh and dwelt among us.[202]

It was repeated again by St. Sophronius of Jerusalem (d. 638), with a notable increase in *maximalism*:

---

[199] *Dan* 3:25.
[200] Cf. TIC: p. 151.
[201] St. Gregory Nazianzen, *In Theophania:* Oration 38. TIC: p. 21.
[202] Alexander, *De inventio Sanctae Crucis.* TIC: p. 29.

Nobody is "blessed" as you, nobody is "sanctified" as you; nobody is "magnified" as you, nobody is "prepurified" as you; nobody is "beaming" as you, nobody is "brilliant" as you![203]

Finally, in a text which, according to Fr. Christiaan Kappes, became the "standard" of Mariology in the subsequent Byzantine tradition, St. John Damascene (d. 749) repeats the doctrine of Mary's prepurification, and refers to Mary as the *Immaculate*:

> O august Immaculate! I will thoroughly describe the infinite power of the Most High, which overshadowed thee, after the Holy Spirit came upon thee, who had been hallowed with respect to soul, and prepurified with respect to body.[204]

In addition to being perhaps the earliest defenders of Mary's Immaculate Conception, the Mariology of the Eastern Church is typified above all by the image of Mary as the *domus* or dwelling place of God—the *Enclosed Garden*, the *Temple*, the *Tabernacle*, and the *Tent* of God; indeed, *Heaven itself*. An early example of this typology can be seen in the Canon of John Damascene on the feast of the Annunciation:

> The overshadowing of the All-Holy Spirit purified her soul and completely hallowed her body, then constructed a temple, having consecrated me as an ensouled container of God, a divinely decorated tent, and the chaste Mother of Life![205]

We have already heard the exclamation of St. John Damascene in which he identifies Mary with Heaven: "O womb [of Anne] in which was conceived the living heaven [Mary], wider than the wideness of the heavens." Indeed, St. John Damascene, Father and

---

[203] St. Sophronius of Jerusalem, *In Sanctissimae Deiparae Annuntiationem*. TIC: p. 31.

[204] St. John Damascene, *In S. Basilium*. TIC: p. 53.

[205] TIC: p. 17.

Doctor of the Church, even says that "this heaven [Mary] is clearly much more divine and awesome than the first" heaven. We have also heard St. Proclus of Constantinople (d. 446 or 447) affirm that Mary is "handmaid and mother, virgin and heaven, the only bridge for God to mankind." His friend, St. John Chrysostom (d. 407), Father and Doctor of the Church, also exclaims:

> Rejoice, mother and heaven, maiden and cloud, virgin and throne, the boast and foundation of our Church. Plead earnestly for us that through you we may obtain mercy on the Day of Judgment and attain the good things reserved for those who love God, through the grace and love of our Lord Jesus Christ, to whom with the Father and the Holy Spirit be glory, power, and honor now and forever and for all eternity. Amen.[206]

This identification of Mary with "Heaven" by the Eastern Fathers has become an integral part of the liturgy of the Eastern Church. In the Ukrainian Greek Catholic Evening prayer (*Vetuniya*) for Saturday, which is called the *Dogmaty*, the faithful pray:

> Let us hymn the whole world's glory, engendered of Adam, who gave birth to the Master, the gate of heaven, Mary the Virgin, the song of the incorporeal Powers, the adornment of the faithful, for She has been proclaimed the Heaven and Temple of the God-head.[207]

We should not be surprised that Mary is called "Heaven" by the Eastern Fathers. The term Heaven is, of course, simply our term for

---

[206] St. John Chrysostom, as quoted in the *Little Office of the Blessed Virgin Mary*, compiled and edited by John E. Rotelle, O.S.A., Catholic Book Publishing Corp., NJ (1988): p. 98 (Thursday Evening Prayer).

[207] From the *Dogmaty*, as quoted by Fr. Francis Marsden, "Breathing with Both Lungs: Some Reflections on Prayer to Mary from the Ukrainian Greek-Catholic Tradition" in *Mary at the Foot of the Cross—III: Mater Unitatis. Acts of the Third International Symposium on Marian Coredemption*, Academy of the Immaculate, New Bedford, MA (2003): p. 433.

the Beatific Vision. That is to say, Heaven is the immeasurable joy, or *beatitude*, that we will experience when we see God face to face. St. John says: "Beloved, we are God's children now, and what we will be has not yet appeared; but we know that when he appears we shall be like him, because we shall see him as he is."[208] Thus, wherever God is there Heaven is also. In view of this fact, it is obvious that in as much as Jesus Christ is Emmanuel, *God with us*, the womb of the Blessed and Ever-Glorious Virgin Mary must *be Heaven*.

However, the Eastern liturgy invites us to go further than that. Mary the Virgin, the Gate of Heaven, the Woman who encompasses the Man,[209] is not only the Temple and Heaven of Emmanuel, God-with-us, while He is on earth. *She has been proclaimed the Heaven and Temple of the Godhead—the whole Trinity.* Thus, Mary's identification with Heaven cannot be limited to the nine months while she carried the God-Man Jesus Christ on earth. Indeed, if we may be so bold as to draw inspiration from the fields of modern psychology and neurophysiology, we learn that, to an unborn child in his or her mother's womb, the subjective experience of "time" or "duration" is inverted in proportion to the child's physical development as he or she ages. Dr. Karl Stern explains:

Everybody knows that with advancing age our subjective experience of duration becomes compressed. For the child, two consecutive summers are separated by an eternity; for an old man, the summers seem to follow each other with accelerating speed. There are indications that the speed of cellular mechanisms is inverted to time experience; as the stretches of subjective time are long in the child, tissue reactions such as the healing of wounds are rapid—and vice versa in the aged. As we extend this back into infancy, it is obvious that we once inhabited a vast time universe;

---

208 *1 Jn* 3:2.
209 Cf. *Jer* 31:22.

and there we lived in an intimate physical and mental fusion with another being.[210]

Putting this fact in the context of the Virgin-Mother Mary and her divine Son, the God-Man Jesus Christ, who was *fully God* and at the same time *fully Man*, we are confronted with an amazing and truly unspeakable mystery: God Himself lived in an *intimate physical and mental fusion* with the Blessed Virgin Mary for a period of time which *seemed to Him like eternity*! What is subjective to God, who is Truth, is objective by definition. Thus, due to the fact (*a posteriori*) of the *Incarnation of the God-Man* Jesus Christ, *Mary is Heaven* in a way that transcends even time itself. In the words of the Thomist philosopher and theologian Charles De Koninck (d. 1965):[211]

> [...] being the origin and Generatrix of God, Mary participates in the reason of the First Principle and is in the root of the universal order [...]. She proceeds from Him Who made her in order that He might proceed from her [...]. She proceeds from the true light, from Him Who is light, in order that from her the indefectible light might arise to the heavens. The Son, who in the bosom of the Father had encompassed all things, including the Virgin, allowed Himself to be encompassed within the womb of the Virgin.[212]

If God once so desired the spiritual and physical space of the Virgin's womb to leap into it and dwell there for nine months, which however brief a time seemed to Him—the Author of time—like eternity, then He must continue to do so eternally, because God never

---

[210] Karl Stern, *The Flight from Woman*, Paragon House, St. Paul, MN (1985): pp. 20–1.

[211] Charles De Koninck was the founder of so-called "Laval Thomism." He was also the mentor of Ralph McInerny, and his son Thomas may have been the inspiration for Antoine de Saint-Exupéry's *Petit Prince*.

[212] Charles De Koninck, *Ego Sapientia*, Surco, La Plata, 1947, pp. 23, 33–4, as quoted by Fr. Carlos Biestro, "The Enclosed Garden" in *Mary at the Foot of the Cross—III: Mater Unitatis. Acts of the Third International Symposium on Marian Coredemption*, Academy of the Immaculate, New Bedford, MA (2003): pp. 173–4.

changes His desires. It follows that Jesus remains in Mary's womb and Heart forever, making her pure body and soul a Temple and truly Heaven for eternity. In the words of St. John Eudes (d. 1680):

> Mary's pure Heart is truly a heaven of which the sky over our heads is a mere shadow and image. It is a heaven exalted above all others, of which the Holy Spirit speaks when He says that the Savior of the World went out from a heaven surpassing all others in excellence, when He came on earth to redeem mankind: *A summo caelo egressio ejus* (*Ps* 19:6). As Our Admirable Mother had formed her Divine Son in her Heart before conceiving Him in her womb, we can truly say that, having remained hidden in her Heart for a little while even as He had been in the Heart of His heavenly Father from all eternity, Our Blessed Savior emerged from it to manifest Himself to men. But just as He went forth from heaven and His Father's bosom, without however relinquishing them: *Excessit, non recessit*, so also is His Mother's Heart a heaven whence He came forth in such a manner that He nevertheless remained and will remain forever in it: "For ever, O Lord, thy word standeth firm in heaven" (*Ps* 119:89).[213]

Moreover, the Blessed Virgin's relationship to us as mother does not end at the end of this earthly pilgrimage, any more than her relationship to her divine Son ends, because He is the Head and we are the members of His Body, the Church.[214] If we are members of

---

[213] St. John Eudes, *The Admirable Heart of Mary*, translated from the French by Charles Di Targiani and Ruth Hauser, P. J. Kenedy & Sons, New York, NY (1948): p. 34 (Part Two, Ch. II).

[214] In the words of Fr. Joaquín Ferrer Arellano: "Pseudo-Augustine calls Mary 'the form of God,' the living mold of the Only Begotten of the Father, firstborn among many brethren, whence is 'formed' from the Woman the Head of the rest of His spiritual descendants. St. Louis-Marie Grignon de Montfort completes this enlightening insight, for centuries attributed to the Holy Doctor St. Augustine, for the rest in perfect harmony with his ecclesiology, in his well-known work *The Secret of Mary* where he writes: 'whoever is shaped in this mold and remains in it shares all the features of Jesus Christ.'" Fr. Joaquín Ferrer Arellano, "Marian Coredemption and Sacramental Mediation" in ibid.: p. 73, footnote 5.

Christ's Body now imperfectly, we will be so perfectly in Heaven. Likewise, if we are Mary's children now imperfectly, we will be so perfectly in Heaven—*the fruit of her womb with Jesus*. It follows that in Heaven we will be *clothed with Mary*, as with a mantle, in her womb. This is why the Virgin-Mother is "the adornment of the faithful." In the words of St. John Damascene:

> Today Eden receives from the New Adam the spiritual paradise, wherein condemnation was abolished, the Tree of Life was planted, and our nakedness was covered. For we are no longer naked and deprived of garments, divested of the splendor of the divine image, deprived of the abounding grace of the Spirit. No longer do we lament our ancient nakedness, saying: "I have already removed my tunic; how can I put it on again?" (*Song* 5:3).[215]

St. Ephrem (d. 373) affirms that Mary is the "garment of the children of Eve":

> By you [Mary], the banished servants come back to enter, that they might obtain once again the benefits of which they had been deprived. May you, who cover their nakedness, be clothed in glory.[216]

Indeed, the Beatific Vision is inseparable from Mary, just as Mary is inseparable from Jesus. In the words of St. Louis-Marie Grignon de Montfort (d. 1716):

> Jesus is altogether in Mary and Mary altogether in Jesus; or rather, she exists no more, but Jesus alone is in her, and it were easier to separate the light from the sun than Mary from Jesus. [...] Glory to Jesus in Mary! Glory to Mary in Jesus! Glory to God alone. [...]

---

[215] St. John Damascene, *Homilia II in Dormitionem B.V. Mariae*, 2, as quoted by Fr. Carlos Biestro, "The Enclosed Garden" in ibid.: p. 189.

[216] St. Ephrem the Syrian, *Hymni de Beata Maria*, XVIII, as quoted by ibid.: p. 191.

Mary is the Paradise and world of God [...] the living mold of God and of the saints [...] she is the Paradise into which the Holy Spirit draws the soul, that it may find God therein.[217]

Essential to both the monastic and liturgical tradition of the Eastern Church is the attitude of *adoring silence*, or "quietude" (*hesychia*), in the face of the divine mysteries, within which the mystery of Mary is ineffably wrapped. This may seem incongruous with the "hermeneutic of doxology"—that is, the ecstatic celebration of Mary as the Panagia and the equally ecstatic celebration of the God-Man Jesus Christ and the Holy Trinity—in the liturgy, hymnography, and homiletics of the Eastern Fathers. But there is no contradiction. The Eastern practice of adoring silence before the divine mysteries is not *muteness* in their regard, but rather the practice of *constant contemplative prayer and recollection.*[218] It would seem that in the tradition of the Eastern Church, the mystery first perceived in an attitude of adoring silence is then proclaimed in a spirit of jubilation! In the words of Pope St. John Paul II:

> Nevertheless this mystery is continuously veiled, enveloped in silence, lest an idol be created in place of God. Only in a progressive purification of the knowledge of communion, will man and God meet and recognize in an eternal embrace their unending connaturality of love. Thus is born what is called the *apophatism* of the Christian East: the more man grows in the knowledge of God, the

---

[217] St. Louis-Marie Grignon de Montfort, *True Devotion to the Blessed Virgin Mary*, No. 247, 265; *The Secret of Mary*, No. 10, 16, 20, as quoted by ibid.: p. 175.

[218] The confusion of contemplation with muteness, which has unfortunately become common in contemporary Western mysticism, seems to arise from a confusion of the "nada" of St. John of the Cross with the "nirvana" of Buddhism (or Hinduism). The latter is indeed akin to "muteness," because it is empty, while the former is filled with Christ. The same distinction holds between the mysticism of the so-called "Eastern religions," which regardless of their human or psychological merit lack Christ, and the mysticism of the Eastern Church, which is eminently Christocentric. As always, the crux is the Cross of Christ. "May I never boast except in the cross of our Lord Jesus Christ, through which the world has been crucified to me, and I to the world" (*Gal* 6:14).

more he perceives him as an inaccessible mystery, whose essence cannot be grasped. This should not be confused with an obscure mysticism in which man loses himself in enigmatic, impersonal realities. On the contrary, the Christians of the East turn to God as Father, Son and Holy Spirit, living persons tenderly present, to whom they utter a solemn and humble, majestic and simple liturgical doxology. But they perceive that one draws close to this presence above all by letting oneself be taught an adoring silence, for *at the culmination of the knowledge and experience of God is his absolute transcendence.* This is reached through the prayerful assimilation of scripture and the liturgy more than by systematic meditation.[219]

The attitude of adoring silence is a path of purification of knowledge and of memory, which leads both to one's growth in the knowledge of God and at the same time to one's perception of His absolute transcendence. This purification is realized precisely in Mary, since, in the words of Fr. Peter Damian Fehlner, "there is no fruition of the greatness (infinite goodness) of God, except via the purity of the Immaculate Heart. Only the pure of heart shall see God (*Mt* 5:8)."[220] This is what St. Germanus of Constantinople (d. 733 or 740) states definitively:

> No one obtains a full knowledge of God except through you, O Most Holy Lady; no one is saved except through you, O Deipara; no one is liberated from perils except by you, Virgin Mary; no one is redeemed except through you, Mother of God.[221]

---

[219] Pope St. John Paul II, *Orientale Lumen*, Apostolic Letter (May 2, 1995): 16.

[220] TTW: p. 213.

[221] St. Germanus of Constantinople, *Oratio VII. In Dormitionem SS Deiparae*, II, as quoted by Fr. Carlos Biestro, "The Enclosed Garden" in *Mary at the Foot of the Cross—III: Mater Unitatis. Acts of the Third International Symposium on Marian Coredemption*, Academy of the Immaculate, New Bedford, MA (2003): p. 177.

Given the fact that the purification of our knowledge depends on our total consecration to and contemplation of Mary, who is the first example of adoring silence,[222] it comes as no surprise that St. Gregory Palamas (d. 1359),[223] the preeminent theologian and defender of the Eastern eremitical practice of *Hesychasm,* or Sacred Quietude,[224] after contemplating her glory in a spirit of adoring silence, exalts the Virgin Mother of God to heights undreamed of—indeed, heights "which, outside of God, no mind can succeed in comprehending fully"[225]—when he asserts:

> She [Mary] is the cause of what came before Her, the champion of what came after Her and the agent of things eternal. She is the substance of the prophets, the principles of the apostles, the firm foundation of the martyrs and the premise of the teachers of the

---

[222] Cf. *Lk* 2:19, 51.

[223] Though long recognized as a saint and doctor in the Eastern Orthodox Church, Gregory Palamas has never been officially canonized by the Roman Catholic Church. However, Gregory Palamas is officially recognized as a saint in both the Melkite Catholic Church and the Ukrainian Greek Catholic Church, and he was repeatedly referred to as a "great writer" and theologian by Pope St. John Paul II: cf. Pope St. John Paul II, *Homily at Ephesus* (November 30, 1979); *General Audience* (November 12, 1997).

[224] One of the central practices of *Hesychasm* is the repetition of the Holy Name of Jesus and the Jesus Prayer: "Lord Jesus Christ, Son of God, have mercy on me, a sinner." The Jesus Prayer must be prayed with the heart—not superficially as simply a group of words or sounds repeated as a "mantra" to aid concentration, but with real meaning and personal longing directed to the Person of Jesus Christ—unceasingly. The practice of *Hesychasm,* or Sacred Quietude, was defended by St. Gregory Palamas in nine treatises called "Triads for the Defense of Those Who Practice Sacred Quietude." The theology of St. Gregory Palamas, sometimes called "Palamism," was adopted as official doctrine (or "dogma") by the Eastern Orthodox Church in a series of councils from 1341 to 1351 having "ecumenical" authority in the Orthodox Churches. This theology distinguishes between the uncreated divine Essence of God, which is absolutely transcendent and therefore essentially unknowable to us as finite creatures, and His (uncreated) divine Energies, which God does in fact allow us to know, and through which God reveals Himself to us. Thus, the goal of the *Hesychast* is the experiential knowledge of God via His divine Energies, which is thought to be the knowledge of God that was enjoyed by the prophets and patriarchs of the Old Testament, who, like Jacob, "saw God face to face" (*Gen* 32:30). Cf. *Gregory Palamas: The Triads* (Classics in Western Spirituality), Paulist Press, Mahwah, NJ (1983).

[225] Bl. Pope Pius IX, *Ineffabilis Deus*, Apostolic Constitution (December 8, 1854).

Church. She is the glory of those upon earth, the joy of celestial beings, the adornment of all creation. She is the beginning and the source and the root of unutterable good things; she is the summit and the consummation of everything holy.[226]

These words of St. Gregory Palamas are certainly striking, containing as they do very precise theological language (e.g., *cause*, *agent*, *substance*, *source*, etc.), and as the fruit of an adoring silence before the mystery of God and the mystery of Mary, they cannot be disregarded as "ecstatic exaggeration"! According to St. Paul, the Incarnation of the God-Man Jesus was ordained before the creation of the world, and before the creation of the first man Adam.[227] By *one and the same decree* (*uno eodemque decreto*), Mary was ordained to be the Mother of God before the creation of the world, and before the creation of the first woman Eve.[228] But this leads us to an amazing logical conclusion. If God created the world on condition of the Incarnation, as Bl. John Duns Scotus holds, and Mary was chosen to be the Mother of Jesus before the creation of the world, then *the creation of the world* in fact depended on Mary's reply to the Archangel Gabriel, when he asked her if she would consent to be the Mother of God. The creation of the universe, "of all things in the heavens and on the earth, things visible and things invisible, whether Thrones, or Dominations, or Principalities, or Powers" depended on Mary's *Fiat*.[229] In fact, as a member of the human race, Mary's *own existence* depended on her *Fiat*. This appears to place Mary, a mere creature and nothing more than the handmaid of the Lord, in a unique category very much like that of God Himself, who declares His Own Existence when He says "I Am Who Am!" However, logically, this observation is inescapable.

---

[226] St. Gregory Palamas, *A Homily on the Dormition of Our Supremely Pure Lady Theotokos and Ever-Virgin Mary* (Homily 37), as quoted by Fr. Paul Haffner, *The Mystery of Mary*, Gracewing (2004): pp. 9–10.

[227] Cf. *Eph* 1:3–10; *Rom* 8:28–30; *Col* 1:15–20.

[228] Bl. Pope Pius IX, *Ineffabilis Deus*, Apostolic Constitution (December 8, 1854).

[229] *Col* 1:16.

Here we have a paradox! How can a creature take part in creation? How can Mary be the cause of what came before her? This is indeed a great mystery! However, perhaps we can shed some light on this mystery by considering the following line of thought: (1) God created the world on the condition of the *fact* of the Incarnation of Christ. (2) Given the observable fact that the world exists, from our point of view as creatures, the Incarnation of Christ was then *necessary*, and thus, again from our point of view as creatures, Mary's *predestination* to be the Mother of God was also *necessary*. (3) Thus, again *from our point of view as creatures*, Mary was *necessarily predestined to say yes* when the Archangel Gabriel asked her if she would consent to be the Mother of God. This seems to the modern eye to deny Mary the use of her free will, which from *God's* point of view would, of course, be unthinkable, since God never rescinds His gift of free will to any human person, least of all His Mother. Here, of course, we have a mystery beyond our human understanding. However, as the Eastern Orthodox theologian David Bentley Hart rightly observes, the modern eye is trained to think of freedom as the ability to choose sin (or not).[230] But this is not true freedom. St. Augustine defines perfect freedom, *not* as being *able* not to sin (*posse non peccare*), but as being *unable* to sin (*non posse peccare*)! Just as God lacks no freedom in being *unable* to sin, Mary could, in perfect freedom, be *unable* to deny the request God made of her. To be *unable* to deny God's proposal, Mary needed to be in possession of *perfect* freedom (as defined by St. Augustine), which means that she needed to be totally free from sin, because sin limits freedom. Thus, in order for God's eternal plan to be free from any contingency, and unchangeable as He is unchangeable, it was absolutely necessary that Mary be totally free from sin, including original sin. Hence, following this line of thought, we perceive the (*a posteriori*) necessity of Mary's Immaculate Conception for the existence of all created things!

---

[230] David Bentley Hart, *Atheist Delusions*, Yale University Press (2010): p. 25.

The "supra-temporal" dimension of Mary's *Fiat* and Immaculate Conception was also recognized by the Swiss Roman Catholic mystic and stigmatic Adrienne von Speyr (d. 1967). In the words of Fr. Donald Calloway:

> What this means is that just as the Immaculate Conception cannot be understood outside of the mystery of the Cross, so all temporal existence (cosmological realities) cannot be understood outside of the common mission exercised by the Immaculate Co-Redemptrix (perfect feminine) and the Incarnate Redeemer (perfect masculine); together they are that through which God creates and redeems because God has paradoxically made each dependent on the other. How can this be? According to Adrienne [von Speyr], this is so because in the mind of God "her [Mary's] Yes is [...] the most certain and most fundamental thing that exists. On the basis of her being pre-redeemed, the Son has her at his disposal from eternity. He can form from her, and from her Yes, whatever he wants, even before she is born." In the omniscient divine mind, "God did not have to worry for a moment whether she would speak this assent, since he had hidden her in himself from all eternity." In other words, just as the Immaculate Conception comes to be, through the anticipation of the certainty of the Cross of Jesus Christ, so redemption *and* creation come to be, by the power of God, through the anticipation of the certainty of Mary's *fiat*.[231]

A hallmark of the Mariology of St. Gregory Palamas and his disciples, such as Mark Eugenicus of Ephesus, is the placement of the Blessed Virgin Mary at the "borderline" between heaven and earth, the infinite and the finite, the eternal and the temporal, the

---

[231] Fr. Donald H. Calloway, M.I.C., "Co-redemption and Cosmology: The Supra-Temporal Dimension of Marian Co-redemption in the Thought of Adrienne von Speyr" in *Mary at the Foot of the Cross—VI: Marian Coredemption in the Eucharistic Mystery. Acts of the Sixth International Symposium on Marian Coredemption*, Academy of the Immaculate, New Bedford, MA (2007): pp. 349–50.

uncreated and the created orders of being, which brings to mind the words of St. Maximilian Kolbe: in the union between the Holy Spirit and the Blessed Virgin Mary "heaven is joined to earth, the whole heaven with the whole earth, the whole of Uncreated Love with the whole of created love: this is *the vertex of love*." Like Bl. John Duns Scotus and St. Maximilian Kolbe, St. Gregory Palamas and Mark Eugenicus believed that Mary is the "divine mind-cause of all creation."[232] Fr. Christiaan Kappes describes Palamite Mariology as follows:

> Mary is the meeting place of the divinity *ad extra*, the borderline between all cosmic perfections and the eternal formally distinct absolute perfections of the divine essence *ad intra*. In Scotistic language, all being falls into one or another disjunctive set: infinite-finite, eternal-temporal, increate-create, etc. For Palamite Christology, Christ is the exception to the rule. He is contradictorily [I would prefer to say *paradoxically*, or in *apparent* contradiction, since God's nature does not admit a *true* contradiction] the being that includes both extremes of every disjunctive *in unum solum Christum*. Mary is the *locus theologicus* for contemplating this unspeakable marvel. She is a marvel for being able not merely to supply the created nature (one of the two sides of the extremes of the disjunctives, viz., the perfect "create"), but she is the *domus* or *locus* of the fusion of two separated worlds. Her excellence is attested to by the fact that the Ephesine [Mark Eugenicus] observes that she alone is not destroyed through containing this incommunicable mystery within her womb.[233]

---

[232] TIC: p. 136.
[233] Ibid.

CHAPTER TWELVE

EROS OR AGAPE?

While Mary has truly been the Air Breathed by Both Lungs of the Catholic Church since the time of St. John the Apostle (and, indeed, since the time of Jesus Himself),[234] there was a certain "flowering" of Marian hyperdulia that began in the West around or shortly after the end of the first millennium following the introduction of the feast of Mary's Immaculate Conception in England and later on the continent. This Marian hyperdulia quickly grew into what would become a sort of "crescendo" during the twelfth century—called the "Marian Century" by historians[235]—when the "hermeneutic of Marian Doxology" in the East became a "hermeneutic of Marian Maximalism" in the West. One striking feature of the Marian Maximalism of the twelfth century in the Western Church is the exegesis of the *Song of Songs* in terms of the relationship between God and the Virgin Mary. For example, the Benedictine Abbot Rupert of Deutz (d. 1130) exclaims:

> "Let him kiss me with the kiss of his mouth" (*Song* 1:2). What is the meaning of such a strong and sudden outburst? O blessed Mary, a flood of joy, and onrush of love, a torrent of pleasure has

---

[234] Cf. Pope St. John Paul II, *Ut Unum Sint*, Encyclical Letter (May 25, 1995). Will the Blessed Virgin Mary—the sweet "Air We Breathe" (cf. Gerard Manley Hopkins)—be the path to true healing and unity between the Eastern and Western Lungs of the Church?

[235] MMA: p. 105.

totally washed over you and taken hold of you; it has made you absolutely drunk; and you have perceived what "eye has not seen, nor ear has heard, nor the heart of man conceived" (*1 Cor* 2:9), and you have said, "Let him kiss me with the kiss of his mouth" (*Song* 1:2). For you said to the angel, "Behold the handmaid of the Lord; let it be to me according to your word" (*Lk* 1:38). [...] You have heard and believed [the angel's words]; and you have made a request on your own behalf, saying, "Let it be to me." And so it was done to you. God the Father covered you over with "the kiss of his mouth." What eye saw this? What ear heard it? Into whose heart did it enter? But to you, O Mary, he revealed himself: the One who kisses, the Kiss, and the Mouth of the One who kisses.[236]

St. Aelred of Rievaulx (d. 1167) also uses the *Song of Songs* to express the ineffable spousal union between God (the Son!) and the Blessed Virgin Mary, by which *the Son has joined the soul of that most Blessed Virgin to His divinity*:

"While the king was on his couch, my nard gave forth its fragrance" (*Song* 1:12). Surely, when he was in the bosom of the Father, even then he smelled the fragrance of her virginity and considered the beauty of her soul. And so today his angel was sent to announce his coming, not only into her heart, but even into her flesh. See, brothers, what kind of marriage this is and how heavenly, in which the bridegroom is God, the bride is the Virgin, and the grooms-man is an angel. [...] But there is an even greater miracle in this marriage. The Bridegroom is the Son, the Bride is the Mother, because the Son has joined the soul of that most blessed Virgin to his divinity, since God himself, made man, came forth from her womb "like a bridegroom leaving his chamber" (*Ps* 19:5). Rightly, therefore, did the angel greet her, saying, "Hail, full of grace, the Lord is with you; blessed are you among women" (*Lk* 1:28, 42).[237]

---

[236] Abbot Rupert of Deutz, *In Canticum Canticorum* I, I. MMA: pp. 129–30.
[237] St. Aelred of Rievaulx, *In Annuntiatione*, sermo 9, 15–16. MMA: p. 169.

In this quote from St. Aelred of Rievaulx, we find one of the most explicit statements of the union (or alliance) of the Two Hearts of Jesus and Mary, a truth of the Catholic-Christian Faith repeated since his time by many saints, including Pope St. John Paul II.[238] In the words of St. John Eudes (d. 1680):

> The holy Heart of Mary was, therefore, always closely united to the Sacred Heart of her Divine Son. She always willed what He willed and also consented to act and to suffer so that the work of our salvation might be accomplished. Hence, the Fathers of the Church plainly assert that the Mother of the Savior cooperated with Him in a very special way in the redemption of mankind. That is why our holy Redeemer told St. Bridget of Sweden, whose revelations have been approved by the Church, that He and His holy Mother worked in perfect harmony, *uno corde*, for our salvation. Thus the Sacred Heart of Jesus is the Heart of Mary. These two Hearts are but one Heart, which was given to us by the Blessed Trinity and by our Blessed Mother, so that we, the children of Jesus and Mary, might have but one Heart with our heavenly Father and our holy Mother and that we might love and glorify God with the same Heart, a Heart worthy of the infinite grandeur of His divine majesty.[239]

It is precisely this union of the Two Hearts of Jesus and Mary that forms the basis for all Marian doctrine, including the doctrine of their joint predestination, their joint mediation, and their joint action in both the objective and subjective orders of redemption—because, in the words of St. Bernardine of Siena, "not only was she [Mary] standing by the cross, but she was also hanging on the cross; for in regard to herself, nothing of herself had remained. She had

[238] Cf. Pope St. John Paul II, *Angelus address* (September 15, 1985); Msgr. Arthur Burton Calkins, "The Alliance of the Two Hearts and Consecration," *Miles Immaculatæ* XXXI (Luglio/Dicembre 1995): pp. 389–407.

[239] St. John Eudes, *The Sacred Heart of Jesus*, translated by Dom. Richard Flower, O.S.B., MA, P. J. Kenedy & Sons, New York, NY (1946): p. 110.

completely entered into the Beloved, and while He was sacrificing His body, she was sacrificing her spirit."[240] It is precisely for this reason that, contrary to what some theologians wrongly assume, Mary's role as Mediatrix of all graces in no way lessens Christ's role as the *One Mediator between God and humanity*;[241] just as the fact that Jesus has placed the *entire order of Mercy in Mary's hands* in no way lessens His own Divine Mercy.[242]

The exegesis of the *Song of Songs* in terms of the relationship between Mary and Jesus brings out a very striking point. We know that Mary is the Mother of Jesus and therefore the Mother of God, and we have also heard St. Francis of Assisi call Mary the Spouse of the Holy Spirit. However, if Jesus is the New Adam and Mary is the New Eve, then Mary can also truly be called the *Spouse of Jesus Christ*: the *Sponsa Christi* par excellence. In the words of Fr. François-Marie Léthel:

> Jesus is the New Adam, the God-Man, the Creator and the only Savior of all men, the Eternal Son of the Father who, by the power of the Holy Spirit, became in a completely virginal manner the Child and the Spouse of his creature, to the point that his creature became truly his Mother and his Spouse. Such is the Mystery of the New Eve in her ineffable communion with the New Adam: she is inseparably Mary and the Church, as Mother of God (*theotókos*) and Spouse of God (*theonúmphos*), Virgin-Mother and Virgin-Spouse.[243]

---

[240] St. Bernardine of Siena, as quoted by Rev. Fr. James Mercer, "St. Bernardine of Siena and Marian Mediation" in *Mary at the Foot of the Cross—VII: Coredemptrix, therefore Mediatrix of All Graces. Acts of the Seventh International Symposium on Marian Coredemption*, Academy of the Immaculate, New Bedford, MA (2008): p. 266.

[241] *1 Tim* 2:5.

[242] Cf. St. Bernard, St. Alphonsus Liguori, St. Maximilian Kolbe, and others.

[243] Fr. François-Marie Léthel, O.C.D., "The Cooperation of Mary and the Church in the Mystery of the Redemption in the light of Saint Thérèse of Lisieux" in *Mary at the Foot of the Cross—II: Acts of the Second International Symposium on Marian Coredemption*, Academy of the Immaculate, New Bedford, MA (2002): p. 382.

Thus, while the Song of Songs describes Mary's spousal union to God, this union is also an icon of the union that we are able to share with Jesus Christ via *transubstantiation into the Immaculate*, which formally defines our membership in the Church, because Mary is the *Virgo Ecclesia Facta*. In the words of Pope Benedict XVI:

> We can thus see how the reception of the *Song of Songs* in the canon of sacred Scripture was soon explained by the idea that these love songs ultimately describe God's relation to man and man's relation to God. Thus the *Song of Songs* became, both in Christian and Jewish literature, a source of mystical knowledge and experience, an expression of the essence of biblical faith: that man can indeed enter into union with God—his primordial aspiration. But this union is no mere fusion, a sinking in the nameless ocean of the Divine; it is a unity which creates love, a unity in which both God and man remain themselves and yet become fully one. As Saint Paul says: "He who is united to the Lord becomes one spirit with him" (*1 Cor* 6:17).[244]

The joint identification of the *Bride* in the *Song of Songs* with the Blessed Virgin Mary and with the Church, both in her entirety and in her individual members, was recognized by the holy writers of the twelfth century. For example, reflecting on the *Song of Songs*, Alain de Lille (d. 1202 or 1203) said:

> As the Church of God is the Mother of Christ in his members, by virtue of grace, just so the Virgin is Mother of Christ the Head, by virtue of his human nature. And as the Church is without spot or wrinkle, even so is the glorious Virgin. And as the Church possesses all gifts in many different individuals, so the Virgin Mary has in herself all charisms.[245]

---

[244] Pope Benedict XVI, *Deus Caritas Est*, Encyclical Letter (December 25, 2005): 10.

[245] Alain de Lille, Migne Patrologia Latina (PL) 210, 60AB. MMA: p. 188.

The Abbot Philip of Harveng (d. 1183) likens Mary's affection for sinners and her effectiveness on their behalf to her two breasts; the milk from which provides the medicine needed to counteract the venomous injections of the serpent:

> She leans down to show compassion to the wretched, as it were, with one breast, while with the other she gives the needy the help he needs. And thus, from these two breasts, that is, from her affection and effectiveness, the Virgin pours out nourishing milk for us, and with her concerned hand she shelters us from the whirlwind and the rain. And, whenever the lion roars, she repulses and checks him with even more powerful threats. With her medicinal milk, she heals whatever the poisonous serpent has injected with his venom.[246]

Sadly, the beautiful and inspiring meditations from this period on the Blessed Virgin Mary as the *Sponsa Christi par excellence* as represented in the *Song of Songs* have been dubbed "erotic" by some Catholic writers of the twentieth century.[247] Not only does this display a surprising lack of appreciation for the way the *Song of Songs* is used in the tradition of Catholic mysticism (as represented, for example, by the poetry of St. John of the Cross), it also displays a sad misunderstanding of *eros*, *agape*, and the language of the Old Testament. In the words of Pope Benedict XVI:

> The Greeks—not unlike other cultures—considered *eros* princi-pally as a kind of intoxication, the overpowering of reason by a "divine madness" which tears man away from his finite existence and enables him, in the very process of being overwhelmed by divine power, to experience supreme happiness. All other powers in heaven and on earth thus appear secondary: "*Omnia vincit*

---

[246] Abbot Philip of Harveng, *In Cantica Canticorum* 4, 14. MMA: p. 184.
[247] Cf. Hilda Graef, *Mary: A History of Doctrine and Devotion*, Sheed and Ward, New York, NY (1964): p. 249.

amor" says Virgil in the *Bucolics*—love conquers all—and he adds: "*et nos cedamus amori*"—let us, too, yield to love.[248]

This view of love, however, is emphatically *not* the view of either the Old or New Testaments. Pope Benedict XVI tells us "that the Greek Old Testament uses the word *eros* only twice, while the New Testament does not use it at all [...]. The tendency to avoid the word *eros*, together with the new vision of love expressed through the word *agape*, clearly point to something new and distinct about the Christian understanding of love. [...] Evidently, *eros* needs to be disciplined and purified if it is to provide not just fleeting pleasure, but a certain foretaste of the pinnacle of our existence, of that beatitude for which our whole being yearns."[249] Pope Benedict XVI continues:

Concretely, what does this path of ascent and purification entail? How might love be experienced so that it can fully realize its human and divine promise? Here we can find a first, important indication in the *Song of Songs*, an Old Testament book well known to the mystics. According to the interpretation generally held today, the poems contained in this book were originally love-songs, perhaps intended for a Jewish wedding feast and meant to exalt conjugal love. In this context it is highly instructive to note that in the course of the book two different Hebrew words are used to indicate "love." First there is the word *dodim*, a plural form suggesting a love that is still insecure, indeterminate and searching. This comes to be replaced by the word *ahabà*, which the Greek version of the Old Testament translates with the similar-sounding *agape*, which, as we have seen, becomes the typical expression for the biblical notion of love. By contrast with an indeterminate, "searching" love, this word expresses the experience of a love which involves a real discovery of the other, moving beyond the selfish character

---

[248] Pope Benedict XVI, *Deus Caritas Est*, Encyclical Letter (December 25, 2005): 4.

[249] Ibid., 3, 4.

that prevailed earlier. Love now becomes concern and care for the other. No longer is it self-seeking, a sinking in the intoxication of happiness; instead it seeks the good of the beloved: it becomes renunciation and it is ready, and even willing, for sacrifice.[250]

Thus, contrary to the opinions of some twentieth century writers, the *Song of Songs* does not ultimately present us with *eros*, but with *agape*! Moreover, while the Hebrew word *dodim* can, in fact, be rendered "lovemaking," this is the very word that God Himself uses to address Jerusalem as her husband: "Your breasts were well-formed [...]. I saw that you had reached the age of lovemaking [*'et dodim*]; so I spread My skirt over you and covered your nakedness. I also swore to you and entered into a covenant with you so that you became Mine."[251] When God enters into a covenant, either with Jerusalem or with the human soul, He does so with perfect *faithfulness*. Thus, the concept of *dodim* as used in the *Song of Songs*, while distinct from *agape* in the sense that it expresses the conjugal love between a man and a woman in both its physical and its spiritual aspects, is nonetheless diametrically opposed to the Greek concept of *eros* understood as a kind of momentary "intoxication" and "overpowering of reason," which is an "apparent exaltation of the body" that "can quickly turn into a hatred of bodiliness."[252] This is precisely because the latter implies irrational abandonment to sexual impulses, which necessarily entails *unfaithfulness*, while the former entails *faithfulness to one person forever*. Again, Pope Benedict XVI explains:

> It is part of love's growth towards higher levels and inward purification that it now seeks to become definitive, and it does so in a twofold sense: both in the sense of exclusivity (this particular person alone) and in the sense of being "for ever." Love embraces the whole of existence in each of its dimensions, including the

---

[250] Ibid., 6.
[251] *Ezek* 16:7–8.
[252] Ibid., 5.

dimension of time. It could hardly be otherwise, since its promise
looks towards its definitive goal: love looks to the eternal. Love
is indeed "ecstasy," not in the sense of a moment of intoxication,
but rather as a journey, an ongoing exodus out of the closed
inward-looking self towards its liberation through self-giving, and
thus towards authentic self-discovery and indeed the discovery of
God: "Whoever seeks to gain his life will lose it, but whoever loses
his life will preserve it" (*Lk* 17:33), as Jesus says throughout the
Gospels (cf. *Mt* 10:39; 16:25; *Mk* 8:35; *Lk* 9:24; *Jn* 12:25). In
these words, Jesus portrays his own path, which leads through the
Cross to the Resurrection: the path of the grain of wheat that falls
to the ground and dies, and in this way bears much fruit. Starting
from the depths of his own sacrifice and of the love that reaches
fulfillment therein, he also portrays in these words the essence of
love and indeed of human life itself.[253]

So finally we must ask ourselves: If bridal imagery can be applied
to the *old* Jerusalem in covenant with God, how can it *not* be applied
to Mary, the *new* Jerusalem, whom God loved before the creation
of the world, and *in whose image* He loved the old Jerusalem? If the
bridal imagery of the *Song of Songs* can be applied to the soul of a
mystic like St. John of the Cross in spiritual union with God, how
can it *not* be applied to Mary, who enjoys a spiritual union with
God more intimate than that of any other creature, and in whose
physical womb the Son of God Himself was *conceived in flesh*? It
would seem that the opinion of those twentieth century writers who
maintain that the twelfth century exegeses of the *Song of Songs* in the
key of Marian Maximalism are somehow "erotic" or inappropriate
can only be more evidence of the strange *miso-Gyny* we have already
mentioned. Indeed, in a vision granted to St. Birgitta (Bridget) of
Sweden, Jesus expressed His own pleasure and delight as well as that

---

[253] Ibid., 6.

of His Father in the beauty of His Virgin-Mother and Spouse, in words that clearly echo the language of the *Song of Songs*:

> Your eyes were so bright and clear in my Father's sight that he could see himself in them [...]. Your ears were as pure and open as the most beautiful windows when Gabriel laid my will before you and when I, God, became flesh in you. Your cheeks were of the fairest hue, white and red, for the fame of your praiseworthy deeds and the beauty of your character, which burned within you each day, were pleasing to me. Truly, God my Father rejoiced in the beauty of your character and never took his eyes away from you. By your love, all have obtained love. Your mouth was like a lamp, inwardly burning and outwardly shedding light, for the words and affections of your soul were inwardly on fire with divine understanding and shone outwardly in the graceful carriage of your body and the lovely harmony of your virtues. Truly, most dear Mother, your divine sweetness never separated me from you, since your words were sweeter than honey and honeycomb. Your neck is nobly erect and beautifully held high [...]. Your breast was so full of every virtuous charm that there is no good in me that is not in you as well, for you drew every good thing to yourself by the sweetness of your character, at the moment when it both pleased my divinity to enter into you and my humanity to live with you and drink the milk from your nipples. Your feet were washed full clean as though with fragrant herbs [...]. Your womb was a spiritual and physical space so desirable to me and your soul was so pleasing to me that I did not disdain to come down to you from the highest heaven and to dwell in you. No, rather, I was most pleased and delighted.[254]

---

[254] Jesus Christ, as quoted by St. Birgitta (Bridget) of Sweden, *Revelations*, Book V, Revelation 4, in *The Revelations of St. Birgitta of Sweden*, translated by Denis Searby with Introduction and Notes by Bridget Morris, Vol. 2, Oxford University Press, New York, NY (2008): pp. 288–89.

It is a principle of Catholic theology that *caro cardo saluti*: salvation hinges on the flesh—that is, on the Incarnation (literally enfleshment) of the Word of God, Jesus Christ, in the womb of the Virgin.[255] If we accept Saint Paul's doctrine of the Primacy of the God-Man Jesus Christ,[256] then, in the eternal foresight of God the Father, the models of all creation, and in particular of all men and women, *must* fundamentally be Jesus and Mary, the *new* Adam and the *new* Eve. This has profound implications on how we must understand ourselves as human beings, particularly in regard to our dual human nature as man and woman. In particular, every aspect of womanhood must be seen in the light of the Blessed Virgin-Mother, and every aspect of human love between a man and a woman must be illuminated by the love between Jesus and Mary, as expressed in the *Song of Songs*. In the words of Ven. Fulton J. Sheen:

> Every man who pursues a maid, every maid who yearns to be courted, every bond of friendship in the universe, seeks a love that is not just *her* love or *his* love but something that overflows both her and him that is called "our love." [...] That ideal love we see beyond all creature-love, to which we instinctively turn when flesh-love fails, is the same ideal that God had in His Heart from all eternity—the Lady whom He calls "Mother." She is the one whom every man loves when he loves a woman—whether he knows it or not. She is what every woman wants to be when she looks at herself. She is the woman whom every man marries in ideal when he takes a spouse; she is hidden as an ideal in the discontent of every woman with the carnal aggressiveness of man; she is the secret desire every woman has to be honored and fostered; she is the way every woman wants to command respect and love

---

[255] Cf. Fr. Nicholas L. Gregoris, "John Henry Newman's Mariology: A Key to Unlocking John Paul II's Theology of the Body" in *The Virgin Mary and Theology of the Body*, edited by Donald Calloway, M.I.C., Ascension Press, West Chester, PA (2007): pp. 99–138.

[256] Cf. *Eph* 1:3–10; *Rom* 8:28–30; *Col* 1:15–20.

because of the beauty of her goodness of body and soul. And this blueprint love, whom God loved before the world was made, this Dream Woman before women were, is the one of whom every heart can say in its depth of depths: "She is the woman I love!"[257]

---

[257] Ven. Fulton J. Sheen, *The World's First Love*, McGraw-Hill Book Company, Inc., New York, NY (1952): pp. 12–13.

CHAPTER THIRTEEN

DAUGHTER ZION

To understand the ubiquity of the imagery and prophecies concerning the Blessed Virgin Mary in both the Old and New Testaments, one must understand a fundamental typology: The Blessed Virgin Mary is *Daughter Zion—the New Israel—the Heavenly Jerusalem*.[258] To perceive the striking correspondence between Our Blessed Mother and the Jewish personification of Israel, one need only read (or preferably hear sung) the words of the *Lekhah Dodi* ("come my beloved"), a Hebrew-language, Jewish liturgical song recited Friday at dusk as a part of the *Kabbalat Shabbat* ("acceptance of Sabbath"):

> Let's go, my beloved, to meet the bride,
> And let us welcome the presence of *Shabbat*.
> "Observe" and "recall" in a single utterance,
> We were made to hear by the unified God,
> God is one and God's Name is one,
> In fame and splendor and praiseful song.
> To greet *Shabbat* let's go, let's travel,
> For she is the wellspring of blessing,
> From the start, from ancient times she was chosen,
> Last made, but first planned.
> Sanctuary of the king, royal city,

---

[258] Cf. Fr. Stefano M. Manelli, F.I., *All Generations Shall Call Me Blessed: Biblical Mariology* (Revised and Enlarged Second Edition), translated by Fr. Peter Damian Fehlner, F.I., Academy of the Immaculate, New Bedford, MA (2005).

Arise! Leave from the midst of turmoil;

Long enough have you sat in the valley of tears

And He will take great pity upon you compassionately.

Shake yourself free, rise from the dust,

Dress in your garments of splendor, my people,

By the hand of Jesse's son of Bethlehem,

Redemption draws near to my soul.

Rouse yourselves! Rouse yourselves!

Your light is coming, rise up and shine.

Awaken! Awaken! Utter a song,

The glory of the Lord is revealed upon you.

Do not be embarrassed! Do not be ashamed!

Why be downcast? Why groan?

All my afflicted people will find refuge within you

And the city shall be rebuilt on her hill.

Your despoilers will become your spoil,

Far away shall be any who would devour you,

Your God will rejoice concerning you,

As a groom rejoices over a bride.

[…]

Come in peace, crown of her husband,

Both in happiness and in jubilation

Amidst the faithful of the treasured nation

Come O Bride! Come O Bride![259]

As a Catholic, if one didn't know better, one would certainly think that this is a hymn to the Blessed Virgin Mary—and one displaying no lack of Marian Maximalism: *For she is the wellspring of blessing. From the start, from ancient times she was chosen, last made but first planned. Sanctuary of the king, royal city…* Indeed, perhaps God has granted in His tender Love and Mercy that every week on the eve of the day that is dedicated to the Blessed Virgin Mary by

---

[259] *Kabbalat Shabbat: Welcoming Shabbat in the Synagogue*, Rabbi Lawrence A. Hoffman, ed., Jewish Lights Publishing, Woodstock, VT (2004).

the Catholic Church our "elder brothers" in the faith of Abraham, His "treasured nation," will sing the glories of the Jewish Woman Mary—*the New Israel—the Heavenly Jerusalem—God's beloved Daughter, Mother, Sister, and Bride*, without even knowing they are doing so! This is possible because, in the words of Pope Benedict XVI (then Cardinal Joseph Ratzinger):

> Israel herself, the chosen people, is interpreted simultaneously as woman, virgin, beloved, wife and mother. The great women of Israel represent what this people itself is. The history of these women becomes the theology of God's people and, at the same time, the theology of the covenant. By making the category of covenant comprehensible and by giving it meaning and spiritual orientation, the figure of the woman enters into the most intimate reaches of Old Testament piety, of the Old Testament relationship with God.[260]

This feminine dimension of the theology of the Old Testament—from the "virgin-earth" out of which God created the first man Adam, to his helpmate Eve, to the Woman of Genesis at enmity with the serpent, to the "woman-savior" stories of Esther and Judith, to the personification of Israel entering into a covenant of love with God, to the feminine Sophia of the Book of Wisdom—becomes embodied concretely in the Immaculate, the Jewish Virgin-Mother, Spouse of the Holy Spirit and Coredemptrix with Christ: Mary. Again, in the words of Pope Benedict XVI (then Cardinal Joseph Ratzinger):

> Thus we can now say the figure of the woman is indispensable for the structure of biblical faith. She expresses the reality of creation as well as the fruitfulness of grace. The abstract outlines for the

---

[260] Pope Benedict XVI (then Cardinal Joseph Ratzinger), *Daughter Zion: Meditations on the Church's Marian Belief,* translated by John M. McDermott, S.J., Ignatius Press, San Francisco, CA (1983): p. 21.

hope that God will turn toward his people receive, in the New Testament, a concrete, personal name in the figure of Jesus Christ. At that same moment, the figure of the woman, until then seen only typologically in Israel although provisionally personified by the great women of Israel, also emerges with a name: Mary. She emerges as the personal epitome of the feminine principle in such a way that the principle is true only in the person, but the person as an individual always points beyond herself to the all-embracing reality, which she bears and represents. To deny or reject the feminine aspect in belief, or, more concretely, the Marian aspect, leads finally to the negation of creation and the invalidation of grace. It leads to a picture of God's omnipotence that reduces the creature to a mere masquerade and that also completely fails to understand the God of the Bible, who is characterized as being the creator and the God of the covenant—the God for whom the beloved's punishment and rejection themselves become the passion of love, the cross.[261]

"Come O Bride!" The Bride Jerusalem in the Jewish liturgy of the *Kabbalat Shabbat* is perfectly mirrored by the Jewish Woman Mary, the Spouse of the Holy Spirit and the Heavenly Jerusalem, in the liturgy of the Catholic Church. As Bl. Pope Paul VI affirms, "When the liturgy turns its gaze either to the primitive Church or to the Church of our own days it always finds Mary."[262] Thus, in the spirit of the *Lekhah Dodi*, we go to greet Mary in the celebration of the Catholic liturgy, ever ancient, ever new: "To greet Mary let's go, let's travel, for she is the wellspring of blessing!" In the words of Pope Benedict XVI (then Cardinal Joseph Ratzinger):

> Mary is identified with daughter Zion, with the bridal people of God. Everything said about the *ecclesia* in the Bible is true of her, and vice versa: the Church learns concretely what she is and is

---

[261] Ibid., 27–28.
[262] Bl. Pope Paul VI, *Marialis Cultus*, Apostolic Exhortation (February 2, 1974): 11.

meant to be by looking at Mary. Mary is her mirror, the pure measure of her being, because Mary is wholly within the measure of Christ and of God, is through and through his habitation. And what other reason could the *ecclesia* have for existing than to become a dwelling for God in the world? God does not deal with abstractions. He is a person, and the Church is a person. The more that each one of us becomes a person, person in the sense of a fit habitation for God, daughter Zion, the more we become one, the more we are the Church, and the more the Church is herself.[263]

Thus, our identity as a member of the Church, and even as a person, depends on our *transubstantiation into the Immaculate*—the mirror and measure of the Church. This is especially true when we receive the Body and Blood of Christ in the Eucharist—*the heart of the liturgy*—since, in the words of St. Maximilian Maria Kolbe:

> Anyone consecrated to the Immaculate totally and without restriction, whenever he makes a visit to Jesus in the Blessed Sacrament, quite apart from his awareness of belonging to Her (to which he may not always advert), will offer the entire visit expressly to the Immaculate, even if only with the invocation "Mary," because he knows this will bring the maximum joy possible to Jesus and because he realizes also that in this instance it is She who accomplishes that visit in him and through him and he in Her and through Her. So, too, there is no better preparation for Holy Communion than to offer it all to the Immaculate (naturally doing on our part all that we can). She will prepare our heart in the best way possible and we can be certain to bring Jesus the greatest joy possible and to show Him the greatest love.[264]

---

[263] Pope Benedict XVI (then Cardinal Joseph Ratzinger), "'Hail, Full of Grace': Elements of Marian Piety according to the Bible" in *Mary—The Church at the Source*, Ignatius Press, San Francisco, CA (2005): p. 66.

[264] St. Maximilian Maria Kolbe, as quoted by Fr. Jerzy M. Domanski, O.F.M. Conv., *For the Life of the World: St. Maximilian and the Eucharist*, translated by

The two titles that St. Francis of Assisi gave to Mary, *Spouse of the Holy Spirit* and *Virgin-Made-Church*, have special significance in this context. Reflecting on the liturgy of the Eastern Church, with his gaze turned "to the *Orientale Lumen* which shines from Jerusalem,"[265] the city where the Word of God, made man for our salvation, a Jew "descended from David according to the flesh,"[266] "died and rose again," Pope St. John Paul II said:

> Participation in Trinitarian life takes place through the liturgy and in a special way through the Eucharist, the mystery of communion with the glorified body of Christ, the seed of immortality.[267] In divinization and particularly in the sacraments, Eastern theology attributes a very special role to the Holy Spirit: through the power of the Spirit who dwells in man deification already begins on earth; the creature is transfigured and God's kingdom inaugurated. [...] On this path of divinization, those who have been made "most Christ-like" by grace and by commitment to the way of goodness go before us: the martyrs and the saints.[268] And the Virgin Mary occupies an altogether special place among them. From her the shoot of Jesse sprang (cf. *Isa* 11:1). Her figure is not only the Mother who waits for us, but the Most Pure, who—the fulfillment of so many Old Testament pre-figurations—is an icon of the Church, the symbol and anticipation of humanity transfigured by grace, the model and the unfailing hope for all those who direct their steps toward the heavenly Jerusalem.[269]

God can truly say to Mary: "All my afflicted people will find refuge within you!" The Lady of All Nations leads all people to

---

Fr. Peter Damian Fehlner, F.I., Academy of the Immaculate, New Bedford, MA (1999): p. 141.

[265] Cf. *Isa* 60:1; *Apoc* 21:10.

[266] *Rom* 1:3; *2 Tim* 2:8.

[267] Cf. St. Gregory of Nyssa, *Catechetical Discourse*, XXXVII: PG 45, 97.

[268] Cf. St. John Damascene, *On Images*, I, 19: PG 94, 1249.

[269] Pope St. John Paul II, *Orientale Lumen*, Apostolic Letter (May 2, 1995): 6.

God—the Father, who is *her Father*, the Son, who is *her Son*, and the Holy Spirit, who is *her Spouse*—as a perfect Mother who loves every one of her children without preference.[270] If all nations will only accept the affection and effectiveness of "the two breasts" of our Virgin-Mother,[271] "coming down out of heaven from God, prepared as a bride adorned for her husband,"[272] then we will surely enter the Heavenly Jerusalem, the Holy City. There we will see God *as He Is*, the fruit of Mary's womb; "And the city shall be rebuilt on her hill."[273] Though we cannot yet fathom the mystery of Heaven—ineffably linked to the mystery of Mary—since "what we will be has not yet been made known,"[274] I believe that Mary will be the air we breathe in Heaven; just as the Jesuit poet Gerard Manley Hopkins likens her to the air we breathe on earth; just as every mother is the air to the child who is folded in her womb:

> Wild air, world-mothering air,
> Nestling me everywhere,
> [...]
> This air, which, by life's law,
> My lung must draw and draw
> Now but to breathe its praise,

---

[270] The apparitions of the Lady of All Nations—"de Vrouwe [which can be translated either as 'the Lady' or as 'the Woman'] van alle Volkeren," as the Blessed Virgin Mary called herself when she appeared to Ida Peerdeman in Amsterdam, the Netherlands, from 1945 to 1959—were approved by the Church on May 31, 2002. On the Feast of Our Lady of Lourdes, February 11, 1951, Mary asked that every person in the world say the following simple prayer in one's own language, preferably before one's own crucifix: "Lord Jesus Christ, Son of the Father, Send NOW Your Spirit over the earth. Let the Holy Spirit live in the hearts of ALL nations, that they may be preserved from degeneration, disaster and war. May the Lady [Woman] of All Nations, [the Blessed Virgin Mary], be our Advocate. Amen." Cf. Fr. Paul Maria Sigl, "God shows the way to true peace through Mary, the Mother of All Nations," *Day of Prayer in Honor of Mary, the Mother of All Nations*, Cologne, Germany, Pentecost Sunday (May 31, 2009).

[271] Cf. Philip of Harveng.

[272] *Apoc* 21:2.

[273] Cf. *1 Jn* 3:2; *Lk* 1:42.

[274] *1 Jn* 3:2.

Minds me in many ways
Of her who not only
Gave God's infinity
Dwindled to infancy
Welcome in womb and breast,
Birth, milk, and all the rest
But mothers each new grace
That does now reach our race –
Mary Immaculate,
Merely a woman, yet
Whose presence, power is
Great as no goddess's
[…]
And men are meant to share
Her life as life does air.
[…]
Be thou then, O thou dear
Mother, my atmosphere;
My happier world, wherein
To wend and meet no sin;
Above me, round me lie
Fronting my forward eye
With sweet and scarless sky;
Stir in my ears, speak there
Of God's love, O live air,
Of patience, penance, prayer:
World-mothering air, air wild,
Wound with thee, in thee isled,
Fold home, fast fold thy child.[275]

---

[275] Fr. Gerard Manley Hopkins, S.J., "The Blessed Virgin Compared to the Air We Breathe" in *Poems and Prose of Gerard Manley Hopkins*, selected with an introduction and notes by W. H. Gardner, Penguin Books (1953): pp. 54–8.

CHAPTER FOURTEEN

THE WOMAN
CLOTHED WITH THE SUN

When the Virgin-Mother appeared to St. Juan Diego Cuauhtlatoa-tzin (whose Nahuatl name means "Messenger Eagle") on the slopes of Tepeyac Hill near Mexico City on December 12, 1531, she appeared as the "Woman clothed with the sun, with the moon under her feet."[276] She identified herself as "Guadalupe," which some believe may be a Spanish "sound spelling" of a Nahuatl word meaning "She who has crushed the head of the serpent."[277] She told St. Juan Diego:

> Know for certain, littlest of my sons, that I am the perfect and perpetual Virgin Mary, Mother of the True God through Whom everything lives, the Lord of all things near and far, the Master of heaven and earth. I wish and intensely desire that in this place my sanctuary be erected. Here, I will demonstrate, I will exhibit, I will give all my love, my compassion, my help and my protection to the people. I am your merciful Mother. The merciful Mother of all of you who live united in this land, and of all mankind, of all those who love me. Here I will hear their weeping, their sorrow, and will

---

[276] *Apoc* 12:1.
[277] Fr. Peter Damian Fehlner, F.I., "Guadalupe, The Immaculate Conception and the Franciscans" in *A Handbook on Guadalupe*, Academy of the Immaculate, New Bedford, MA (2001): p. 159.

remedy, and alleviate all their multiple sufferings, necessities and misfortunes.[278]

Remarkably, the location where Our Lady chose to appear to St. Juan Diego had previously been the site of a temple dedicated to the Nahuatl goddess Tonantzin, meaning "Our Lady-Mother." Moreover, Mary incorporated in her own clothing many of the native symbols associated with "deity." The blue-green color of Our Lady's mantle was a color reserved for the Aztec creator god and goddess couple Ometecuhtli and Omecihuatl, and the four-petaled "flower of the sun," Nahui-Ollin, that appears over Our Lady's womb represented the entire universe (the four compass directions).[279] Indeed, the placement of the whole universe at Mary's womb is very fitting since, according to St. Maximilian Kolbe, St. Gregory Palamas, and St. Basil of Seleucia, *it is in Mary herself, the created Immaculate Conception, that the entire created universe is joined to heaven!*[280] "Who is she that cometh forth as the morning rising, fair as the moon, bright as the sun, terrible as an army set in array?"[281] In the words of St. Lawrence of Brindisi:

How noble did Mary appear in the heaven of the Divine Plan! *A great sign appeared in heaven: a woman clothed with the sun.* No more brilliant or splendid figure can be created by the mind of mortal man. Mary was not merely predestined for grace and glory with the holy angels and the elect of God and chosen for the greatest measure of grace and glory after Christ. She was also selected

---

[278] The Blessed Virgin Mary, as quoted by Msgr. Angel Garibay, "The Spiritual Motherhood of Mary" in ibid.: pp. 9–10.

[279] Janet Barber, I.H.M., "The Sacred Image is a … Divine Codex" in ibid.: p. 72; and Eric Wolf, "The Virgin of Guadalupe: A Mexican National Symbol," *The Journal of American Folklore*, Vol. 71, No. 279 (1958): pp. 34–9.

[280] Cf. SK 1318; TIC: p. 136; GOM: pp. 326–7. Cf. SK 1318; TIC: p. 136; GOM: pp. 326–7. Cf. also Jonathan Fleischmann, "The Vertex of Love," *Homiletic & Pastoral Review* (October 8, 2012).

[281] *Song* 6:10.

to fill the role of Mother of God, for she indeed is the God-bearer, the truly natural Mother of the Only-Begotten Son of God.

She was the predestined Mother of Christ, having been predestined before all creatures (cf. *Col* 1:15, 17), together with Christ, the firstborn of every creature. For Christ had been predestined to be the Son of Mary, just as Mary had been predestined to be the Mother of Christ. The light of the sun reflects the dignity of motherhood, which God had ordained for her. With a radiance surpassing that of the moon, her position above the moon signifies the excellence of her grace. The crown of stars bespeaks the dignity of her special glory. For to these three things had Mary been predestined: motherhood, grace, and glory. What a truly noble act of predestination, a selection so unique and ineffable that words cannot express it aptly![282]

The *Apostolic Doctor* goes further:

Christ showed His glory to His chosen apostles on the holy mountain when He *was transfigured before them. And His face shone as the sun and His garments became white as snow* (cf. *Mt* 17:2). Still, He was not exalted above the moon. In other passages, as in the *Apocalypse,* we often read that Christ appeared to John in glory, His face shining like the sun (cf. *Apoc* 1:13–6). At one time He appeared to John in the midst of seven golden lamp-stands and stars (*Apoc* 1:13–6); at another time crowned with a rainbow (*Apoc* 4:2–3); at still another time surrounded with many crowns (*Apoc* 4–10). And yet never did He appear with a glory such as this. What then is this? Is the glory of the Virgin greater in heaven than the glory of Christ, than the glory of God? By no means! It is customary, at marriages and public solemnities in the courts

---

[282] St. Lawrence of Brindisi, *Mariale,* S. 2, "On the Nobility of the Virgin Mother of God," as quoted in WOM.

of princes and kings of this world, that the queen, because of her beauty and sex, enters glittering with gold and adorned with such splendid and costly garments, that she appears more glorious than even the king or prince, the king's son. So Mary appeared in heaven surrounded with a glory greater than that which even God or Christ has ever appeared.[283]

Our Lady of Guadalupe appeared in the clothing of a goddess, but not because she wanted to deceive St. Juan Diego and the native people of the New World. How could the most Perfect Daughter of God the Father, the Creator of heaven and earth; the Virgin-Mother of Jesus Christ, the Eternal Word and Logos (meaning) of the universe; the Immaculate Spouse of the Holy Spirit, the Giver of Life; how could *this* woman, who is the Woman loved by the Thrice-Holy Trinity before the creation of the world, deceive anyone? Indeed, she is the Woman who crushes the head of the serpent—the deceiver! Why would this woman appear like a goddess? It can only be because, in Mary's *perfect humility*, she appeared to St. Juan Diego *exactly* as God Himself saw her and wished her to be seen: exalted above all other women on earth, the one "highest after Christ and also closest to us,"[284] who "shines with a purity greater than which none can be imagined, except for God's,"[285] and who possesses "that fullness of holy innocence and sanctity than which, under God, one cannot even imagine anything greater, and which, outside of God, no mind can succeed in comprehending fully."[286] In the words of St. Lawrence of Brindisi, once again reflecting on St. John's vision of the *Woman clothed with the sun* in the Apocalypse:

---

[283] St. Lawrence of Brindisi, *Mariale*, S. 1, "On the Excellence of the Virgin Mother of God," as quoted in WOM.
[284] LG 54.
[285] St. Anselm of Canterbury, *De Conceptu Virginali et de Originali Peccato*, 18.
[286] Bl. Pope Pius IX, *Ineffabilis Deus*, Apostolic Constitution (December 8, 1854).

By this heavenly vision the Lord wished to show John how great and precious was the treasure He had entrusted to his keeping, the treasure in which are contained all the riches and glories of heaven. Through John He wished to show the universal Catholic Church, all the faithful of Christ, how exalted is the Virgin in the sight of the angels and elect of God in paradise. He did this lest we might perhaps think that Mary has been spurned by God, for the Holy Spirit has graced her with a certain holy obscurity in Sacred Scripture. [...] By this heavenly vision God wished, as far as possible, to show the true Church the divine splendors of Mary and to unfold to the faithful the things that lie hidden in the Virgin. This He did that all might know, from the things written concerning her, how great and wonderful is the Virgin's glory.[287]

For, as St. Alphonsus Liguori tells us:

"God endowing her in the highest degree," as Blessed Albert the Great asserts, "with all the general and particular graces and gifts conferred on all other creatures, in consequence of the dignity granted her of the divine maternity": [...] She was a Virgin without the reproach of sterility. She was a Mother, but at the same time possessed the precious treasure of virginity. She was beautiful, even most beautiful, as Richard of St. Victor asserts, with St. George of Nicomedia, and St. Denis the Areopagite, who (as it is believed) had the happiness of once beholding her beauty; and he declared that had not faith taught him that she was only a creature, he should have adored her as God.[288]

Indeed, Mary's exaltation is such that *her own soul magnifies* the greatness of the Lord! Yet, at the same time, her spirit rejoices in God *her Savior*. She proclaims: "My soul doth magnify the Lord. And my

---

[287] St. Lawrence of Brindisi, *Mariale*, S. 1, "On the Excellence of the Virgin Mother of God," as quoted in WOM.
[288] GOM: pp. 368–9.

spirit hath rejoiced in God my Savior. Because he hath regarded the humility of his handmaid."[289] Thus, while Mary appears to St. Juan Diego in the clothing of a goddess, standing *in front of* the sun with the moon *under* her feet; her eyes are downcast, because she can rightly say with St. John the Baptist that *there is One still greater than she.* The idea that Mary could provide "competition" to God is inherently flawed, because no matter how high we "lift" our understanding of Mary, by heaping on her an *infinity* of rightly deserved praise, we find that we have only "lifted" our understanding of God higher still, since we know that He is transcendently greater than any creature. In the final analysis, it is Mary's *humility* more than any other quality which defines her greatness.

> Hence Bernardine de Bustis says that "Mary merited more by saying with humility, *Behold the handmaid of the Lord!* than all pure creatures could merit together by all their good works." Thus, says St. Bernard, this innocent Virgin, although she made herself dear to God by her virginity, yet it was by her humility that she rendered herself worthy, as far as a creature can be worthy, to become the Mother of her Creator. "Though she pleased by her virginity, she conceived by her humility." St. Jerome confirms this, saying that "God chose her to be his Mother more on account of her humility than all her other sublime virtues. Mary herself also assured St. Bridget of the same thing, saying: "How was it that I merited so great a grace as to be made the Mother of my Lord, if it was not that I knew my own nothingness, and that I had nothing, and humbled myself."[290]

For, in the words of St. Lawrence of Brindisi:

> It was from the Child in her womb that Mary received all her glory. He clothed her with the sun, rolled the moon beneath her

---

[289] *Lk* 1:46–8.
[290] GOM: pp. 359–60.

feet, and set upon her head a crown of twelve stars. The Virgin Mother of God had this glory not from herself, but from God, the Creator of heaven, Who had made the sun, the moon, and the stars. She had her glory from Christ, her Son, through Whom all things, even Mary herself, have been made (cf. *Jn* 1:3). Christ was not only a son to Mary, but also a father who had created her, and adorned her with every virtue and blessing. He was her Lord, her true and supreme God.[291]

Thus, in her *humility*, Mary consents to the desire of the Triune God—Who is at once her Son, Spouse, and Father—to "display" and publicly rejoice in her beauty (in a way which every devoted son, husband, or father can well understand, but which every humble woman shuns). Why? Because, just as Jesus tells us that the voice of the Father from heaven was not for His sake, but for the sake of His disciples,[292] the vision of Mary as the *Woman clothed with the sun* is not for her sake, but for ours. In the words of St. Lawrence of Brindisi:

> Mary was seen clothed with the sun that we may know that she is like the sun which, although one, illumines and warms each man as if it had been created by God for him alone, for *there is no one that can hide himself from his heat* (Ps 19:6). So the Virgin Mother of God is both the mother of all men and the mother of each individual man. To all she is a common mother; to each his own personal mother. As the one sun can be seen in its entirety by each and every man (for every man at the same time sees a complete outline of the sun), so every one of the faithful, who from his heart devotes himself entirely to the Virgin, may enjoy her complete

---

[291] St. Lawrence of Brindisi, *Mariale*, S. 6, "The Sorrows of the Virgin Mother of God," as quoted in WOM.

[292] Cf. *Jn* 12:30.

love as if he were her only son. For this reason Christ spoke to Mary in the singular when He said: *Woman, behold thy son.*[293]

Here we discover yet another affinity between the Two Pierced Hearts of Jesus and Mary.[294] With His *Fiat*,[295] Jesus consented to the will of His Father to be "lifted up from the earth,"[296] to be "displayed" for the sake of "the many,"[297] like the bronze serpent that God commanded Moses to set up in order that the people who were bitten by the fiery serpents might be healed:[298]

> And as Moses lifted up the serpent in the desert, so must the Son of man be lifted up: That whosoever believeth in him, may not perish; but may have life everlasting. For God so loved the world, as to give his only begotten Son; that whosoever believeth in him, may not perish, but may have life everlasting.[299]

Likewise, with her *Fiat*, Mary consented to the will of her Father to be "lifted up from the earth," viz., above the moon and among the stars of heaven, as the Woman clothed with the sun, and the Woman of Genesis at enmity with the evil serpent;[300] to be "displayed" for the sake of "the many," like Jesus, so we might know that *we have a Mother in heaven* whose intercessory power on behalf of sinners is *omnipotent*.[301] When the Son of God is lifted up from the earth for the satisfaction of *Divine Justice,* "there is no beauty in him, nor comeliness: and we have seen him, and there was no sight-

---

[293] St. Lawrence of Brindisi, *Mariale*, S. 1, "On the Excellence of the Virgin Mother of God," as quoted in WOM.

[294] Cf. Fr. Dwight Campbell, "The Pierced Hearts of Jesus and Mary: Redeemer and Coredemptrix" in OLG: pp. 73–100.

[295] *Mt* 26:42.

[296] *Jn* 12:32.

[297] *Mt* 26:28.

[298] *Num* 21:6–9.

[299] *Jn* 3:14–6.

[300] Cf. *Lk* 1:38; *Apoc* 12:1; *Gen* 3:15.

[301] Cf. GOM: p. 181.

liness, that we should be desirous of him."[302] When the Mother of God is lifted up from the earth for the satisfaction of *Divine Mercy* she "shines with a purity greater than which none can be imagined, except for God's," and she appears "surrounded with a glory greater than that which even God or Christ has ever appeared." Yet, despite this apparent difference, and despite the Father's *infinite Love* for both His Son and His Daughter, both *Fiats* entail immeasurable suffering on the parts of Jesus and Mary, for, though on account of her *virginitas in partu*, Mary was spared the pains of physical childbirth while on earth,[303] this is no longer true when she has been lifted up from the earth:

> And being with child, she cried travailing in birth, and was in pain to be delivered. And there was seen another sign in heaven: and behold a great red dragon, having seven heads, and ten horns: and on his head seven diadems: And his tail drew the third part of the stars of heaven, and cast them to the earth: and the dragon stood before the woman who was ready to be delivered; that, when she should be delivered, he might devour her son.[304]

---

[302] *Isa* 53:2.

[303] Cf. Fr. Paul Haffner, *The Mystery of Mary*, Gracewing (2004): pp. 150–9. "Before she was in labor, she brought forth; before her time came to be delivered, she brought forth a man child" (*Isa* 66:7). "My sister, my spouse, is a garden enclosed, a garden enclosed, a fountain sealed up" (*Song* 4:12). Commenting on the east gate of the sanctuary that "shall be shut, it shall not be opened, and no man shall pass through it: because the Lord the God of Israel hath entered in by it, and it shall be shut" (*Ezek* 44:1–3), St. Ambrose says: "Who is this gate, if not Mary? Is it not closed because she is a virgin? Mary is the gate through which Christ entered this world, when he was brought forth in the virginal birth, and the manner of His birth did not break the seals of virginity (quando virginali fusus est partu, et genitalia virginitatis claustra non solvit)," *De institutione virginum*, as quoted by Msgr. Arthur Burton Calkins, "Our Lady's Virginity in Giving Birth," *Mother of all Peoples: De Maria Numquam Satis Amoris* (December 16, 2011). Fr. John Saward explains: "According to the Fathers, God the Word treats Mary's womb with infinite courtesy and gentleness [emphasis added], leaving, as he enters, without breaking its maidenly seal. It is God's inviolable sanctuary, and, like the Temple in Jerusalem, says St. Ambrose, its gate remains shut." Fr. John Saward, *Redeemer in the Womb*, Ignatius Press, San Francisco, CA (1993): p. 48.

[304] *Apoc* 12:2–3.

Pope St. Pius X explains:

"A great sign," thus the Apostle St. John describes a vision divinely
sent him, appears in the heavens: "A woman clothed with the sun,
and with the moon under her feet and a crown of twelve stars
upon her head" (*Apoc* 12:1). Everyone knows that this woman
signified the Virgin Mary, the stainless one who brought forth our
Head. The Apostle continues: "And, being with child, she cried
travailing in birth, and was in pain to be delivered" (*Apoc* 12:2).
John therefore saw the Most Holy Mother of God already in
eternal happiness, yet travailing in a mysterious childbirth. What
birth was it? Surely it was the birth of us who, still in exile, are yet
to be generated to the perfect charity of God, and to eternal happiness. And the birth pains show the love and desire with which
the Virgin from heaven above watches over us, and strives with
unwearying prayer to bring about the fulfillment of the number
of the elect.[305]

Mary's children "brought forth in pain" are the individual members of Christ's Mystical Body, the Church;[306] and even as she brings
each one of them forth to new life in grace, she prepares herself to
defend each of them against the dragon that stands waiting to devour
them. Still, the birth pangs suffered on behalf of every one of us
poor sinners individually, and the painful visibility associated with
her being "lifted up," cannot compare with the pain that the Mother
of God suffered when she beheld her divine Son Jesus suffer and die,
as He was "lifted up" on the Cross: "Despised, and the most abject
of men, a man of sorrows, and acquainted with infirmity."[307] It was
then that Mary's Immaculate Heart was pierced and broken;[308] and

---

[305] Pope St. Pius X, *Ad Diem Illum Laetissimum*, Encyclical Letter (February 2,
1904): 24.
[306] *Gen* 3:16.
[307] *Isa* 53:3.
[308] Cf. *Lk* 2:35.

the Virgin-Mother felt the birth pangs of the *whole Church*, as she associated herself with her divine Son Jesus in the objective Redemption of humankind.

CHAPTER FIFTEEN

HIGHEST AFTER CHRIST
AND ALSO CLOSEST TO US

The irresistible attraction of the Virgin-Mother lies precisely in the fact that she is "highest after Christ and also closest to us." Mary's infinite and unspeakable glory (by grace) does not entail any essential *separation* between her and every other human being (by nature). In this way, the Blessed Virgin Mary is the most perfect icon of "what God can do," or to quote Bl. John Duns Scotus, the "perfect fruit of a perfect redemption by a perfect Redeemer."[309] In the words of Fr. Peter Damian Fehlner:

> The "unlikeness" with all else in the world, in particular with every other human being and every other woman qua woman is not absolute in the sense Mary does not belong to our human family, but is a difference resulting from a unique likeness to the triune God: the Holy Virgin Mary, before time (creation) and prior to original sin, is uniquely similar to God the Father, like the Son who will become her Son, therefore daughter and handmaid of the most high Father and King, and so uniquely at the Father's disposition to be Mother (begetter) of that same Son in time. Mary in some way, not by nature, but by grace, reflects both the

---

[309] Bl. John Duns Scotus, *Ordinatio*, III, d. 3, as quoted by Fr. Maximilian Mary Dean, F.I., *A Primer on the Absolute Primacy of Christ*, Academy of the Immaculate, New Bedford, MA (2006): p. 47.

personal features of Father and Son, that is, reflects these because the grace in question is that of spouse of the Holy Spirit or Immaculate Conception, icon of the love in which Father and Son are one, of the love by which the members of Christ share that same unity (cf. *Jn* 17).[310]

Thus, though unquestionably worthy of unbounded admiration as *the perfect Woman*, Mary is not a "woman on a pedestal" doomed to be admired only. (Indeed, the Virgin-Mother would surely find this *unbearable*.) Rather, the Blessed Virgin is the teacher and example *par excellence* to be imitated by each individual member of the Church. In the words of Bl. Pope Paul VI:

> Mary is not only an example for the whole Church in the exercise of divine worship but is also, clearly, a teacher of the spiritual life for individual Christians. The faithful at a very early date began to look to Mary and to imitate her in making their lives an act of worship of God and making their worship a commitment of their lives. As early as the fourth century, St. Ambrose, speaking to the people, expressed the hope that each of them would have the spirit of Mary in order to glorify God: "May the heart of Mary be in each Christian to proclaim the greatness of the Lord; may her spirit be in everyone to exult in God."[311] But Mary is above all the example of that worship that consists in making one's life an offering to God. This is an ancient and ever new doctrine that each individual can hear again by heeding the Church's teaching, but also by heeding the very voice of the Virgin as she, anticipating in herself the wonderful petition of the Lord's Prayer—"Your will be done" (*Mt* 6:10)—replied to God's messenger: "I am the handmaid of the Lord. Let what you have said be done to me" (*Lk* 1:38). And Mary's "yes" is for all Christians a lesson and example

---

[310] PDF: pp. 66–7.

[311] St. Ambrose, *Expositio Evangelii secundum Lucam* 11 26: CSEL 32, IV, p. 55: S. Ch. 45, pp. 83–4.

of obedience to the will of the Father, which is the way and means of one's own sanctification.[312]

And in the words of Pope St. John Paul II:

Feminine perfection, as it was fully realized in Mary, can at first sight seem to be an exceptional case and impossible to imitate, a model too lofty for imitation. The unique holiness of Mary, who from the very first moment received the privilege of the Immaculate Conception, is sometimes considered unreachably distant. However, far from being a restraint on the way of following the Lord, Mary's exalted holiness is destined in God's plan to encourage all Christians to open themselves to the sanctifying power of the grace of God, for whom nothing is impossible. Therefore, in Mary all are called to put total trust in the divine omnipotence which transforms hearts, guiding them toward full receptivity to his providential plan of love.[313]

According to Pope St. John Paul II, receptivity is central to femininity, along with sensitivity, generosity, and maternity.[314] However, *receptivity* must not be confused with *passivity*. The ideal of feminine receptivity implies an *active response*, as exemplified in the Virgin-Mother *Coredemptrix*, while the ideal of feminine passivity is *unresponsive*. The ideal of feminine passivity is expressed, for example, in the so-called (and poorly named) *marianismo-machismo* gender role dichotomy typically associated with Latin American folk culture in academic (feminist) literature.[315] Regardless of whether or not such a gender role dichotomy actually exists in Latin America from a sociological point of view, the ideal of feminine passivity expressed in

---

[312] Bl. Pope Paul VI, *Marialis Cultus*, Apostolic Exhortation (February 2, 1974): 21.

[313] Pope St. John Paul II, *General Audience* (November 29, 1995).

[314] Cf. Pope St. John Paul II, *Mulieris Dignitatem*, Apostolic Letter (August 15, 1988).

[315] Cf. Evelyn P. Stevens, "Marianismo: The Other Face of Machismo" in *Confronting Change, Challenging Tradition: Women in Latin American History*, edited by Gertrude M. Yeager, SR Books, Oxford (2005): pp. 3–17.

"marianismo" is in fact a very poor representation of the personality of the Blessed Virgin Mary, both as she appears in Scripture and as she is venerated in the Sacred Tradition of the Catholic Church.

Far from being an artifact of a womanly ideal that has lost its place in modern society, the *Woman clothed with the sun* has no "expiration date." Again, in the words of Bl. Pope Paul VI:

> Thus, the modern woman, anxious to participate with decision-making power in the affairs of the community, will contemplate with intimate joy Mary who, taken into dialogue with God, gives her active and responsible consent,[316] not to the solution of a contingent problem, but to that "event of world importance," as the Incarnation of the Word has been rightly called.[317] The modern woman will appreciate that Mary's choice of the state of virginity, which in God's plan prepared her for the mystery of the Incarnation, was not a rejection of any of the values of the married state but a courageous choice which she made in order to consecrate herself totally to the love of God. The modern woman will note with pleasant surprise that Mary of Nazareth, while completely devoted to the will of God, was far from being a timidly submissive woman or one whose piety was repellent to others; on the contrary, she was a woman who did not hesitate to proclaim that God vindicates the humble and the oppressed, and removes the powerful people of this world from their privileged positions (cf. *Lk* 1:51–3). The modern woman will recognize in Mary, who "stands out among the poor and humble of the Lord,"[318] a woman of strength, who experienced poverty and suffering, flight and exile (cf. *Mt* 2:13–23). These are situations that cannot escape the attention of those who wish to support, with the Gospel spirit, the liberating energies of man and of society. And Mary will appear

---

[316] LG 56.
[317] Cf. St. Peter Chrysologus, *Sermo* CXLIII: PL 52 583.
[318] LG 55.

not as a Mother exclusively concerned with her own divine Son, but rather as a woman whose action helped to strengthen the apostolic community's faith in Christ (cf. *Jn* 2:1–12), and whose maternal role was extended and became universal on Calvary.[319]

These words of Bl. Pope Paul VI vividly and accurately represent Mary as the true model and example for the whole Church, which, in the words of Pope Francis, is "called to come out of herself and to go to the peripheries, not only geographically, but also the existential peripheries: the mystery of sin, of pain, of injustice, of ignorance and indifference to religion, of intellectual currents, and of all misery."[320] Mary is the antithesis of a "sick and self-referential" Church, because Mary's love is completely self-emptying. Mary's concern for her children on the periphery is neither pharisaical nor condescending. Rather, it is like the concern of Bl. Mother Teresa of Calcutta—a true image of the Blessed Virgin in our own times—when she relates:

> One evening, we went out and we picked up four people from the street. And one of them was in a most terrible condition. [...] So I did for her all that my love can do. I put her in bed, and there was such a beautiful smile on her face. She took hold of my hand, as she said one word only: "thank you"—and she died. [...] Then there was a man we picked up from the drain, half eaten by worms, and, after we had brought him to the home, he only said, "I have lived like an animal in the street, but I am going to die as an angel, loved and cared for." Then, after we had removed all the worms from his body, all he said, with a big smile, was: "Sister, I am going home to God"—and he died.[321]

---

[319] Bl. Pope Paul VI, *Marialis Cultus*, Apostolic Exhortation (February 2, 1974): 37.

[320] Pope Francis (then Cardinal Jorge Mario Bergoglio), speech delivered during the pre-conclave General Congregation meetings (March, 2013).

[321] Bl. Teresa of Calcutta, address given at the National Prayer Breakfast in Washington D.C. (February 3, 1994).

In fact, Bl. Mother Teresa of Calcutta frequently pointed to Mary's cooperation in the work of redemption as an example for her daughters to follow in their work as Missionaries of Charity, so that they might become *contemplatives at the foot of the Cross.*[322] She advised them: "Stay very close to Our Lady. If you do this, you can do great things for God and the good of people."[323] It was Our Lady herself who asked Mother Teresa to go to the poorest of the poor. In a vision in 1947, Mary said: "Take care of them—they are mine. Bring them to Jesus—carry Jesus to them. Fear not. Teach them to say the Rosary—the family Rosary and all will be well. Fear not—Jesus and I will be with you and your children."[324]

Mary's concern for her children on the periphery is like the concern of Jesus Himself, who, when he saw the crowds, "had compassion on them, because they were harassed and helpless, like sheep without a shepherd";[325] and who "went forth, and saw a great multitude, and was moved with compassion toward them, and he healed their sick."[326] With Jesus, Mary says to the crowd: "how often I have longed to gather your children together, as a hen gathers her

---

[322] In 1993, Bl. Mother Teresa of Calcutta wrote the following concise letter of support for a dogmatic definition of Mary's role as Coredemptrix, Mediatrix of all graces, and Advocate: "Mary is our Coredemptrix with Jesus. She gave Jesus his body and suffered with him at the foot of the cross. Mary is the Mediatrix of all grace. She gave Jesus to us, and as our Mother she obtains for us all his graces. Mary is our Advocate who prays to Jesus for us. It is only through the Heart of Mary that we come to the Eucharistic Heart of Jesus. The papal definition of Mary as Coredemptrix, Mediatrix, and Advocate will bring great graces to the Church. All for Jesus through Mary." Cf. Dr. Mark Miravalle, "Historical Highpoints of the Title of Mary Coredemptrix" in *Mary at the Foot of the Cross—IV: Mater Viventium (Gen. 3, 20). Acts of the Fourth International Symposium on Marian Coredemption*, Academy of the Immaculate, New Bedford, MA (2004): p. 268.
[323] Bl. Teresa of Calcutta, as quoted by Fr. Joseph Langford, M.C., *Mother Teresa: In the Shadow of Our Lady*, Our Sunday Visitor Publishing Division, Huntington, IN (2007).
[324] Ibid., 20.
[325] *Mt* 9:36.
[326] *Mt* 14:14.

chicks under her wings, but you were not willing."[327] In the inspired words of Caryll Houselander (d. 1954):

> There was always the Crowd.
> Even when he
> lay folded in the darkness
> of Mary's womb,
> she carried him
> into the crowded city of Bethlehem
> to be born.
> [...]
> There was always the crowd,
> thronging the mountain side
> and the sea shore
> and the wilderness,
> to hear the word.
> And she was always there
> as one of the crowd,
> she, who had heard,
> the first cry,
> and taught the Word
> his first word,
> and stored
> all his words in her heart.
> [...]
> When he died on the Cross
> the crowds were there,
> climbing the hill,
> as they did when first he came
> from Nazareth,
> to utter the word
> of his Father's love

---

[327] *Mt* 23:37.

in the broad, speech,
of a Nazarene.
But now they came to deride,
to mock at him and to curse,
they came to silence the Word!
Mary,
his Mother,
stood at the foot of the Cross.
She heard the seed
that had shone in her womb
falling into the ground,
and the sound
of a great wind
sweeping the red harvests
from end to end of the world–
And she heard
the sound of his blood,
that was hers,
like the sound of a great sea
[...]
And she saw the crowds,
coming again to the mountain side
from the ends of the earth,
and the end of time.
She saw
the cities of all the world,
and the glory of them
from the mountain
where he had died.
And she sought
for her son who was lost,
and found him there
in the crowd.

[…]
And then
the Word
was silent.
The sound of the great wind
and the sea
became
the silence of the Word.
She heard
only the sound of the little stream
that broke from his side.
But mankind
born again
was laid in her arms,
in the body of her dead child.[328]

---

[328] Caryll Houselander, *A Rocking Horse Catholic*, Catholic Way Publishing, London (2013): pp. 87–92.

CHAPTER SIXTEEN

QUEEN OF MARTYRS

Mary indeed experienced suffering—so much that there is none other than her divine Son Jesus Christ who has ever, or can ever, suffer more—and thus with reason she is called the Mother of Sorrows and the Queen of Martyrs. The suffering of the divine Mother, experienced throughout her life and continuing until the end of time, reached its climax in union with her divine Son Jesus at the Foot of the Cross, on Calvary. In words that pierce the soul of a sinner, St. Louis-Marie Grignon de Montfort (d. 1716) describes the torture and martyrdom of Mary:

> Let us contemplate our Mary so afflicted
> Near her Savior's cross,
> Her blessed soul transpierced
> By sword of living pain.
> She groans and sighs
> From love's inspiration,
> Suffering great martyrdom
> Not visible to human eye.
> Jesus dying is her torture,
> Love her greatest torment.
> Offering her heart in sacrifice,
> O my God, how great her torment.
> Beholding her love's object

Hanging on a gibbet
She suffers more within her soul
Than any martyr ever.
The same pains she feels
As her beloved dying Son:
His the very echo of her suffering,
True portrait of her torment.
Tears flow in abundance,
She trembles and turns pale,
Her body quite exhausted,
Her great love sustains her still.
We sinners by our crimes
Make Jesus and Mary
Two innocent victims.
Ah! Ah! Ah! Let us never sin again.[329]

These words of St. Louis de Montfort, striking both for their beauty and their brutal accuracy, are confirmed by Mary herself, who described the Passion of her Son to St. Birgitta (Bridget) of Sweden (d. 1373) in a vision:

I was standing nearby and, at the first lash, I fell down as if I were dead. When I revived, I could see his body whipped and scourged to the ribs. What was even more horrible was that when they pulled the whips back, the weighted thongs tore his flesh, like earth before a plow. [...] Once he was sentenced, they placed the cross on him to carry. [...] When I reached the place of the passion with him, I saw all the instruments of his death ready. [...] Then his cruel executioners seized him and stretched him out

[329] St. Louis-Marie Grignon de Montfort, *Canticle of the Blessed Virgin at the Foot of the Cross*, as quoted by Fr. Bertrand de Margerie, S.J., "Mary and John at the Foot of the Cross—Under the Guidance of St. Louis-Marie Grignon de Montfort: Canticle 74" in *Mary at the Foot of the Cross—II: Acts of the Second International Symposium on Marian Coredemption*, Academy of the Immaculate, New Bedford, MA (2002): pp. 291–2.

on the cross, [...] when the first nail was driven into him, that first blow shook me so much that I fell down as if dead, my eyes covered in darkness, my hands trembling, my feet unsteady. In the bitterness of my grief I was not able to watch until he had been fastened entirely to the cross.[330]

St. Birgitta goes on to describe the Virgin-Mother at the Foot of the Cross:

Full of grief after I had witnessed their cruelty, I then saw his most sorrowful mother lying on the ground, trembling as though half-dead. John and her sisters were comforting her. [...] She stood there [*stabat Mater Dolorosa*], held up by her sisters, completely dazed, as though dead but alive, transfixed by a sword of pain.[331]

It was in this culminating moment at the Foot of the Cross that Mary *truly merited* to become the most worthy Coredemptrix and Mediatrix of all graces, Reparatrix of the lost world, Dispensatrix and Distributrix of the graces purchased for us by the infinite merit of the Passion and Death of her divine Son. In the words of Pope St. Pius X:

Hence that uninterrupted community of life and labors of the Son and the Mother, so that of both might have been uttered the words of the Psalmist: "My life is wasted with grief and my years in sighs" (*Ps* 31:10). When the supreme hour of the Son came, beside the Cross of Jesus there stood Mary His Mother, not merely occupied in contemplating the cruel spectacle, but rejoicing that her Only Son was offered for the salvation of mankind, and so entirely participating in His Passion, that if it had been possible "she

---

[330] The Blessed Virgin Mary, as quoted by St. Birgitta (Bridget) of Sweden, *Revelations*, Book I, Ch. 10, v. 17–24, in *The Revelations of St. Birgitta of Sweden*, translated by Denis Searby with Introduction and Notes by Bridget Morris, Vol. 1, Oxford University Press, New York, NY (2006): pp. 67–9.

[331] St. Birgitta (Bridget) of Sweden, *Revelations*, Book VII, Ch. 15, v. 13–6, in ibid., Vol. 3 (2012): p. 235.

would have gladly borne all the torments that her Son bore."[332] And from this community of will and suffering between Christ and Mary "she merited to become most worthily the Reparatrix of the lost world"[333] and Dispensatrix of all the gifts that Our Savior purchased for us by His Death and by His Blood.[334]

How was it possible for Mary to "rejoice" in this moment of supreme pain, united with Christ as His helpmate—the New Eve standing beside the New Adam—at the Foot of the Cross? The answer lies in Christ's own joy in the midst of His supreme pain, and in the union of the Two Hearts. The Seraphic Doctor, St. Bonaventure, explains:

> The sixth star [in Mary's crown of twelve stars] is communication of the act of noblest charity, which was the redemption of the human race via the passion; in which glorious act of highest charity, according to the witness of Him (Christ) who said: "Greater love has no man, etc.," *she merited* [emphasis added]. The Father of mercies and the Mother of mercies knew Him to have carried out this (work), effect of highest mercy; but He was helped by her to consummate what was said prophetically of Him, Genesis, chapter 2: "Let us make a helpmate like him." For she, in the likeness of her Son, under the Cross and by the Cross, had a supreme joy and supreme sorrow, like that of the Son on the Cross and through the Cross. He had a supreme natural sorrow of death and a supreme rational joy for the redemption of the human race. [...] So also the Blessed Mother—from Christ's death upon which she gazed—endured a supreme, natural sorrow in virtue of her love for her Son. But with the manifestation of her Son's charity she had a supreme rational love for what He did to redeem the human race.[335]

---

[332] St. Bonaventure, *I Sent.* d. 48, ad Litt. dub. 4.

[333] Eadmer, *De Excellentia Virg. Mariae*, c. 9.

[334] Pope St. Pius X, *Ad Diem Illum Laetissimum*, Encyclical Letter (February 2, 1904): 12.

[335] St. Bonaventure, *Sermo VI de Assumptione*, as quoted by Fr. Peter Damian M. Fehlner, F.I., "Total Consecration to the Immaculate Heart and the Mariology of

Nevertheless, Mary's joy did not lessen the torture of her Immaculate Heart, which simultaneously contains and is contained in the Sacred Wounds of Jesus. Indeed, this torture transcends human understanding. In the inspired words of the *Goad of Love* (*Stimulus Amoris*):[336]

> [Y]our whole heart, Lady has been tortured by the passion of your Son. O wondrous thing, you are totally in the wounds of Christ; the whole Christ crucified is in the innermost parts of your heart. How can this be that the container is in the contained? O man, wound your heart, if you wish to understand the question. Open your heart with nails and lance, and the truth will enter in. The Sun of Justice does not enter a closed heart. But O wounded Lady, wound our hearts and in our hearts renew the passion of your Son. Join to our heart your wounded heart, that with you we might be wounded with the wounds of your Son.[337]

On account of her *Fiat*—uttered once at the moment of the Incarnation and uttered a second time in union with her divine Son Jesus at the Foot of the Cross, on Calvary—Mary courageously shoulders her unique and inestimable share of the *incomprehensible burden of the Redemption of the human race* with her divine Son, by suffering an indescribable martyrdom of compassion (or Co-Passion) with Him, and by willingly offering Him and herself to the Eternal Father in satisfaction of divine justice. In the words of St. Pio of Pietrelcina (d. 1968):

St. Bonaventure" in OLG: pp. 321–2.

[336] The *Stimulus Amoris* or "Goad of Love" was written in the late thirteenth century. It was among the most popular spiritual texts of the Middle Ages, being translated from Latin into many vernacular languages: Middle High German, Middle Low German, Dutch, French, Italian, Spanish, Polish, Swedish, Danish, and Middle English (the "Prickynge of Love," possibly translated by Walter Hilton c. 1380). Long attributed to St. Bonaventure, it is now attributed to a Franciscan monk named James of Milan.

[337] James of Milan, *Stimulus Amoris* 15 (Meditation for Good Friday), as quoted by Fr. Peter Damian M. Fehlner, F.I., "Total Consecration to the Immaculate Heart and the Mariology of St. Bonaventure" in OLG: pp. 326–7.

Oh, if all people would but penetrate this martyrdom! Who could succeed in suffering with this, yes, our dear Coredemptrix? Who would refuse her the good title of Queen of Martyrs?[338]

Thus, we can well understand the following words of St. Catherine of Siena (d. 1380), Doctor of the Church:

O Mary [...], bearer of the light [...], Mary, Redemptrix of the human race because, by providing your flesh in the Word, you redeemed the world. Christ redeemed with his Passion and you with your sorrow of body and mind.[339]

For, in the words of Pope Benedict XV (d. 1922):

Mary suffered and, as it were, nearly died with her suffering Son; for the salvation of mankind she renounced her mother's rights and, as far as it depended on her, offered her Son to placate divine justice; so we may well say that she with Christ redeemed mankind.[340]

St. Thérèse of Lisieux, Doctor of the Church, likens Mary standing at the Foot of the Cross to a priest at the altar:

Mary, at the top of Calvary standing beside the Cross
To me you seem like a priest at the altar,
Offering your beloved Jesus, the sweet Emmanuel,
To appease the Father's justice...
A prophet said, O afflicted Mother,

---

[338] St. Pio of Pietrelcina, as quoted by Fr. Stefano Manelli, F.I., "Marian Coredemption in the Hagiography of the 20th Century" in *Mary at the Foot of the Cross: Acts of the International Symposium on Marian Coredemption*, Academy of the Immaculate, New Bedford, MA (2001): p. 218.

[339] St. Catherine of Siena, as quoted by Msgr. Arthur Burton Calkins, "Mary Co-Redemptrix: The Beloved Associate of Christ" in *Mariology, a Guide for Priests, Deacons, Seminarians, and Consecrated Persons*, Seat of Wisdom Books, Queenship Publishing, Goleta, CA (2007): p. 370.

[340] Pope Benedict XV, *Inter Sodalicia*, Letter (May 22, 1918).

"There is no sorrow like your sorrow!"

O Queen of Martyrs, while remaining in exile

You lavish on us all the blood of your heart![341]

Through this joint sacrifice of the God-Man Jesus and the Woman Mary, offered, as it were, with one will and with one united Heart, the Redemption of all created things was accomplished, and the "knot of Eve's disobedience was untied by Mary's obedience."[342] Jesus, our Redeemer, renounced His power as God and offered Himself as a holocaust to the Heavenly Father, thus "satisfying for our sins"; and Mary, our Coredemptrix, renounced her maternal rights as Mother of God and offered herself and her Son as a holocaust to the Heavenly Father, thus "obtaining the application of this satisfaction to us."[343] In the words of Ven. Pope Pius XII (d. 1958):

> She [Mary] it was who, immune from all sin, personal or inherited, and ever most closely united with her Son, offered Him on Golgotha to the Eternal Father together with the holocaust of her maternal rights and motherly love, like a new Eve, for all the children of Adam contaminated through this unhappy fall.[344]

In the words of the Benedictine Abbot Arnold of Chartres (d. after 1156), the friend and biographer of St. Bernard of Clairvaux:

> [...] the Virgin died without dying [...] she stands as a living host, pleasing to God, and a holocaust that comes from the depths of the heart. She herself sets on fire this holocaust, her sole instrument

---

[341] St. Thérèse of Lisieux, "Why I Love You, O Mary!" in *The Poetry of Saint Thérèse of Lisieux*, translated by Donald Kinney, O.C.D., ICS Publications, Washington, DC (1996): p. 220.

[342] St. Irenaeus of Lyons, *Adversus Haereses*, 3:22. MFC: p. 54.

[343] GOM: pp. 401–2.

[344] Ven. Pope Pius XII, *Mystici Corporis*, Encyclical Letter (June 29, 1943).

the love of her heart, sacrificing herself silently on the altar of her soul, reuniting the wood, the flame and the water.[345]

Thus, not only did Mary offer her Son Jesus and consent to His immolation on Calvary, she also offered *herself*, associating herself with His Sacrifice. This Sacrifice *of both the Son and the Mother*, the New Adam and the New Eve, is renewed in the Eucharistic sacrifice of every Mass. In the words of Pope St. John Paul II (d. 2005):

> Born of the Virgin to be a pure, holy and immaculate oblation, Christ offered on the Cross the one perfect Sacrifice which every Mass, in an unbloody manner, renews and makes present. In that one Sacrifice, Mary, the first redeemed, the Mother of the Church, had an active part. She stood near the Crucified, suffering deeply with her Firstborn; with a motherly heart she associated herself with his Sacrifice; with love she consented to his immolation (cf. *Lumen Gentium*, 58; *Marialis Cultus*, 20): she offered him and she offered herself to the Father.[346]

Since, as Pope Leo XIII (d. 1903) observed, the Eucharist is the prolongation of the Incarnation in time and space,[347] *both of Mary's Fiats*, and especially her second *Fiat* uttered in a silent union of hearts and wills with her divine Son Jesus on Calvary, are re-pronounced in every Catholic Mass until the Parousia. Moreover, in every Catholic Mass, the words that Jesus spoke to His beloved disciple are repeated to us: "Behold your mother!"[348] Again, in the words of Pope St. John Paul II:

---

[345] Abbot Arnold of Chartres (of Bonneval), *De VII Verbis Domini in Cruce*, as quoted by Mother Abbess Elizabeth Marie Keeler, O.S.B., "The Mystery of Our Lady's Cooperation in our Redemption as seen in the Fathers of Benedictine Monasticism from the VI to the XII century" in *Mary at the Foot of the Cross—III: Mater Unitatis. Acts of the Third International Symposium on Marian Coredemption*, Academy of the Immaculate, New Bedford, MA (2003): p. 290.

[346] Pope St. John Paul II, *Angelus address for the Feast of Corpus Christi* (June 5, 1983).

[347] Pope Leo XIII, *Mirae Caritatis*, Encyclical Letter (May 28, 1902).

[348] *Jn* 19:27.

In a certain sense Mary lived her *Eucharistic faith* even before the institution of the Eucharist, by the very fact that *she offered her virginal womb for the Incarnation of God's Word.* The Eucharist, while commemorating the passion and resurrection, is also in continuity with the Incarnation. [...] In the "memorial" of Calvary all that Christ accomplished by his passion and his death is present. Consequently *all that Christ did with regard to his Mother* for our sake is also present. [...] Experiencing the memorial of Christ's death in the Eucharist also means continually receiving this gift. It means accepting—like John—the one who is given to us anew as our Mother.[349]

---

[349] Pope St. John Paul II, *Ecclesia de Eucharistia*, Encyclical Letter (April 17, 2003): 55, 57.

CHAPTER SEVENTEEN

WOMAN OF THE EUCHARIST

In his encyclical *Ecclesia de Eucharistia*, Pope St. John Paul II identifies Mary as the "Woman of the Eucharist." Following the thought of Pope St. John Paul II, we may distinguish three modes of Mary's Eucharistic life, which correspond to what might be called Mary's "three Fiats." First, her reception of Jesus-Hostia: "be it done to me according to Thy word."[350] In the words of Pope St. John Paul II:

> At the Annunciation Mary conceived the Son of God in the physical reality of his body and blood, thus anticipating within herself what to some degree happens sacramentally in every believer who receives, under the signs of bread and wine, the Lord's body and blood. As a result, there is a profound analogy between the *Fiat* which Mary said in reply to the angel, and the *Amen* which every believer says when receiving the body of the Lord.[351]

Second, her life of faith, prayer, and service as the "living tabernacle" of Jesus-Hostia: "my soul doth magnify the Lord [...] because He that is mighty hath done great things to me; and holy is His name" and "do whatever He tells you."[352] In the words of Pope St. John Paul II:

---

[350] *Lk* 1:38.
[351] Ibid., 55.
[352] *Lk* 1:46, 49; *Jn* 2:5.

Mary also anticipated, in the mystery of the Incarnation, the Church's Eucharistic faith. When, at the Visitation, she bore in her womb the Word made flesh, she became in some way a "tabernacle"—the first "tabernacle" in history—in which the Son of God, still invisible to our human gaze, allowed himself to be adored by Elizabeth, radiating his light as it were through the eyes and the voice of Mary.[353]

Third, her participation in the sacrifice of Jesus-Hostia: "there stood by the cross of Jesus, His Mother."[354] In the words of Pope St. John Paul II:

> Mary, throughout her life at Christ's side and not only on Calvary, made her own *the sacrificial dimension of the Eucharist*. [...] In her daily preparation for Calvary, Mary experienced a kind of "anticipated Eucharist"—one might say a "spiritual communion"—of desire and of oblation, which would culminate in her union with her Son in his passion, and then find expression after Easter by her partaking in the Eucharist which the Apostles celebrated as the memorial of that passion.[355]

These three modes of Mary's Eucharistic life, which are identified by St. Peter Julian Eymard (d. 1868) as (1) her hidden life, (2) her interior life, and (3) her life of sacrifice, continued after the Ascension of Jesus during Mary's life on earth, in uninterrupted union with the Eucharistic life of her divine Son Jesus in the Most Blessed Sacrament. First, Mary's hidden life was lived in union with Jesus-Hostia, in the words of St. Peter Julian Eymard:

> Jesus leads a hidden life in the Most Blessed Sacrament. [...] Such was the life of Mary after the Ascension of her divine Son. She retired to the Cenacle, on Mount Sion, and she wrapped herself up

---

[353] Ibid.
[354] *Jn* 19:25.
[355] Ibid., 56.

in obscurity and oblivion [...] at the foot of the adorable Eucharist in the habitual exercise of a humble and self-effacing adoration.[356]

Second, Mary's interior life was lived in union with Jesus-Hostia, in the words of St. Peter Julian Eymard:

In the Most Blessed Sacrament, Jesus lives an entirely interior life. [...] In the Eucharist, Jesus continues His poverty. [...] In the Eucharist, Jesus continues His obedience, [...] In the Eucharist, Jesus continues His life of prayer; [...] Such is the contemplative life of Jesus; such also was the life of Mary. She honored in herself the everyday virtues of Jesus, and made them live anew by imitating them perfectly.[357]

Third, Mary's life of sacrifice was lived in union with Jesus-Hostia, in the words of St. Peter Julian Eymard:

But it was in sharing the immolation of Jesus in the Most Blessed Sacrament that the strength of Mary's soul and the perfection of her conformity with Jesus were greatest. Mary adored her dear Son on this new Calvary where His love crucified Him. She offered Him to God for the salvation of her new family. The remembrance of Jesus on the Cross with His gaping wounds renewed in her soul the martyrdom of her compassion. She seemed to see her Jesus crucified once more at Holy Mass, shedding streams of blood in the midst of great suffering and of insults, abandoned by man and by His Father, and dying in the supreme act of His love.[358]

By uniting ourselves with Mary, Our Eucharistic Mother, we can *console the Heart of Jesus* with her in a *life of Eucharistic adoration*. In the words of St. Peter Julian Eymard:

---

[356] St. Peter Julian Eymard, *A Eucharistic Handbook*, Congregation of the Blessed Sacrament, Cleveland, OH (1948): pp. 124–5.
[357] Ibid., 126–7.
[358] Ibid., 129.

At the sight of His holy Mother immolating herself with Him, Jesus was consoled over the desertion of man. [...] Mary was compensation enough for everything, and His love found an unspeakable satisfaction in accepting her prayers and her tears for the salvation of the world. Let adorers therefore learn to unite themselves with Mary to the Sacrifice of Jesus in order to be themselves a source of consolation to the august Victim. Let them make room in their lives for a suffering that is voluntary and embraced out of love. Let them become saviors with Jesus by completing in themselves what is lacking to His Eucharistic Passion.[359]

St. Peter Julian Eymard teaches us that if we unite ourselves to the Sacrifice of Jesus with Mary, the perfect adorer, then we, like Mary, can become "co-saviors" with Jesus,[360] but according to a divinely established hierarchy: Jesus Christ, the Head; then Mary, uniquely united to Christ; then Joseph, uniquely united to Mary; and so on. This is the mystery of the Church as the Body of Christ, through which we complete what is lacking in the sufferings of Christ.[361] All of "our theology"[362] *a posteriori* hinges on the ineffable union of the Two Hearts of Jesus and Mary—indeed, the union of

---

[359] Ibid., 130.

[360] Cf. Dr. Mark Miravalle, "Co-Redeemers in Christ: the Church as Type of Mary Co-Redemptrix" in *Mary at the Foot of the Cross—IX: Mary: Spouse of the Holy Spirit, Coredemptrix and Mother of the Church. Acts of the Ninth International Symposium on Marian Coredemption*, Academy of the Immaculate, New Bedford, MA (2010): pp. 237–57.

[361] Cf. *1 Cor* 12:27–8; *Col* 1:24.

[362] The term "our theology" (cf. PDF: p. 3; p. 178) is used by Bl. John Duns Scotus to refer to what is possible for us (as creatures) to know about God, as opposed to what God knows about Himself (but which is unknowable to us as creatures). The absolute predestination of Jesus and Mary in the mind of the Eternal Father before the creation of the universe, as the paradigms and "divine mind-cause" of all creation (cf. St. Gregory Palamas), implies that the intelligibility of creation to us as creatures depends on the union of the Two Hearts of Jesus and Mary. Thus, in order to be intelligible to us, "our theology" must (*a posteriori*) be Christology, and Christology must (*a posteriori*) become Mariology (and vice versa) in order to be as radical as the faith of the Church requires (cf. Pope Benedict XVI), and both must (*a posteriori*) include Ecclesiology as the prolongation of the Incarnation in time and space (cf. Pope Leo XIII). Or to put it more simply, "our theology" hinges on the Incarnation.

the *Three Hearts* of Joseph, Jesus, and Mary: icons of the Father, Son, and Holy Spirit. This "interpretive key" of creation is reflected in the Eucharistic mystery. When we receive the Body of Christ—the Spotless Host—we receive the *real food* prepared by the Virgin-Mother Mary from her own Immaculate flesh, like milk from her abundant breasts.[363] In the words of Fr. Stefano Maria Manelli:

> With heavenly insight St. Augustine illustrates still better how Mary makes Herself our own and unites Herself to each one of us in Holy Communion. He says: "The Word is the Food of the angels. Men have not the strength to nourish themselves with this Heavenly Food; yet, they have need for it. What is needed is a mother who may eat this super-substantial Bread, transform it into her milk, and in this way feed her poor children. This mother is Mary. She nourishes herself with the Word and transforms Him into the Sacred Humanity. She transforms Him into Flesh and Blood, i.e., into this most sweet milk, which is called the Eucharist."[364]

And in the words of St. Thérèse of Lisieux, Doctor of the Little Way:

> This Dew hides in the sanctuary.
> The angels of Heaven, enraptured, contemplate it,
> Offering to God their sublime prayer.
> Like Saint John, they repeat: "Behold."
> Yes, behold, this Word made Host.
> Eternal Priest, sacerdotal Lamb,

---

[363] Cf. *Jn* 6:55; *Isa* 66:11.

[364] Fr. Stefano M. Manelli, F.I., *Jesus Our Eucharistic Love*, Academy of the Immaculate, New Bedford, MA (1996): p. 111. The quote from St. Augustine appears in Abbot Guéranger, O.S.B., *The Liturgical Year*, translated by Dom Laurence Shepherd, Vol. 10, Bk. I, Stanbrook Abbey, Worcester (1879): p. 375. Abbot Guéranger cites St. Augustine's *Confessions*, vii, 18, though a comparison of the texts suggests that the quote is more of a reflection by Abbot Guéranger inspired by St. Augustine rather than a literal quotation.

The Son of God is the Son of Mary.
The bread of Angels is Virginal Milk.[365]

As Bl. James Alberione said: "She prepared the Host for sacrifice; and now behold her offering and immolating it on Calvary." This is why Pope St. John Paul II said:

> At the root of the Eucharist, therefore, there is the virginal and maternal life of Mary, her overflowing experience of God, her journey of faith and love, which through the work of the Holy Spirit made her flesh a temple and her heart an altar: because she conceived not according to nature, but through faith, with a free and conscious act: an act of obedience. And if the Body that we eat and the Blood that we drink is the inestimable gift of the Risen Lord, to us travellers, it still has in itself, as fragrant Bread, the taste and aroma of the Virgin Mother.[366]

---

[365] St. Thérèse of Lisieux, "The Divine Dew, or The Virginal Milk of Mary" in *The Poetry of Saint Thérèse of Lisieux*, translated by Donald Kinney, O.C.D., ICS Publications, Washington, DC (1996): p. 38.

[366] Pope St. John Paul II, *Angelus address for the Feast of Corpus Christi* (June 5, 1983).

CHAPTER EIGHTEEN

WHAT IS PROOF?

We have so far quoted a panoply of Catholic saints, all of whom must, I think, be admitted to be Marian Maximalists. These saints are from both the Eastern and Western traditions of the Catholic Church, and their lives span her entire history, from the first to the twenty-first century. We could have quoted many more. We have shown that—given the almost unanimous testimony of the saints that *Mary has a glory greater than which none can be imagined, except for God's*—it follows with logical certainty that the fullness of Mary's glory is "unutterable" (to use the terminology of St. John Damascene), or to use the more traditional Latin expression: *De Maria numquam satis*—About Mary we can never say enough! Given all of this, what have we actually *proven*? To answer this question, we must consider the notion of proof itself.

In fact, the notion of proof is not as straightforward as it may at first seem. Even in the secular world, the notion of proof varies significantly from discipline to discipline. Consider, for example, a typical "proof" in physics (or any of the empirical sciences). If one wishes to prove a scientific hypothesis, one performs a series of experiments that are carefully designed ("controlled") in such a way that the number of free variables are limited as far as possible so that they bear only on the hypothesis to be proven. If one performs, say, one thousand experiments of this kind, and all of these experiments support the scientific hypothesis to be proven, then one typically is satisfied that the hypothesis *has been proven*. In practice, one is often satisfied with fewer than one thousand successful experiments, depending on how well the experiments have been controlled to eliminate extraneous free variables, but for the purposes of the point we intend to make the actual number of experiments is immaterial (i.e., it could be one million, or any finite number—however large).

Consider, on the other hand, a typical "proof" in mathematics. If one wishes to prove that a property holds for *all* natural numbers, then it is hardly sufficient to prove that the property holds for the first one thousand natural numbers (or the first one million, or any finite number—however large). Neither is it sufficient to prove that the property holds for one thousand randomly picked natural numbers. Rather, if one wishes to prove that a property P holds for *all natural numbers* n, then one must prove first that P holds for the first natural number 1, which we may write formally as "P(1)," and then *prove the rule* that "for any natural number n, if P(n) holds, then P(n+1) holds." Thus, according to this method of *mathematical induction*, a *single inductive rule* is sufficient to prove that the property P holds for *all natural numbers*.[367]

What is the difference between these two methods of proof? One could simply say that the first (that of physics) is *a posteriori*, while the latter (that of mathematics) is *a priori*. However, this picture is a bit oversimplified. Consider again the notion of proof in physics, and suppose for the sake of argument that we are performing an experiment that demands the observation of sub-atomic particles (which are very small, and therefore very hard to characterize, but which, also

---

[367] A similar method also works for a set that contains uncountably many elements. Like the set of natural numbers, which is called countable, an uncountable set contains infinitely many elements, but is incommensurate with the set of natural numbers in the sense that no bijective relation can exist between them. To prove that a property P holds for all members of an uncountably infinite set, one typically either invokes Zorn's Lemma or uses transfinite induction on infinite ordinal numbers. The crux is getting the inductive rule to work for the so-called limit ordinals. Similar inductive methods work for well-founded sets that are not linearly ordered, such as infinitely branching "trees."

for the sake of argument, we will assume are truly particles—rather than waves, or wave-like particles, or particle-like waves) that travel at speeds relatively close to the speed of light (about three hundred million meters per second). Actually, it would be more accurate to speak of a sub-atomic *event* rather than a sub-atomic particle, the *effect* of which propagates at speeds very close to the speed of light. According to Einstein's theory of relativity (which may or may not be strictly correct), information in the universe cannot travel faster than the speed of light. Thus, whether we imagine that we can "look" at these sub-atomic particles with some (imaginary) super-microscope, or whether we speak (more accurately) of measuring the effects of sub-atomic events, the fact remains that we can never observe the particle's location and speed, along with its direction of motion, before it has moved somewhere else entirely. This may seem like a rather amusing anecdote, but it really illustrates a very basic problem in sub-atomic physics, sometimes called the Heisenberg uncertainty principle, which has been verified again and again in different ways in the field of quantum mechanics. Really, this principle has nothing to do with relativism or a denial of absolute existence (as it is sometimes popularly represented), but rather with basic limitations of *observability* at this scale.[368]

If one is suspicious of very small things like sub-atomic particles (which is reasonable, since it is hard to say anything very definite about them), one can see the same phenomenon in satellite motion. In the absence of the physical constraints placed on objects on the surface of the earth, a satellite in space is particularly susceptible to a phenomenon called *chaos* (which is studied in a mathematical field

---

[368] A physicist might object that quantum-scale uncertainty arises not from the inherent limitations of observability, but rather from the mathematical formulation of the wave-particle duality of sub-atomic matter itself. However, this objection would be a logical fallacy, since the mathematical theory that characterizes sub-atomic particles or events—whether it is based on quantum mechanics or string theory or some as yet undeveloped theory—is itself based on observation of these sub-atomic particles or events, and, as such, the theory cannot be used as a norm for itself without introducing a vicious circle.

called chaos theory). Once again, despite popular representations to the contrary, chaos in a dynamical system simply refers to a condition in which the *ultimate behavior* of an object is so sensitive to initial conditions (such as the object's initial position, orientation, and speed) that the ultimate behavior of the object is nearly impossible to predict, because it is nearly impossible to ascertain (or prescribe) the initial conditions with sufficient accuracy. For satellites, the only way around this difficulty is to design the satellite in such a way as to avoid chaos, which can be done in a variety of ways, such as including mechanisms for energy dissipation within the satellite (a sloshy fluid will work).

The phenomena of uncertainty in physics, both large and small scale, point to a problem inherent to the whole notion of scientific proof. Namely, we can never really be sure that our observations are sufficiently precise to justify our conclusions. We may *believe* that the accuracy of our measurements are sufficient for the application we have in mind (which differs from case to case), but the scientific method *itself* does not tell us where to draw the line. In particular, the scientific method alone *cannot* provide the norm for *applying* our "proven" scientific theory to reality. These are not problems that exist merely because of the current state of our technology (i.e., these problems will not go away when we have more powerful instruments of measurement or more effective means of observation). Rather, these are problems that are inherent to the very *idea* of physical observation.

What of the notion of proof in mathematics? Here, it might seem, we at least know that our notion of proof is "self-sufficient," since it relies on nothing outside of logic… but is this really true? In fact, we have already shown in an earlier section that this is not true, since, if mathematics could rely solely on itself to prove, for example, its own consistency, then it would be like Baron Münchhausen lifting himself (and his horse) out of the mud by his own hair. As we have already mentioned, the fact that mathematical logic *cannot* prove its own consistency was proven formally by Kurt Gödel in 1931. We may go further, however, and ask if mathematics itself is really *a priori*. L.E.J. Brouwer maintained that mathematics depends on our intuition of sequence, which is a primitive concept external to logic, and must be experienced. Other mathematicians prefer a more Platonic view. In practice, the Intuitionistic view of mathematics can be treated simply as a restricted version of the Platonic view of mathematics, and both have their applications. But whether mathematics is regarded in the strictly Platonic-ontological sense of completed ideal entities existing outside of our minds, or in the Intuitionistic-epistemological sense of ongoing mental constructions, the fact remains that mathematics cannot prove its own consistency, and so it *must* of necessity depend on something outside itself. In particular, for a mathematical proof to have any meaning at all, we must at least *believe* (without mathematical proof) that mathematics itself is consistent.

We may add to these examples yet another notion of proof that exists in the secular world: the notion of proof in jurisprudence. Even a cursory observation of court proceedings shows that in the case of criminal law, proof depends not so much on the quantity of physical evidence (as in the empirical sciences), or on the rules of logical deduction or induction (as in mathematics), but above all on *personal testimony*. Thus, in criminal law, even when physical evidence is offered, it must be explained and presented to the jury via the personal testimony of an expert. Any fan of Erle Stanley Gardner's character Perry Mason knows that the direct, personal testimony of a single eyewitness to a crime means more in a courtroom than any amount of hypothetical, logical reasoning or circumstantial evidence, and that the ultimate norm for success or failure of a proof in the courtroom depends solely on whether or not the jury is convinced!

Thus we come finally to the case of theology. What is a "proof" in theology? Clearly, as the greatest "science," theology must be at least as rigorous as any of the lesser sciences (and more so). Indeed, if we consider the method of proof used by the scholastics, such as Bl. John Duns Scotus, we see employed all three of the *proof paradigms* that we have just observed in the typical secular disciplines of physics, mathematics, and law: namely, observable evidence (*a posteriori*), logic (*a priori*), and personal testimony (the testimony of the saints—and even the testimony of God Himself via divine revelation). However, *more is still needed*. Even in the comparatively "finite" sciences of mathematics and physics, the applicability of a formal proof to reality always lies outside the scope of the formal proof system itself.[369] If this is true even of the lesser sciences, then it is certainly no less true of the greatest "science": theology! Thus, the final step of any proof, secular or religious, is the act of *assent*. This act of assent, which must be taken every time the proof is read or the theory is applied, always depends on the will of the individual, and it is always formally distinct from the method of proof or the logical reasoning preceding it. In the words of Bl. John Henry Newman:

> I lay it down, then, as a principle that either assent is intrinsically distinct from inference, or the sooner we get rid of the word in philosophy the better. If it be only the echo of an inference, do not treat it as a substantive act; but on the other hand, supposing it be not such an idle repetition, as I am sure it is not,—supposing the word "assent" does hold a rightful place in language and in thought,—if it does not admit of being confused with concluding and inferring,—if the two words are used for two operations of the intellect which cannot change their character,—if in matter of fact they are not always found together,—if they do not vary with each other,—if one is sometimes found without the other,—if one is strong when the other is weak,—if sometimes they seem even in conflict with each other,—then, since we know perfectly well what an inference is, it comes upon us to consider what, as distinct from inference, an assent is, and we are, by the very fact of its

---

[369] Cf. Rossella Lupacchini and Giovanna Corsi (Eds.), *Deduction, Computation, Experiment: Exploring the Effectiveness of Proof*, Springer-Verlag Italia, Milano (2008).

being distinct, advanced one step towards that account of it which I think is the true one.[370]

Hence, whenever we are faced with a proof in theology, we must ultimately say with St. Anselm (echoing St. Augustine): "I believe in order to understand."[371] When we say this, we are in no way committing ourselves to the error of *Fideism*, which maintains that the knowledge of our faith depends on divine revelation alone. If this were the case, then the necessity of belief or assent would apply only to the notion of proof in theology, and not to the notions of proof in the secular cases of physics, mathematics, and law. But we have already shown that the act of assent is necessary for the notion of proof in physics, since physical observations are inherently uncertain. Similarly, the act of assent is necessary for the notion of proof in mathematics, since mathematical logic cannot prove its own consistency. The same is true of the notion of proof in law, since the final criterion for success of a proof in the courtroom relies on the "assent" of the jury. What then, have we proved so far about Marian Maximalism? That must be left to the reader to decide, since it depends ultimately on his or her *assent*.

---

[370] Bl. John Henry Newman, *An Essay in aid of a Grammar of Assent*, Longmans, Green, and Co., London (1903): p. 166.

[371] St. Anselm of Canterbury: "Neque enim quaero intelligere ut credam, sed credo ut intelligam. Nam et hoc credo: quia 'nisi credidero, non intelligam' (*Isa* 7:9)," *Proslogion*, 1.

CHAPTER NINETEEN

A FOX IN THE HEN HOUSE?

Sadly, we must admit the existence of a few groups who at first *appeared* to be "Marian" but later *did* become heretics. One such group is the "Army of Mary" (not to be confused with the Blue Army or the Militia Immaculata), also called the "Community of the Lady of All Nations" (not to be confused with the approved apparition of Our Lady of All Nations to Ida Peerdeman in Amsterdam, the Netherlands, from 1945 to 1959), founded by the supposed visionary Marie-Paule Giguère in Quebec in 1971. While the group originally advocated the praying of the Rosary and other pious activities, Marie-Paule Giguère seems to have lost her mind in the end, since in 1978 she came to believe that she was the reincarnation of the Blessed Virgin Mary herself! The group was formally declared heretical in 2001, after repeated censures from the Congregation for the Doctrine of the Faith beginning in 1987 under the authority of then-Cardinal Joseph Ratzinger. However good the intentions of the members of the "Army of Mary" were at the outset, ultimately this group can hardly be called "Marian" since they ended not by worshipping the Blessed Virgin Mary at all (which would, of course, be wrong in itself) but by worshipping Marie-Paule Giguère![372]

---

[372] In 2006, several members of the "Army of Mary," including Fr. Jean-Pierre Mastropietro, attempted to perform invalid priestly ordinations against the will of the Church, and as a result incurred automatic excommunication. In 2007, the Congregation for the Doctrine of the Faith issued a formal declaration of excommunication for anyone who continues to associate with the movement. In the presence of even the possibility of confusion regarding the piety of a group

Clearly, it was groups like the "Army of Mary" that the Fathers of Vatican II had in mind when they urged "theologians and preachers of the word of God to be careful to refrain as much from all false exaggeration as from too summary an attitude in considering the special dignity of the Mother of God."[373] This balance called for by the Council Fathers will be maintained if we never separate the Virgin-Mother Mary from the God-Man Jesus Christ:

> Following the study of Sacred Scripture, the Fathers, the doctors and liturgy of the Church, and under the guidance of the Church's magisterium, let them rightly illustrate the duties and privileges of the Blessed Virgin which always refer to Christ, the source of all truth, sanctity, and devotion.[374]

Any human being is capable of error, and indeed as fallen humans we are greatly prone to it. Thus, the very fact that it is *difficult* to find any honest devotee of Mary—a group in which I do *not* include the likes of Marie-Paule Giguère and any others who think they are reincarnations of the Blessed Virgin Mary—who is also guilty of significant error regarding the Faith says a great deal concerning the protection that Mary gives to her devoted children. However, while I truly believe that one cannot in justice speak of a "Marian heretic," this does not mean that a devotee of the Blessed Virgin Mary cannot make mistakes. Indeed, if it were possible to claim that one *could not make a mistake* based on any finite rule, including the finite rule of being (nominally) "devoted to Mary," then that would be analogous to mathematical logic proving its own consistency—an impossibility due to the inherent trap of the "liar's paradox." Indeed, it is precisely because *one can never give Mary enough praise* that no such finite rule regarding Marian devotion can be made. In other words, the

---

or society, unequivocal actions against the authority of the Church—such as attempting to perform invalid ordinations—help to clarify the situation greatly. "God does not trick us," and neither does our Heavenly Mother!

[373] LG 67.
[374] Ibid.

mistakes that are made by honest Marian Maximalists can never be held against Marian Maximalism as such, since even Mary's most honest devotees can never be devoted to her *enough*.

One such honest Marian Maximalist who seems to have made mistakes in his enthusiasm was the Franciscan Conventual theologian Fr. Angelo Volpi (d. 1647),[375] whose incomplete magnum opus *Summa Theologiae ad mentem Scoti* was condemned by the Holy Office in 1659 *donec corrigatur*—until corrected. This correction has not yet been systematically undertaken. Actually, it seems to be possible to "rescue" much of what Fr. Angelo Volpi wrote, provided the substance of his meaning is correctly appreciated and his formulations are amended accordingly.[376] However, it is certain that Fr. Angelo Volpi made mistakes, for example when he said:

> The early scotistic school would [say] that Christ was Redeemer of His Mother in the preservative sense and, therefore, would deny that she would have been Coredemptrix. We, on the contrary, reply that by eternal divine election, according to the postulates of the supreme order of the hypostatic union, both Christ and His Mother should be born in the state of original justice: Christ, as a postulate springing from the hypostatic union, Mary as a right deriving from her divine Maternity.[377]

At first it is seems quite shocking that Fr. Angelo Volpi would in good faith maintain that Christ was *not* the Redeemer of His Mother in a preservative sense! However, in fairness, it should be noted that he lived several centuries before the solemn definition of the dogma of Mary's Immaculate Conception, so he did not have the

---

[375] "Volpi" means "Fox."

[376] Cf. Fr. Alessandro M. Apollonio, F.I., "The Coredemptrix and the Church in Angelo Volpi" in *Mary at the Foot of the Cross—IX: Mary: Spouse of the Holy Spirit, Coredemptrix and Mother of the Church. Acts of the Ninth International Symposium on Marian Coredemption*, Academy of the Immaculate, New Bedford, MA (2010): pp. 345–89.

[377] Fr. Angelo Volpi, O.F.M. Conv., as quoted by ibid.: p. 377.

benefit—as we do—of the precise wording of that dogma. Neverthe-less, whatever the merit of his motivation for writing what he did in the interest of defending Mary's role as Coredemptrix (for which it is certainly *not* necessary to deny Mary's preservative redemption by Christ!), it is clear that on this point he erred—in formulation at least, if perhaps not in substance. However, since Fr. Angelo Volpi never *persisted in error* in the face of censure from the Magisterium of the Catholic Church (which came after his death), he can only be accused of *error*, and not of *heresy*. A similar error was made by Fr. Joseph Lebon (d. 1957). According to Dr. Gloria Falcão Dodd:

> Lebon thought that, since the divine maternity was not for Mary's personal sanctification, the divine maternity was a gift directly from God, not given by the merits of Christ. Lebon proposed that, in her association to Christ, Mary's cooperation in the redemption, by her renunciation of her maternal rights, *did not pass through the intermediacy of Christ* [emphasis added]. Lebon's novel concept of Mary's independence of Christ only fueled the controversy over Mary's universal mediation.[378]

To ascribe merit *de condigno* to the Blessed Virgin Mary in the work of Redemption is one thing, and it is indeed important to do so in order to defend Christ from the heresy of monotheletism, if for no other reason, as we have already argued. To say, however, that Mary obtained her merit *independent of Christ* is quite another thing!

Did Fr. Volpi and Fr. Lebon make mistakes regarding the Blessed Virgin Mary? Yes! Were Fr. Volpi and Fr. Lebon devoted *enough* to the Blessed Virgin Mary? Definitely not—since no one can be devoted enough to the Blessed Virgin Mary! Thus, does Fr. Volpi or Fr. Lebon provide a counterexample to our thesis? No! Indeed, I do not believe that one can say Fr. Volpi and Fr. Lebon were giving Mary *too much* praise in the cases we have cited. It is only our (fallen) human way

---

[378] Gloria Falcão Dodd, *The Virgin Mary, Mediatrix of All Grace*, Academy of the Immaculate, New Bedford, MA (2009): p. 228.

of thinking that equates autonomy with glory. In fact, the desire to make the Blessed Virgin Mary autonomous, or *independent of Christ*, does not give her *more* glory, but *less*, because nearness to Christ, who is God-in-Person, is the very *definition* of Mary's glory! Mary's glory is like the ultimate "limit ordinal," greater than which none can be imagined, except for God's. That is why she is closest to God and also closest to us, and why we can never give her too much praise: *De Maria numquam satis*!

CHAPTER TWENTY

Conclusion

In conclusion, unless the entire company of saints and holy writers, including Fathers and Doctors of the Church, from the *first to the twenty-first century* are heretical (which is a contradiction in terms, and therefore impossible), it seems to be a gross misrepresentation to speak of *anyone* being a Marian heretic, witting or unwitting, pious or impious, or to speak of *any truly Marian devotion* as being exaggerated or excessive, provided that such devotion never separates Mary from Christ.[379] Indeed, if St. Maria Faustina Kowalska and the rest of the saints throughout the history of the Church were right in believing that "nothing is too much when it comes to honoring the Immaculate Virgin," then clearly exaggerated or excessive Marian devotion is impossible, and a "Marian heretic" is a contradiction in terms (unless the heretic were so in virtue of giving too *little* honor to Mary), provided that this Marian devotion is based on sound doctrine and a true understanding of *who Mary is* and *Who God Is*. As Bl. John Henry Newman said with incisive precision:

---

[379] Note that LG 67 cautions the clergy and laity only against false exaggerations, which are, by definition, not truly Marian. We will never commit the sin of "false exaggeration" in our devotion to the Blessed Virgin Mary so long as we never separate the Virgin-Mother Mary from the God-Man Jesus Christ; that is, so long as we see Mary as God Himself sees her, and see all of Mary's glories as flowing to her from Christ, the one Mediator. To desire autonomy from God—either for our Heavenly Mother or for ourselves—is the very antithesis of what it means to be truly Marian.

But surely when [God] became man, He brought home to us His incommunicable attributes with a distinctiveness, which precludes the possibility of our lowering Him merely by our exalting a creature. He alone has an entrance into our soul, reads our secret thoughts, speaks to our heart, applies to us spiritual pardon and strength. […] Mary is only our mother by divine appointment, given us from the Cross; […] Woe is me, if even by a breath I sully these ineffable truths! But still, without prejudice to them, there is, I say, another range of thought quite distinct from them, incommensurate with them, of which the Blessed Virgin is the centre. If we placed our Lord in that centre, we should only be dragging Him from His throne, and making Him an Arian kind of God; that is, no God at all. He who charges us with making Mary a divinity, is thereby denying the divinity of Jesus. Such a man does not know what divinity is.[380]

Far from putting us in the danger of heresy, Mary is called the *Destroyer of All Heresies* in the Liturgy of the Catholic Church, because she continually draws our eyes to the God-Man Jesus Christ, who "draws all things to himself."[381] This is why we can never honor the Virgin-Mother enough, because we can never honor her as much as she is honored by her Son, *the Alpha and the Omega*, whom we must love and also *imitate* with all our heart, all our soul, all our strength, and all our mind.[382] As Pope Benedict XVI (then Cardinal Joseph Ratzinger) famously said to Vittorio Messori:

As a young theologian in the time before (and also during) the Council, I had, as many did then and still do today, some reservations in regard to certain ancient formulas, as, for example,

---

[380] Bl. John Henry Newman, "A Letter Addressed to the Rev. E. B. Pusey, D.D., on Occasion of His Eirenicon" in *Certain Difficulties Felt by Anglicans in Catholic Teaching Considered*, Vol. 2, Longmans, Green, and Co., London (1900): pp. 83–5.

[381] *Jn* 12:32.

[382] Cf. *Lk* 10:27.

that famous *De Maria numquam satis*, "concerning Mary one can never say enough." It seemed exaggerated to me. So it was difficult for me later to understand the true meaning of another famous expression (current in the Church since the first centuries when—after a memorable dispute—the Council of Ephesus, in 431, had proclaimed Mary *Theotokos*, Mother of God). The declaration, namely, that designated the Virgin as "*the conqueror of all heresies.*" Now—in this confused period where truly every type of heretical aberration seems to be pressing upon the doors of the authentic faith—now I understand that it was not a matter of pious exaggerations, but of truths that today are more valid than ever.[383]

One thing is certain: As a perfect human mother who at the same time holds *all the love of creation* (according to St. Maximilian Kolbe) and is an *omnipotent intercessor before God* (according to St. Josemaría Escrivá), our Blessed Mother will *never* allow the child who loves her to be led astray by the evil one.

St. Anselm says, "that as it is impossible for one who is not devout to Mary, and consequently not protected by her, to be saved, so is it impossible for one who recommends himself to her, and consequently is beloved by her, to be lost." St. Antoninus repeats the same thing and almost in the same words: "As it is impossible for those from whom Mary turns her eyes of mercy to be saved, so also are those towards whom she turns these eyes, and for whom she prays, necessarily saved and glorified."[384]

---

[383] Pope Benedict XVI (then Cardinal Joseph Ratzinger), as quoted by Vittorio Messori, *The Ratzinger Report: An Exclusive Interview on the State of the Church*, Ignatius Press, San Francisco, CA (1985): pp. 105–6.
[384] GOM: p. 221.

AFTERWORD

Dr. Fleischmann's study of the old axiom: *De Maria numquam satis*, is a wonderful testimony not only to the fact of *Marian maximalism*, but to the need of it in striving to be "perfect as our heavenly Father is perfect" (Mt 5:48). Saints from every place and age have made this extraordinarily clear. And all of them have clearly distinguished between a maximalism which is phony and one which is genuine, one which brings together the love of the Father of the Word Incarnate with that of His Mother in the mystery of the Incarnation. In terms of divine law the relation between the first and second tablets of that law could not be more perfectly realized than when we strive as much as we can with Jesus to exercise maximal love of Mary, matching His unmatchable love of her. And with this brief observation we can begin to contemplate the reason why such unlimited love of the Virgin Mother by her children, the brothers and sisters of Jesus, is needed to attain during their pilgrimage on earth the perfection and sanctity prerequisite for admission to the life to come.

In his classic *My Ideal, Jesus Son of Mary*, Fr. Emile Neubert explains the reason why there is no limit on the love and praise we should shower on the Virgin Mary. She is the one whom the Father has chosen from all eternity before the foundation of the world (cf. Eph 1:3 ff.) to be both Mother of his dearly beloved Son and our Mother.

To become perfect in love as our heavenly Father is perfect in love it is not enough to love our spiritual Mother in natural ways, however good these may be. All of these ways are limited, not maximal. To be counted as brothers and sisters of Jesus we must love Mary as He does: without limit before the foundation of the world.

For from all eternity Jesus thought of her and loved her, from all eternity seeing in her His future Mother. He thought of her as He formed the earth and the human race, as He pronounced sentence against our first parents and as He revealed Himself to the ancient patriarchs and prophets. Out of love He heaped privileges upon her, each of which exceeds the greatest of His bounties toward other creatures.

He exempted her from laws to which the whole human race is subject: her alone did He make Immaculate in her Conception, free from all concupiscence, unsullied by any imperfection, more full of grace than all the angels and saints, Mother of God and ever a Virgin, glorified in her body, even as He was, before the general resurrection. Such is our maternal Mediatrix: through her and in her Jesus comes to us; and through her and in her we go to Him.

This fully deliberate love, then, of Mary by Jesus, a love without limit, is the measureless limit of that love which will make us saints, viz., the brothers and sisters of Jesus because children of Mary, as Jesus became a Child of Mary for our salvation. That salvation consists in loving Mary as Jesus did, sharing His filial love for Mary so far as to being obedient to her. In striving to imitate Jesus in this, an imitation which places no limit on His filial love for Mary, we become more and more one with Jesus in holiness by loving Jesus as Mary does. Without this maternal mediation of Mary there is no other way of being transformed into the image and likeness of our Incarnate Savior. This filial love of Mary in us is far from being perfect as we begin to live as members of Christ's Body. We must strive continually to perfect this love in us by removing obstacles, by generous effort in acquiring the thoughts, sentiments, desires, will and activity of Jesus in regard to His Mother. In a word, we must fill up what is lacking of His filial love in us toward His and our Mother.

And how is this to be done? By loving her as Jesus does. We must love her because He loves her in this way, with the selfsame love as He loves her. When not only we love Mary as our Mother who in begetting us in the order of grace bestows on us everlasting life, but when that love is identical with the love of Jesus for Mary in each of us, then we are truly becoming saints. It is at this point that our love for Mary, or better, the love of Jesus not only in Himself but in and through us, transcends the limits of natural love for Mary and Jesus.

It is this love which is maximal. Or, as Fr. Neubert explains, we honor Mary in the name of Jesus as well as of our own, honoring her for those who do not honor her: for pagans who have no knowledge of her, for heretics who blaspheme her, for bad Christians who fail to pray to her, for consecrated souls who show themselves lukewarm in her service. In a word, we should strive to honor her to the limit of our power, for she is beyond all praise and we will never sufficiently praise her: *de Maria numquam satis*. We can honor her with no fear of excess, because we will never honor her as much as Jesus does and as much as He wants her to be honored by us.

O Jesu dulcis, O Jesu pie, O Jesu, fili Mariae.
O sweet Jesus, O loving Jesus, O Jesus, Son of Mary
[From the Marian Eucharistic hymn *Ave verum corpus natum de Maria Virgine*]

Fr. Peter Damian M. Fehlner, F.I.

THE ACADEMY OF THE IMMACULATE

The Academy of the Immaculate, founded in 1992, is inspired by and based on a project of St. Maximilian Kolbe (never realized by the Saint because of his death by martyrdom at the age of 47, August 14, 1941). Among its goals the Academy seeks to promote at every level the study of the Mystery of the Immaculate Conception and the universal maternal mediation of the Virgin Mother of God, and to sponsor publication and dissemination of the fruits of this research in every way possible.

The Academy of the Immaculate is a non-profit religious-charitable organization of the Roman Catholic Church, incorporated under the laws of the Commonwealth of Massachusetts, with its central office at Our Lady's Chapel, POB 3003, New Bedford, MA 02741-3003.

AcademyoftheImmaculate.com

Special rates are available with 25% to 60% discount depending on the number of books, plus postage. For ordering books and further information on rates to book stores, schools and parishes: *Academy of the Immaculate, P.O. Box 3003, New Bedford, MA 02741, Phone/FAX (888)90.MARIA [888.90.62742], E-mail academy@marymediatrix.com.* Quotations on bulk rates by the box, shipped directly from the printery, contact: *Franciscans of the Immaculate, P.O. Box 3003, New Bedford, MA 02741, (508)996-8274, E-mail: fi-academy@marymediatrix.com. Website: www.marymediatrix.com.*